"He's got what it takes to be a significant voice in urban literature. Biz details the harsh realities of the urban community. It would've been great to release this book under the G Unit books imprint. Maybe part two."
—Curtis(50cent)Jackson
Jamaica Queens

"I rarely read books that are not associated with Teri Woods Publications, but I read BE LIKE THAT SOMETIMES and loved the way the story takes you on a consistent incline of drama. I was all over my couch and floor reading this book."
—Teri Woods
Virginia

"A lot of action. Several times things would seem calm for a minute then bam!!! Something else would be jumping off again. I can't believe this is Biz's first book."

—Supreme
New York

"He's a new writer out the hood and off the block with a pen game like Eric Jerome Dickey, except better because Dickey can't take you in the hood and on the block."

—Terrance(Gangsta)Williams
Original Hot Boy
New Orleans

"It's a great storyline… the story flows continuously without losing you, which is a good thing… in the beginning the characters are not that recognizable but as you read on they take form and speak for themselves… The Last Big Mama is allllright by me."

—Namond Williams
Baltimore

"The story is very interesting. Told in a very smart and compelling way. A real page turner... the story evoked a range of emotions from laughter to pity to rage... full of suspense. I was caught off guard quite a few times... on a scale from 1 to 10. I give it a 10+... a very talented writer."
—Kenny Willis Sr.
Orlando

"I think it is amazing the way the author articulates Big Mama's accent throughout the book. It emphasizes her character. Every time Big Mama appeared in the story I smiled."
—Gethel Gil
Los Angeles

"After reading the first part of this trilogy, I feel recently well fucked. Just what I needed… very satisfying. If I smoked I would have a cigarette right now. That was soooooo good. I can't believe Biz writes so well. I did not want to stop reading. I barely did any work today. I lived a lifestyle I would have never known, thru his characters. All I can say is DAMN Biz is good!! He raps, he writes, makes ya wonder—what other talents does he have?!!"
—Teri Clay
Pheonix

Biz Nolastname
The Last Big Mama

Be Like That Sometimes

Beverly Hills, CA.
Biz Nolastname
The Last Big Mama
Copyright © 2015 by
Biz-e-Bee Book Group
Beverly Hills, California
All Rights Reserved
Printed and Bound in the United States of America
Published by:
Biz-e-Bee Book Group
8549 Wilshire Blvd. #139
Beverly Hills, California. 90211
www.bebpub.com
Cover Design: Biz-e-Bee Book Group
Formatting: Biz-e-Bee Book Group
First Printing, April 2008
10 9 8 7 6 5 4 3 2 1
ISBN #978-0-9817074-5-7
Library of Congress Cataloging-in-Publication Data
Biz Nolastname
Distributed by:
Professional Publishing House.
1425 W. Manchester Ave., Suite C
Los Angeles, California 90047
www.professionalpublishinghouse.com
drrosie@aol.com
(323) 750-3592

Publisher's Note
No part of this book may be reproduced, stored in a retrieval system or transmitted by any means, electronic, mechanical, photocopying, recording, or otherwise, without written permission from the author. This book is a work of fiction. The names, characters, places and incidents are either the product of the author's imagination or used fictitiously, without intent to describe actual conduct of any persons living or dead. Any resemblance is purely coincidental.
Sale of this book without a front cover is unauthorized. If this book is without a cover, it may have been reported to the publisher as "unsold or destroyed" and neither the author nor the publisher has received payment for it.

The Last Big Momma

ACKNOWLEDGEMENTS

I thank God for sending me the route in life he did. From the struggle, the hunger, the voids in my home, the shootouts on the street, baby momma drama and more jails in more jurisdictions than the average criminal, to the good life of getting fast money, new cars, condos, houses and the females that come with it. Traveling across more states than the 10 Freeway, all while eating and drinking good. It's a fuzzy line where my experiences cross over into my imagination.

I thank God that all of that bleeds through my pen in a desirable art form. There are characters in this book that are true to life. If you know me then you know who they are. Thank you for being you.

I wanna thank the niggas that sent the detectives at me. (Thank God it wasn't a dope case.) I'll never forget that night 20 unmarked cars with that single red light in their windshield chased me down on the 405 Freeway. I only ended up with a 20 month federal probation violation, but thank you bitch ass niggas because it gave me time to discover that I could push a pen.

I thank my kids for not letting me forget that I have responsibilities that I need to stay out for and find something legal to do. This is the new dope game and I got that work!!! Now snitches "go run-tell-that!" like Martin Lawrence said.

One thang for sure and two thangs for certain, either you gonna hate me or love me.

Thank you, to everybody who truly give a fuck about me.

Holla at yuh boy!!!

West Coast Biz

The Last Big Momma

BE LIKE THAT SOMETIMES
A NOVEL

THE LAST BIG MAMA

The Last Big Momma

PROLOGUE

If he reach, I'm downin' 'im. Mannish thought to himself.

The detective said, "What's that you got there, are you on parole?"

"No, I maxed out."

"I'll be watching you."

"Only way you gonna be able to do that is if you take a picture right now."

Mannish managed to beat a very high profile DEA agent's murder on a technicality. He did a two year violation and had been home for a couple of months. Mannish never forgot, while he was locked up, his friend told him that with a million dollar investment, the profits from appreciation of market value and the completion of development projects could retire any savvy hustler. It had only been a couple of months but Mannish's game was already back in swing.

Big Mama's health is fading. A family get-together and cook out was the occasion. The house was full of family. How many families do you know that have a gangbanger, a stripper, a crackhead, a hustler and a college graduate in them? Life was normal for now, at least for this family anyway, but as usual, things change.

CHAPTER ONE

"Mannish!" Big Mama yelled.

"Yeah Momma, here I come." Mannish responded, remembering growing up, just hollering from another room without getting up and being on your way would get you slapped upside your head. He was twenty-five years old and hadn't gotten hit in a long time, but Mannish never forgot when Big Mama called, it meant come and come right now.

"I knew you was hea' cause I seent yuh kids runnin' tru' hea' like lil bats outta hell. Dem an' Mable's gran' kids. Dey lil feet jussa pitty pattin.'" Big Mama said grinning.

Mannish is tall, dark and handsome. He has a muscular frame and has thin locks growing from his head at a rapid pace. He has two sons by two different women.

"Where Aiyana at, she witchu?" Big Mama asked.

"Yeah, she in the backyard helping Kaitlynn with the bar-b-que."

"Yuh know yuh otha baby momma hea', but I done sent her ta da' sto' ta get me some mo' brown shuga. She be back direkly. Now you know I dont want no mess 'tween dem girls. I dont 'spose she gon' ack no fool in my house, but I'm tellin' yuh anyways cause yuh know dat Cherise, she a good momma ta yuh son, but she half crazy. Yuh hea' me?"

"Yes Ma'am."

"What yuh autta do is juss choose one an' be done wit it."

"It's not easy as you say Momma, cause every time I do that, the other one will do something for me to show that she a good woman. When I'm ready to make a serious choice something will happen and I'll end up in jail. The one I was about to leave will be the first one to come see me and that means a lot when you're locked up, cause for real, nobody in my family ever came to see me."

The thought of it almost brought a tear to his eye. But as a man who's been doing time and accepting life's challenges head on, he didn't even let his eyes water. What he said was true, but he shrugged it off and thought to himself.

I guess cum is thicker than blood.

"Well I aint talkin' bout yo famly, I'm talkin' bout dem girls. You dont watch out dey gon' link up an' boff of 'em gon' kill yuh."

The way it came out of her mouth made Mannish laugh.

"I'm serious." Big Mama said, laughing too.

It was a nice moment. Mannish cared less what the topic of the conversation was or the cause for the laughter. He was enjoying his mother. It was a moment he wanted to capture forever, and forever live in it. As far back as he could remember she never really seemed too interested in what he did as long as he didn't bring any trouble home. And when he did he got his ass whooped thoroughly for it. From his perspective, neglect at home is what fueled his quest to acquire a sense of importance elsewhere.—The Streets.

"Gon' make sure dem kids dont tear up my house." Big Mama suddenly said.

His time was up. His look put his emotions on display, love then dejection. Mannish walked into the living room and saw his older sister Shawna and her husband Travis just sitting down on the couch. They were looking like two lanes of two miles of bad road.

When Shawna saw him she jumped up. "Mannish! Can your big sister get a hug?"

"Always." Mannish responded hugging her. After the embrace he stepped back and said, "You looking good." he lied.

"I'm...we're doing better." she lied.

Shawna is a medium brown complexion. Her limbs resembled match sticks. Her hair was permed and badly damaged. Her eyes were bloodshot with bags under them.

Her husband Travis was stocky for a crackhead. He wore his hair in a small afro. His face was pockmarked and he was about a week overdue for a shave. Travis stood up from the couch and extended his hand. Mannish's smile did a somersault and got stuck upside down.

He looked Travis in the eyes and said, "Handshakes is for men and you ain't no fucking man. A bitch ass nigga is what I see! You got my sister on that shit and you up in here looking like shit. Put your fucking hand down! You ain't no man. Y'all lost Shawna's son Ty to the system. Good thing Big Mama went and got him. I've been always wanting to catch up to you. You lucky we up in Big Mama's house right now, plus this fool love you for some reason and she grown so..."

"Yeah, I'm grown." Shawna said, stepping between them. "How you doin'? How long you been out?" she asked him trying to change the subject.

Ignoring her, he sidestepped to reconnect his devil's gaze on Travis. "I'ma be around, you feel me, brother in law!" Mannish said.

Travis looked toward the door, contemplating getting on the other side of it with the speed of the crackhead he was, then he thought better of it. Instead he sat down and studied the dirt on his shoes.

In another attempt to defuse the situation, Shawna got in front of her brother again.

"You was in there hittin' them weights huh?" Shawna said, wrapping her frail arms around Mannish's body.

Bringing his attention back to her, Mannish

smiled and said, "Yeah you know how it go. You talk to momma yet?"

"Naw I was just about to sit down for a minute and have a drink, you know." she said, motioning to a can of beer she had wrapped in a paper bag as she sat back down.

"Naw, I don't know. You better go in there and holla at yo momma."

Immediately, Shawna got up and without a word of defiance, she was headed for the kitchen.

"Hi Momma."

Big Mama raised her head up from the steaming pots and looked at Shawna. "Hey, come gimme' a hug. Chile you look like you aint ate in a month a Sundays. I know a place dat can help."

She spoke while reaching for a card she had stuck on the refrigerator under a magnet of a contorted black man playing an instrument.

She handed it to Shawna and said, "Remembuh dat boy Bone whut come up down da street, an' had got inta dem' drugs an' went ta breakin' in peoples houses an' stealin' anythang wudnt nailed down? Anyways after so many years, I guess he got tired an' went ta dat dere place on dat card. He doin' real good now. I didnt know he was dat handsome under all dat filth, he bout yo age. Call dem peoples on dat dere card. Iffen you aint gots no money whichen I know you aint, I'll pay for it Chile."

"I'll call them, I promise." Shawna responded

heading back to her spot in the living room. It was the only room in the house Big Mama would let her enter since she first got hooked on drugs and things began to come up missing.

"You muss got dat no good man sittin' in my house, well let 'im sit. Come back hea', I aint finish talkin' ta yuh. Yuh son Ty is juss as grown as he wanna be. Did yuh see him out dere on da porch? Did he tell yuh he got 'spended from school fa havin' a gun? No matta whut I tell 'im he juss wont do right. I thank he even done joined a gang. Matta fack, go get 'im."

Shawna left out the kitchen and in a few seconds she came right back alone.

"He said he'll come when he finish his game."

"Whut! Tell 'im I said come hea' now!" Big Mama yelled.

Shawna stepped back out on the porch.

"Domino Mutha Fucka!" Ty hollered.

Ty's homeboy Swiss yelled. "That ain't domino! Where that otha bone at nigga? I sent you to the boneyard! You thought I forgot! Cough it up out yuh ass fool!"

"You smokin' crack fool! I hollered domino for a reason, count mine!"

Mike and Swiss threw their dominoes on the table suspiciously.

"Tyshon, your grandmother said come right now." Shawna said, interrupting his flow.

Her son looked at her scornfully while getting up on his feet.

"Shake 'em Jake 'em." he rapped to Mike and went in the house with his mother in tow.

"You wanted me Big Mama?" Ty asked when he reached the kitchen.

"Yeah yall boff sit down, I want yall ta undastand me when I say if yuh dont straighten yuhselves out, yuh goin' ta hell. Da Bible tell yuh all dat mess is of da world an Lord knows I raised yall betta den dat. But I dont know whuts goin' on. Da devil is a busy body an' he got his hands in 'erthang from da drugs ta da music. We is truly in da last days and yuh bess be tryna get yuh butts back in church. But you dont wanna do nuthin' less dem boys in dem videos say its cool. If dat hoodlum boy, whut his name is? Da one got shot an' stabbed an' seem mad at da world. I dont know why but if he say he goin' ta church den all you gon' wanna go. Follow 'im anywhere like a fool. I calls yuh fools cause right now he on his way ta hell an' you fools is right behind him. Oh yeah, his name 50 percent. Dat autta tell yuh sumthin' right dere, God is 100 percent. An' Shawna, dem drugs aint neva did nobody no good. Worst thang coulda eva happen ta black folks was dem drugs, make it where you dont want nuthin', nuthin' but ta hurt da people yuh love. Anyways I done said my piece, gon' back in dere wit yo man.Tyshon see how Kaitlynn comin' long wit da bar-b-que."

With that, they exited, happy she didn't pull out the Bible. The kids were in the backyard being kids. Throwing dirt rocks at the dog next door and jumping up and down on Grampa's old Buick, oblivious to the drama in the world.

"How's the grub comin' Auntie?" Ty asked Kaitlynn.

"You tell me." she said, lifting the lid of the pit, inundating the backyard with flavorful smoke.

Grabbing a piece of chicken with his bare hands was Ty's mistake. "Ooh ah, ooh ah!!" was the sounds he made while switching the smoking bird from one hand to the other, blowing his fingers in between and jumping from one foot to the other. "Damn! This shit hot!"

He smartened up and dropped the meat on a plate sitting on the table. When he looked up he realized Kaitlynn had her hand over her mouth trying to hold her laugh in.

The little people were pointing with one hand and holding their stomachs with the other laughing too. Ty couldn't help but laugh himself. Aiyana was standing to the side cracking up too.

"What yall laughin' at?" Ty said, directed at his little cousins and their friends. Ty grabbed the water hose and quickly turning on the faucet, he chased the Be-Be's kids down the driveway until he ran out of hose.

"Ha ha you can't catch us!" they shouted, throwing dirt rocks at him.

When he got up to the front he heard, Slam!

A domino hit the table on the porch.

"I'm tryna figure out how many titties seven and a half bitches got." Swiss said.

"What?" Mike asked confused.

"Fifteen, nigga give me fifteen and domino when I go. Lemme' get them bones cause you can't count and I needs all mines." Swiss said, reaching for Mike's dominoes.

"Hold up! I know yall ain't playin' wit out me, wit my shit, and at my house too!" Ty snapped.

"One monkey don't stop no show." Swiss retorted.

"Nigga you been gone a cool minute. I ain't wit all that waitin'. How long you wanted us to wait? I started feelin' like I was at the county building wit my momma and shit." said Mike.

"Mutha fucka I was in the house choppin' it up wit my G-moms!"

Just then Cherise (Mannish's baby momma) pulled up in front of the house, exited her vehicle and sashayed up the walkway with a bag from the store for Big Mama in her hand.

Ty said, "Cherise don't trip, watch that crack in the ground." he continued, "When you gonna let me push tha Cadillac truck?"

"When you get a license." knowing it would be at least a year before he would be the legal driving age of sixteen.

"You serious, I get a license you gonna let me dip?" he asked, thinking about the Mexicans downtown that made fake California driver's licenses for a hundred bucks. He pictured himself on Crenshaw stunting for the hoochies as soon as next week.

"Yeah boy I ain't trippin', as long as you be responsible. Holla at me next year."

"Huh?" His cheesy smile did a handstand. "Next year?!"

Cherise entered the house and went into the kitchen to give Big Mama her brown sugar. Mannish took his cellphone conversation into Ty's bedroom. A few minutes later two hands reached around Cherise's waist from the back coupled with soft kisses on the back of her neck. She knew it could be none other than the love of her life and baby daddy.

Cherise is one of those girls with a big onion booty and small breast. She always shows off her pretty feet. This particular day she had on pink strap up sandals with four inch heels, tight white Capri pants and a pink blouse.

"Mannish."

"Hey Babygirl."

"Where were you last night?"

Big Mama gave him a conspiratorial look and stuck her head in a pot.

"You know them streets be calling me. I'm a creature of the night. You know me and Dracula blood brothers." he said. He started laughing at his own corny joke. "Get it, Dracula, blood?"

"Are you going to answer my question?" she said with a hand on her hip.

"Yeah, check it out, my boy up at the barber shop on Crenshaw, The New Millenium, he got some money for me, about five racks and I need you to go get it."

He told her to call him when she got in front of the barber shop so he could tell his boy Q-Tip to bring the package out. While Mannish talked he walked Cherise to the door.

"I saw your son outside. Is Aiyana here?" Cherise asked, already knowing the answer.

"Yeah, I guess she around here somewhere if you seen lil Naj running around, unless she dropped him off."

"Ain't that her Dodge Magnum across the street?"

He looked at the car as if he hadn't just gotten out of it twenty minutes prior.

"Yeah that's it."

"So she here then?"

"Yeah I guess, look, I need you to go get my money for me and stop at Chambers and pick up my Gator boots. And if you want to, you can get yourself something from the mall."

He knew that last comment would pacify her and end her relentless inquiries of Aiyana's presence. He also knew that his tactic was obvious but still it would work. It would give him some time. He would deal with the love triangle later. This house was the only place he ever had to be a master at his chess game, playing with two queens.

CHAPTER TWO

"Bitch what you doin'?" Cherise chirped into Vallawn's Boost twoway phone without warning.

Vallawn answered, "Damn bitch, what if I was in church?"

"Bitch please, either you on your back or on your knees."

They both laughed.

"Either he gonna drop a stack, pay this mortgage or car note, but it's gonna be some fees." said Vallawn.

They laughed some more.

Cherise told Vallawn that she was on the way to pick her up so they could go to the mall. They had been hanging together for a few months, ever since they met at the beauty shop and found out how much they seemed to have in common. They just seemed to click.

Cherise made a left behind the Normandie Club on Vermont and Rosecrans. When she got to the building she called and told Vallawn to come out.

Vallawn stepped out of her condo looking scrumptious as usual. Her skin was a sun baked, honey complexion. She had jet black, wavy hair that used her shoulders as a couch to rest on. The rest laid down her back. Her titties were a little bigger than what could be cupped by two grown man hands. They sat up though she wore no bra. She could do a support bra commercial without a bra. Serious bizness. Her ass was ghetto fabulous, meaning it was the biggest it could be and still look good. Anymore would put her in another category. It was perfect. She sat it down in the passenger seat and they rolled out.

When they got in front of the barber shop, Cherise made her presence known with 50 cent blasting out of the truck, telling the females to come enjoy his amusement park.

Her man's homeboy came stepping out wearing a fresh white Biz-e-Bee Apparel tee shirt, some Five Four jeans and a pair of Creative Reaction shoes that haven't hit the stores yet.

"Hey Q-T (Cutie)." Vallawn pronunciates flirtatiously.

"What's up ladies?" he says casually.

"What's up Q-Tip?" responds Cherise. "You got something for me?"

"Yeah I got something for you." *A lil doggy style action and a lot-a-dick.* he thought to himself.

While he fantasized about "it" for a minute,

the pregnant pause had everybody just hanging quiet. Then after a few seconds he shook off the suicidal thoughts. Q-Tip knows that Mannish has no problem going back to jail. You don't play with his money or his baby mommas.

"Yep, here." Q-Tip said, throwing a Gucci pouch in Cherise's lap.

It landed heavy with money. The pouch still had the $400 price tag on it.

"You keep that." He had contemplated for a second before he said it, and decided. *Fuck it. Men flirt, playas play, it's lowkey flirting the playa way.*

Vallawn, the wise beauty, read his eyes and caught his every gesture. She knew what was up. She actually wanted them to fuck.

Cherise sung a "Thank you."

She had matching pieces. Purses, belts, boots, etc. but she had never seen a pouch like the one she had in her hand.

"What you got for me?" whined Vallawn, then she boldly reached deep into Q-Tip's pockets.

His reflexes automatically grabbed her arm above the wrist, since her hand and wrist were already deep in his pocket. He held her arm right where it was.

"Ooh!" Her eyes bucked at what she felt.

"Pick one bill and whatever it is you can have it." he told her.

She felt through a stack that seemed too big to fit into Q-Tip's pocket. Then she pulled out two

Benjamin's stuck together with the dead president peeking out of both sides.

Placing them in the cupholder she uttered a sweet "Good lookin' out playa."

"That's gonna cost you." he said.

"Money spent, services rendered. I felt your dick and it was hard as a sista tryna find a good man. Anything more gonna take the rest of that you got in your pocket playa. Time to go. Bye Q-T (Cutie)."

"Bye Q-Tip." came from Cherise.

Gear in drive, foot on gas, truck in motion.

Q-Tip went back into the shop and into the smiling face of his homeboy Thugsta, who was just getting out of Tracen's barber's chair.

"Who was them females?" another barber named Estevon asked.

"That was Mannish's girl and her partner. Them bitches is crazy, they cool though." he told him as he walked through the shop.

There was a pool table and an air hockey game in the middle of the hardwood floor. The floor looked just like a half of a basketball court, with all the lines and a goal hanging ten feet in the air. There were jerseys hung along the four walls near the top and big mirrors everywhere.

The whole place had the Lakers theme. Everything was decorated in purple and gold. It even had purple and gold cushioned bleachers sitting on the side up against one wall.

The front had ten stations where you could get

your hair cut by some of the cities finest barbers. On any regular day you could be sitting next to any Laker or Clipper that lived in the town and wasn't scared to hang in the hood. The middle room is where the females did their magic. Most were Belizean hairstylist and they knew how to hook some hair up. Francine and Princella were two of the best. Pretty girls went in and came out bad bitches. Mudducks came out counterfeit dimes.

A barber named J Bird and a few more did their thang in the back room and kept the PlayStation 3 Madden competition popping on the big screen. The most anticipated rapper in the city had a station back there. They call him Trenseta.

Q-Tip and his boy stepped out the back door where everything went on that didn't need to be broadcasted in the front, dice games, weed being sold, rolled and smoked. The local baIlers hung back there just to kick the shit and show off to each other their jewelry, clothes, whips, whatever was freshly acquired.

Everybody watched the Cadillac truck snaking through the parking lot with the soundz bumping. Cherise and Vallawn were going around through the back way. They were in the truck singing.

"This is why I'm hot..."

Q-Tip waved them down. He walked up to Vallawn's window and told her he forgot to give her something while throwing a XL Magnum condom into her lap.

"While you out see if you can find me something bigger. Those fit kinda tight." He strolled away smiling.

One of the guys said to Q-Tip. "The one driving, what's her name? I think I seen the one driving on BET uncut videos."

"Naw homie, not her. That's Mannish's baby momma."

"Yeah dog, I swear that's her."

CHAPTER THREE

Just as Cherise was going into Chambers, her Boost chirped. It was Mannish.

"Hey Honey." she spoke into the speaker.

"What's up, you ain't got to the barber shop yet?"

"What's my name?"

"Cherise."

"And Cherise handles her bizness right? I already picked that up from Q-Tip and I'm picking up your boots right now."

"Aight cool, but I told you to call me. Come back when you leave there."

"Okay, Vallawn is wit me."

His dick got hard immediately.

"That's cool, she can cum too, I guess." he said nonchalantly trying to downplay his excitement.

On the way back to Big Mama's house, Cherise and Vallawn took the back streets like the avenues and 48th Street. They did that when they weren't really trying to be flirted with. They noticed a fine brother. He was six feet tall, wearing a wife beater allowing his muscles, moist with a light sweat, to glisten in the sun. That initially caught their attention, then, they noticed that he was helping what may have been his grandmother up the walkway.

With his assistance, she slowly made her way up to the front door. She was a diminutive, little woman with a hunched over posture and long, silky, silver hair. Her face adorned infinite wrinkles. She also carried a smile that was highly contagious. The girls in the truck smiled their biggest smile of the day, yet reminiscing on both of their grandparents which had already returned to earth.

The short emotional discussion on the way back to the house, reminded both of them that their grandparents were their family's foundation, that since they were gone, the glue that held the family together was gone too.

They sat in front of the house, hugged and cried. They let the moment pass, gained their composure, dried their eyes and hopped out the truck like "What!"

Cherise noticed that the Dodge Magnum was gone.

When they got in the house the girls hugged Big Mama in unison interrupting her favorite soap opera.

"Whut's goin' on, whut yall done done?"

Their only answers were kissing her on her cheeks.

The food was done but everybody was doing their own thing. The kids were in the backyard finding bugs to drop onto the hot coals in the smoldering bar-b-que pit.

Mannish was walking in circles around the house talking some bizness on his cell phone. Shawna and Travis sat in the same spot they were in when Cherise left. Kaitlynn was upstairs on the computer researching grant programs that she might qualify for before she graduated. That's what she told Cherise when she came downstairs in answer to the question "What's up girl?" after their sisterly embrace.

Kaitlynn treated both of her brother's son's mothers the same. She observed all the drama they went through but she never got involved. It's her sixth year in higher learning. She will be handed a Master's degree in May.

She knows that Mannish loves her and is proud of her although he never gets to express it. He's either in jail or caught up in his own complexity in the street life. Kaitlynn is always preoccupied with her academic world.

Kaitlynn sat on the couch inbetween Cherise and Vallawn.

"What's up with you two?" she said to Vallawn and Cherise.

"Nothing." Vallawn answered.

"Leanin' back." Cherise responded, eyeing Mannish casually talking on his cellphone and trying to figure out if he was talking to a female.

"Momma aren't you ready to eat? I know I

am." came from Kaitlynn.

Big Mama was so engrossed in her daytime drama on television that she hadn't heard a word Kaitlynn had said.

Kaitlynn scanned the room. Shawna and Travis looked hungry but then that was kind of a permanent look for them. She looked in the direction of her brother, then his baby momma, then her friend.

"Are you guys ready to eat?"

Mannish shook his head.

Cherise said, "Uh huh."

Vallawn said. "For sure, you know I love to eat."

Kaitlynn realized the time. Where is Jacob? her older brother.

He should've been here by now, knowing that white woman keeps his butt punctual. I should call him, or should I? If he doesn't come, then he just doesn't come. Hmmp. Let me go call this man. Everybody's here, even Mannish is here and Jacob should be here just the same. He knows Momma has been having a hard time with her heart lately.

Kaitlynn went into Big Mama's bedroom to use the phone. She called but Jacob didn't answer his phone at home. His home sits on the side of a hill in Laguna Hills.

People in the ghetto view white people that move to the hills as trying to get away from black folks and they view black people who move there as running from their damnselves. If man was meant to live on the side of a hill we wouldn't have gravity.

She called Jacob's cellphone. It went unanswered also.

I know he ain't trying to play his family out.

Another try to both numbers, same result.

Screw it.

Time to eat. Kaitlynn came out of the bedroom and asked about Ty's whereabouts.

"Probly up ta no good." Big Mama said.

"I saw him up the block when I was driving up a little while ago." said Cherise.

Kaitlynn went out to the sidewalk and looked down the block. Her heart almost jumped out of her chest. She blinked and focused in, hoping she wasn't seeing correctly. Hoping that someone else had on a shirt similar to the powder blue and white Biz-e-Bee Apparel shirt Ty was wearing.

No. It was him!

Ty had busted a 40 oz. bottle of beer on another boy's face. The boy was dazed so Ty put his face on the curb, positioned his teeth on the edge and jumped up and down on his head. From down the street Kaitlynn could see the boy's teeth get crunched on the concrete.

"Ty!" Kaitlynn screamed.

Ty stopped and looked up the block then threw his hands in the air innocently like "What's up Auntie?"

That couple of seconds of distraction was all that the other boy needed. He pulled a .32 caliber pistol out of his jacket, pointed and squeezed. Ty fell down and scrambled behind a parked car and ran towards the house. The boy squeezed until the gun clicked. Kaitlynn ran into the house, thinking about how the innocent bystanders always get hit.

Not today!

Everyone in the house jumped to their feet. They'd heard the shots but they were so accustomed to it that it didn't click until Kaitlynn ran into the house. Before anyone could fix their mouths to say "What's going on?" Ty busted through the front door and ran through the house, straight to his room. Everyone's neck swung in unison.

They didn't know if he just got shot or just shot someone or what had happened.

"Whut da hell is goin' on?!" Big Mama yelled.

No one had an answer.

Kaitlynn yelled "Mannish!" in a tone that was understood to mean "Handle this!" He went to open Ty's room door. It was locked. "Ty!" he yelled, at the same time noticing blood on his hand from the doorknob. With one strong thrust from his muscular shoulder, the door gave.

The lights were on, the room was empty and the window was open. A few moments later three shots echoed in the air outside. A few more moments later Ty came bolting back into the house and collapsed on the living room floor.

CHAPTER FOUR

Sirens were rapidly getting louder. In the ghetto you hear sirens so often, you could tell whether it belonged to an ambulance, fire truck or police car. By the sound of it, there was an ambulance and three police cars, one of the police cars was an unmarked detective car. Yeah, you can tell all that by the sounds when you grew up in it.

Ty's clothes were increasingly turning to a dark red hue and soaking wet. His breathing was labored. All the females in the house were screaming. Mannish noticed the 9mm Berretta in Ty's hand but no one else did, because Ty laid with one arm under his body. Mannish retrieved it and put it in his waistband. Mannish was pulling his shirt down over it just as a detective walked in. First the officer scanned the room and made a mental head count. He did a double take when he saw Vallawn. Then he gave everyone a second look over, then he said, "I'm gonna need everybody to step back away from the suspect of the shooting death up the street."

Every face in the house looked at the officer as their jaws fell open. The only sound in the house came from the television. Everyone's mind raced to try to imagine what the scene down the street looked like. Then the silence was interrupted by Big Mama.

"No such a lie! Dis boy aint done nuthin' like dat! Look at 'im, he da one got shot!" Big Mama looked at Kaitlynn. "Get a doctor from outside fast baby!"

Without hesitation Kaitlynn ran to get help, bumping into Mannish and almost making the gun fall down his pants. The officer eyed him suspiciously. It didn't go unobserved by Mannish.

If he reach I'm downin' him. Mannish thought.

He went upstairs and stashed the gun in the ceiling. Afterwards, he sat down on the bed for a minute and tried to collect his thoughts. He was the man of the family.

He had to remain cool and in control. Mannish was a thinker. Even though he had been to jail enough times to be considered a convict, repeat offender, jail bird or any other derogatory name you could come up with to label a loser. Anyone who knew him would always be left to wonder how he happened to end up in jail again. He was a chance taker true, but he was calculated even more so.

He thought. *Okay the women will see to it that*

Ty gets taken care of.

Mannish did notice that Ty was only hit in the arm.

What he needed to do was get outside and peep what was going on down the block. He needed to find out who supposedly got killed like the detective claimed and why.

He also needed to know who shot his nephew. Mannish climbed out of the upstairs window, jumped down on the old Buick and went over the back gate. He went through the yard behind the house and came out on 47th. Place. He walked around the corner and came back onto 48th Street.

The street was lit up. There was another ambulance and what seemed like twenty more police cars. Lights on the top of every vehicle flashed silently blue and red. People were standing all about being nosey and chattering from porches to the middle of the street. There was a crackhead with a brand new video camera talking about, "I got that exclusive footage." He was pushing buttons at random until something caught Mannish's attention.

"Lemme' see that!" Mannish said, snatching the device out of the crackhead's hand and pushing rewind on the touch screen. It was an electronical testimony he held in his hand. The whole incident was captured on video.

While Mannish studied the video he maneuvered across the street and down a few houses to where no one was standing. The crackhead was right on Mannish's heels and in his ear.

"Give me twenty dollars for it." the crackhead

said.

Mannish ignored him and kept moving and studying the images on the camera.

"Don't be trying to walk off... where you going?... you can look at it right here... I tell you what, gimme' ten dollars now and the next time I see you gimme' the other ten... you know that's a top of the line camera right there."

"Shut the fuck up!" Mannish yelled at him.

"Oh what, you gonna rob me in front of the police? I could take that video to the newspaper and get thousands or more for it, but I'm trying to work with you... how much you got on you, you got five dollars, and you won't owe me nothing."

Mannish wanted to punch him in the mouth. That'll shut 'im up. But if he hollered and the police got involved and got their hands on the camera...

He thought better of it and said. "Here's fifty dollars."

Before the crackhead could run off to the nearest dope spot, Mannish said. "Ay, you never saw nothing. I'm buying your memory of the last thirty minutes. You never saw nothing, you understand?"

"I gotcha boss but thirty minutes of my memory gonna run yuh a hundred dollars."

Mannish flinched like he was going to throw a punch and stomped his foot.

"Get the fuck outta here!"

The crackhead scurried down the block.

From the video Mannish ascertained that no one else was around except a couple of Ty's homeboys, who clearly didn't hang around when the police showed up.

I gotta go see how Big Mama is handling this.

Mannish walked through all the excitement. As he approached the house the same detective from inside the house stepped to him.

"I need to talk to you." the detective said.

"You mean you would like to talk to me." Mannish responded.

"Yes, I would like to talk to you."

"Well people in hell would like ice water but just like them, you ain't got nothing coming."

"Are you on parole?"

"Nah, I maxed out."

"What did you do, jump out the back window or something? That's strange behavior. I'm going to be watching you."

"Only way you gonna be able to do that is if you take a picture right now." Mannish said, as he continued into the house.

"What's that you got there in your hand?"

"Personal property." Mannish answered without even turning around.

CHAPTER FIVE

In the house the hysteria had calmed because the paramedics informed the family that Ty's injury wasn't life threatening. They also told them that no one could accompany him in the ambulance because he was being taken to the hospital ward in the jail.

The police gave no information on what transpired down the street because evidently, they still had to investigate. They just knew that somebody had been shot.

All the women screaming led them to Big Mama's house.

The police left the number to the jail so the family could check on Ty. It was a Friday. There was a possibility he would go to court the next week.

It was all too much excitement for Big Mama, so she fixed everybody a plate and sent them on their way. She told 'em "You aint gotsta go home but you gotsta get da hell up outta hea. I needs some peace an' quiet."

Shawna and Travis was the first to leave. They called a cab and were out. When the cab got to their apartment Travis told the cab driver, "My wife is going to get the money from inside, she'll be right back."

Shawna looked at him with suspicion. The look said, "Fool, you know we ain't got no money up in there."

He nudged her. "See you in a minute honey. I'll wait right here. Here take the food with you."

She did as her husband said. After five minutes Travis called inside the apartment to the landline that will be cut off by morning with a cellphone that he picked out of an unsuspecting passenger's pocket on the bus on the way to Big Mama's house earlier that day.

"Hello." Shawna said, answering the phone.

Travis said, "Hey baby what's up, what's taking you so long?" loud enough for the cab driver to hear.

"Taking me so long? Ain't no money up here to pay for..."

"Oh you was talking to my boss." Travis interrupted.

"Huh?" she replied confused.

"Oh okay I'll just go up to my job then. Okay I'll call you later." Travis said.

Shawna started to totally think about all the stuff her family said about Travis and how her life had spiraled downward since getting with him. Figuring he was up to something underhanded she just said, "Okay bye."

Travis told the cabbie to take him a mile up the boulevard to a Denny's Restaurant. When they got there he told him, "Hold on a sec... how much I owe you... I'ma get it from my boss."

Travis walked inside the restaurant and went to the restroom to take a piss. He came back out playing with five one dollar bills he'd already had in his pocket. As he approached the driver's door, the cabbie let down the window to receive his pay. Suddenly, Travis grabbed him by the collar and pulled the man halfway out the car window, put him in a headlock and demanded his money.

In his heavy accent the cabbie said, "Here take it, whatever you want, I will comply."

The cabbie reached into his pocket and pulled out about seventy five dollars in ones, tens and fives. Hurriedly, trying to hand it over and rid himself of his current dilemma, he overreacted and handed the money off to the air. It rained to the ground and blew through the parking lot in the wind. Travis, true to his dopefiend nature chased after every single bill as the cabbie burned rubber out of the parking lot.

Travis looked up and saw a bunch of people that were dining in Denny's gazing through the window at him in awe due to his antics. He flipped them the bird and ran to the dope spot.

He stepped up to the back door and rang the doorbell. One of the youngsters named J-Stone looked out the peep hole.

"Ay, it's Travis' bitch ass."

He opened the door and told Travis to come in.

Travis immediately got apprehensive.

Why did I even come here?

The youngsters always fucked with him but he would always return because they always had that good dope.

As Travis stepped in, he remembered last month when he had asked for credit, two of them had wrestled him down and hog tied his hands and feet behind his back, filled up the bath tub with cold water and ice and put him in it. They were in the other room playing Grand Theft Auto while Travis screamed and hollered until his body shut down. He shivered just thinking about it.

"What you want Travis?"

"A five-O." he said proudly.

J-Stone looked around. "It's five of us. We all can give you ten."

Three of them tackled Travis and held him bent over. They took turns kicking him in the ass ten times each. When they were done and let him go, Travis collapsed to the floor and scrambled to the corner.

He was grateful to leave with some dope and his money. When they tortured him he wouldn't have to pay for any dope. He figured in a weird kind of way they liked him.

When Travis made it back to the apartment Shawna was on the phone with Big Mama. She had been on the phone since he pulled off in the cab an hour before. They had been discussing her re-evaluation of her current state of existence. Shawna had decided to leave Travis and check into the rehab. She was done with all the bullshit. She would smoke no more crack. Her mind was made up. She would pack her bags as soon as she got off the phone and she would tell Travis it was over.

"I'll talk to you later Momma, Travis just walked in." Click.

"Look what I got." he said as he dropped fifty dollars worth of crack on the table. Then he took out an ounce of powder he'd managed to steal while getting his ass kicked.

Shawna's eyes bucked wide open at the site of it all. She got her pipe out of her purse, melted a big chunk of crack on it and took a big hit. She held it in until almost all the smoke dissipated in her lungs and there was nothing to blow out. She tried to speak but her mouth twitched too much. Then she heard something and went to peek out the window. Finding no one out there, she looked in the closet. Coming up empty in the closet, she checked to see if somebody was under the couch. Convinced no one was lurking about, she laid back high as hell.

Travis picked up the pipe and took a blast. Bells rang in his ears. The cocaine stimulated his sex drive. He laid on top of her and kissed her. He worked her dress up. She assisted by unzipping his pants and pulling his dick through. He moved her panties to the side and slid into her. The sensation was sensational to say the least due to the drugs. They would always get high and have sex. The crack was their aphrodisiac. They worked up a sweat and came out of their clothes piece by piece. Every couple of minutes they would get overheated, take off another item of clothing and take another hit. Then Travis would plunge back into Shawna's wet and waiting pussy. These sessions are what made it all worth it, what made the habit attractive.

It was all good during these moments, but when the dope was gone then their fucked up reality would set back in. They'd worry about that later. Right now they had dope and plenty of it. They cooked up a gram at a time telling themselves they were being conservative.

All this went on for three days. The house phone had been cut off as well as the stolen cellphone. So no one had spoke with them all weekend. It wasn't unusual for them not to be heard from for long periods of time, but it was just that this was the first time Shawna had made Big Mama a promise and sounded sincere about quitting.

Big Mama called Mannish and told him to go over there and check on her.

Travis had just taken a blast when Mannish knocked on the door. His head popped up and his eyes popped out like a cartoon character. He choked on the smoke but dared not make a sound. He whispered to his wife, "That's the police."

There was another knock at the door, a more aggressive knock. Shawna watched Travis run into the bedroom, stash the pipe under the mattress and jump out of the second story window.

Shawna ran to the window and looked down. He laid flat across the dirt and gravel behind the building.

Oh my God! He killed hisself!

Shawna hollered his name. Without even looking to see who was calling his name, he automatically assumed it was the police and hightailed it down the alley.

That man is crazy.

Another knock at the door.

"Shawna!"

She opened the door.

"Hey Mannish what brings you around here?" she asked, nervous as hell trying not to look as fragile or physically broke down as she was. She saw pity in his eyes when he looked her over. The pity was coupled with rage.

"Where dude at?"

"He not here right now."

She meant his body was not here in this apartment and his mind wasn't even on the planet. She stepped outside and closed the door, embarrassed at her living conditions and afraid he would smell crack smoke in the air.

"Aww what's up, I can't come in?" he complained, figuring she was probably hiding the chump inside.

"Ahh, I just sprayed the place with Raid. There were a lot of ants." she lied. He knew, but let it go.

"Momma said you checking into the program today or something."

"Yeah, but I don't know if I'ma make it today."

He knew her hesitation had something to do with her man.

"What did he have to say about it?"

"Ah, um, he's all with it." another lie.

"Aight sis, whatever, I gotta go."

"How's Tyshon?"

"He's taking it like a soldier. The doctor patched his bullet wound up. He go to court in a week. The other dude was a youngster from the neighborhood, stay a few blocks over. His name is Derrick. He got hit in the shoulder and once in each leg. He's charged with the same thing Ty is because he shot Ty too. But anyway I gotta go."

Before Mannish pulled off he looked in his rear view mirror. He saw Travis in the bushes a few apartments down peeking out at him. He couldn't help but laugh.

Right now he had no time for Travis. He had something more important on his agenda.

A former crime partner of his transferred his hustle skills to the real estate game. He kept in touch with Mannish while he was locked up. Mannish never forgot the time his friend told him that with a million dollar investment, the profits from appreciation of market value and completion of development projects could retire any savvy hustler.

CHAPTER SIX

Gear shift to drive, gas pedal to the floor.

The Dodge Magnum burned rubber all the way down the street. The music was setting off car alarms a hundred yards before he got to them. Mannish made a right on La Brea and went to Interstate 10. As he entered westbound his cellphone vibrated in his pocket.

"What up." he answered.

"What you doin'?" It was Cherise.

"I'm on my way to the Valley."

"What you bout to do?"

"I'm bout to go see Nunya."

"Nunya, who is that?"

"None yuh damn bizness." He chuckled and hung up the phone.

She called right back. He threw the phone on the passenger seat and let it vibrate.

The Mexican named Hector he dealt with, his connection for cocaine, liked to call himself "Professional." He didn't want to see any unfamiliar faces and if Mannish was more than ten minutes late he wouldn't answer the door or the phone. Mannish would just be stuck on stupid. He understood Hector had his ethics, but he was always straight up with Hector and thereso Mannish didn't want to deal with any bullshit.

Don't be having me out here wasting my time and lookin' like a fool.

This was his second trip in two days because the day before Mannish was thirty minutes late. He got caught up helping his son with his homework.

Before he exited the freeway he made a quick call.

"Where you at?" Mannish said into the phone.

"I'm where you told me to be, on Sherman Way in the supermarket parking lot." Jay answered.

"Aight, hold tight I'ma hit you right back."

"Aight nigga, hurry up."

Hector was standing in the front yard. Mannish stopped at the house and got out of the car.

"What the fuck kinda car is that holmes?" Hector asked.

"Oh, you ain't know? This that new Dodge Magnum Biz-e-Bee Limited Edition with that supped up Hemi motor. Peep the interior, even my leather got leather trim. And the music feel like you at a concert." Mannish said, while opening the passenger door.

Hector leaned in. As he admired the upholstery Mannish got in the driver's side. Mannish pushed a button on the radio. A screen slid out and flipped up showing West Coast Biz's new music video. Hector sat down to get a good view of the video.

"Close the door." Mannish said.

Hector complied.

"What you know about the Hemi motor Hec?"

The car took off down the street like a rocket. They gave each other high fives as the car performed down a series of streets. Suddenly, there was a loud gun shot. It sounded like it was in the music, maybe part of the video.

No. This was real. Up close and personal. There was the smell of gunpowder in the air, a gun in Mannish's hand, a hot sensation in Hector's side, Hector had just gotten shot. Hector's face turned red and there was a sharp pain in his left side. Mannish cut the music off. What was happening clicked in Hector's mind. The look in Mannish's eyes were evil.

He told Hector. "Okay mutha fucka, I got sixteen more where that one came from. Call your house and tell your boys to fill my boy car up wit that shit!"

Hector made the call while Mannish made his call.

"Ay Homie, drive around to that house I showed you last night." Mannish told his boy Jay.

Once Jay called back to say he had the load and was getting on the freeway, Mannish put

Hector out of the car and burned rubber up the freeway onramp.

They went to "The Spot" on Adams and Crenshaw. The apartment unit was called "Tha Spot" but nothing got sold out of it. It was a safe house where Mannish and Jay kept everything.

They counted fifty kilos and two hundred grand.

Mannish felt like it was a good come up and would put him that much closer to his goal. But he really didn't care how much it was, he was teaching Hector a lesson in ethics.

Mannish gave Jay ten keys and fifty grand. He didn't want to give him that much because he knew Jay would just fuck it off on dumb shit, but Jay had worked for it.

Mannish was already calculating. *With the five kilos I already have in the streets plus this new come up, I plan on taking it slow and parlaying this come up into a means to an end. I could be out of the life of crime for good if I make the right moves.*

Jay was already on the phone telling a female he met at the club the week before, that he was going to take her to the mall, as he flipped through the pages of a XXL Magazine. He was trying to figure out which rapper he was going to out stunt when he sold his dope.

Mannish decided it was time for him to find a safe house only he knew about. He had moved up and had to make sure he "B-More Careful." He left the apartment and drove off to find a new spot. He thought as he drove. He thought about all the drama that had went down over Big Mama's house the week before. He knew he too, had put Big Mama through a lot of trouble when he was growing up. He thought about when he was ten years old.

I had stolen a snake from the pet store and brought it home. I hid it in my bedroom closet. The next day when I came home from school I couldn't find it. I figured it must've gotten out of the house and went on about it's business. Until two o'clock in the morning, when Big Mama and Paw-Paw went running out the house butt naked and screaming.

Mannish sure got his ass whooped for that one. He overheard Big Mama on the phone the next day talking to her friend Mable about how her and Paw Paw had just finished getting busy and she was rubbing on what she thought was his penis. She was marveling at how large it seemed, causing her to pull back the cover.

Big Mama told Mannish that he was grounded for six months that time. But as usual his privileges were restored a week later.

Mannish's cellphone vibrated in his pocket. It brought him back to the here and now. He threw it on the back seat.

Maybe I'll check some outskirt cities.

Mannish headed east on the 91 freeway towards Cerritos. His mind drifted back off. When he was twelve he was introduced to Bruce Lee movies.

I started flipping off of beds and couches. I got Big Mama's old thick broom and cut the stick up and made some nunchucks. One day in the living room trying to mimic The Kung Fu legend, I shattered her sixty gallon fish tank. Fish, glass, rocks and water were everywhere. I spent the next hour cleaning up the evidence. When Big Mama came home she said the house looked clean, more spacious for some reason but she didn't realize why. I was outside praying that she just keep not noticing. My stupid ass cousin Paula asked Big Mama what had happened to the fish tank. Everybody was in the house but me and by the reaction of everybody's face it was obvious they had no clue to what happened. Big Mama waited patiently for me to come in that evening. I wasn't ten feet in the door when I caught a flurry of lashes from a switch made of three braided tree branches. My brain didn't even think to deny it. There was just a chorus of sopranic "I'm sorry Mommas." She whipped me until she had to sit down and catch her breath.

Exiting the freeway Mannish smiled to himself.

Big Mama the enforcer, ha!

He wondered if he expended all of her energy to kick ass because Kaitlynn nor Ty ever got their butts whipped.

In Cerritos, Mannish found an upscale building with lots of units. He liked it because he figured there would be too much coming and going for anyone to be worried about his schedule, or lack of one for that matter. In a week he was moved in but he continued to hang at The Spot like nothing changed.

He was at home watching the movie Heat when Kaitlynn came by. She yelled over the TV. "Dang, fool I could hear that noise up the street and how come that's the only scene you always watching."

"Cause it's the best scene ever. Them mutha fuckas had they shit together. They hit that bank in broad daylight. I'd say they got every dime in there!" Mannish's face lit up while he talked. "And when Val Kilmer seen the Feds…." Mannish jumped up to his feet and aimed his imaginary fully automatic weapon. "d.d.d.d.d.d. It was on and popping! That's the best shootout scene ever! Fuck that, I'm bout to watch this again! Wanna see it? Sit down right here. These surround sounds have you thinking you right there!"

"No thank you, I'll pass. Where is Aiyana?"
"She's in the bedroom."

Kaitlynn went that way. She knocked and opened the door at the same time. "Hey what's up?"

"Girl you can't be coming in here like that, I could've been giving my boyfriend some head or something."

"Pleeease, your man is in the living room."

"I know where my man is, I said my boyfriend." Aiyana said jokingly.

When Kaitlynn caught on to the joke her jaw

dropped.

She covered her mouth with her hand and pointed at Aiyana with the other hand. "You crazy, if I busted you like that, Mannish would kill you, dude and me."

"You ain't never lieing girl."

"Where is my nephew at?" Kaitlynn asked.

"You didn't see him in the front? I told his little ass to stay in the yard."

Aiyana grabbed the Boost twoway radio off of the nightstand and flipped it open. She pushed a button on the side and started hollering into it.

"Naj! Where you at boy?!"

When Naj's phone squawked it startled him and his little buddy Shavoree. He quickly covered it with his hand but it was too late.

"Hey, what was that?" said the man, breaking his stride of pumping and sweating on top of the prostitute in the back seat of his Lincoln Town Car. The kids had noticed the car bouncing up and down and snuck up to it. They had been peeking in on a real live porno scene. The man's face appeared in the window.

"Oh shit!" the boys gasped in unison.

They ran up someone's driveway and through a gap in the back wooden fence. They emerged on the next block.

As Naj stepped up onto his porch he answered his mom's next summons.

"Boy, where are you at?"

"On the porch Momma."

"Come in here."

He entered the house and went into his mother's room looking innocent. Aiyana gave him a look to tell him that she knew him, while he was standing there acting like she didn't. But she merely said, "Your Auntie wanted to see you."

"Hi Auntie Kaitlynn." Naj said, giving her a hug.

"What were you doing?" Kaitlynn asked him.

"Nothing."

"Wanna go with me?"

"Where?"

"I gotta run some errands. We can eat whatever you want."

"What if what I want to eat is only sold at Six Flags Magic Mountain?"

"Then you gonna be wanting. You wanna come with me or what?"

"Yeah, lemme' change my clothes real fast."

He ran to his room and took off the soiled jeans and t-shirt he was wearing. He put on his favorite red and white Biz-e-Bee Apparel sweat suit and matching Air Jordans. He tied a doo rag on his head and tilted his ball cap to the side and came back.

"Okay I'm ready Auntie."

As they were headed out through the living room, they looked at Mannish sleeping in his big fat Lazy Boy recliner. The television had a frozen frame of several police cars riddled with bullet holes.

CHAPTER SEVEN

While navigating through the quiet community in her Range Rover, Kaitlynn asked Naj how things were going in school. He didn't answer right away because he was distracted by the sight of the Town Car on a different street but still bouncing up and down. A big smile was on Naj's face.

"What's that big smile about? Is school going that well?"

He just looked at her. He thought about school. Last week me and my friend wrote up an anonymous love letter addressed to the Principal. *I handed it to the Principal personally, sealed of course, so that it would seem I didn't know what was in it. Although, I made sure to hint that it came from one of the prettiest staff members. It was hilarious to us how the principal acted after that. His style of dress had improved. His old dirt covered car was blingy, blingy.*

"Yeah, I like school."

"What's your favorite subject?"

"P.E. of course."

"Okay you got me there. But I'm talking about academically."

"Aca what?"

"Academically. You know, knowledge you gotta get out of books."

"Oh, well that's gotta be math, cause when I get older, I'ma have to be counting all my daddy's money for him, cause he gonna be too old."

They stopped at Office Depot. Kaitlynn replenished her supplies of paper, printer ink, staples, paper clips, a couple highlighters and a few pens. She made a run to Kinko's and the post office.

"You don't get tired of school sometimes Auntie?" Naj asked.

"Yeah, I do but I also see the big picture. Lots of people just hope everything's gonna be alright. You have to take chances in life, but you would be smart to go where the odds are on your side. The chances are that if you stay in school you'll do good in life."

"My teacher said he went to college to be a engine or something..."

"A mechanic?"

"No, I think he said engine. He said he was gonna be rich..."

"Oh, you mean an engineer."

"Yeah that. He said he was supposed to be rich, but he just ended up being a school teacher and they don't pay him anything."

She had to laugh at what Naj was thinking.

"They have to pay him something. There's a law that says there is a minimum your job has to pay you. It's about $8 an hour and I'm sure he gets more than that. But compared to what he was dreaming of getting as an engineer, it probably feels like nothing. Like I said, it's what the odds are, which means some people aren't going to make it, but most will. There are odds to everything. Like most drug dealers get killed or go to jail but a few make it work for them. And maybe your teacher was thinking about the money instead of having a love for what he chose to do with his life."

Naj was nodding his head. Kaitlynn knew she put something on his mind. Mission accomplished. She always tried to spill something on the kids whenever it was appropriate.

They went to her dorm at the university. Kaitlynn shared it with a white girl named Meagan from Europe that was on an exchange student program. Meagan was fascinated with the thugs at the school. She was on her seventh boyfriend. She was getting the total urban experience.

When Kaitlynn and Naj walked in, Meagan's newest boyfriend was laid back on the couch with his feet up on the coffee table, eating some Chinese food with some chopsticks. Kaitlynn looked at the rice he was spilling on the floor with disgust.

"It's obvious you're not domesticated, but I'ma tell you anyway." Kaitlynn was waving her index finger back and forth between the rice and the floor and his feet on the table. "This is unacceptable."

"Oh I'm sorry Ma."

"I know you are and don't call me Ma."

Kaitlynn went to her room to fill out some forms and prepare some other papers. The thirty minutes that it took her, Naj spent playing X Box with Meagan's boyfriend. Needless to say, Naj won every game. Afterwards Kaitlynn gave Naj a tour of the school campus on the way to the administration building. The landscaping was impressive. The student traffic was light.

Everyone was dressed down as usual. Jeans, sweatshirts or t-shirts and sneakers was the common dress code. There were students parked all over campus reading and conversing in groups. Kaitlynn's heart quickened when she saw a glimpse of one of the male students going into the gym.

On a Tuesday? Kaitlynn thought to herself.

She and Naj got some food from the cafeteria and had a picnic in the grass area.

An hour later Kaitlynn was in Mannish's driveway dropping Naj off. She watched him walk into the house.

There were other eyes behind tinted windows parked a few houses up. When Kaitlynn pulled off, the Grand Marquis pulled from the curb and headed the other direction.

CHAPTER EIGHT

Aiyana snuggled her head back into her man's chest to finish watching a bootleg DVD of an unreleased movie after letting Naj in. When the movie went off Mannish grabbed his keys and headed for the door.

"Where are you going?" she asked already knowing there was nothing she could say to impede his mission.

She also knew he would be evasive.

"Gotta make a run Baby, be back."

That didn't mean tonight. It just simply meant "be back."

He hopped in his newly purchased INFINITI QX56 SUV. It had a snow white paint job and matching 26" rims that looked like they weren't spinning when the truck moved. They were called Floaters. There was no one else in the city with them, so he was the man. The new INFINITI was a show stopper alone, plus while the ballers were still spinning when they stopped, his wheels never moved even if he was speeding. He hit the Crenshaw strip, a must, even if it was out of your way. That's how it's done in the City of Angels when you're shining.

If you were on 135th Street and you were going to 77th Street, the playa way would be to go all the way to the westside, hit Crenshaw to see and be seen, then take the closest main street to 77th Street back to the eastside.

Mannish's destination was Cherise's house. She lived on 79th Street and Crenshaw Blvd. He parked in the driveway and used his key to catch her off guard. She was in the bedroom lotioning up after her bath. Ashanti's CD played in the background. Aromatherapy candles burned and faintly lit the room.

"Now that's ass." Mannish said, startling her.

"Oh, boy, you scared me. Where you been?"

"You know I make a lot of moves."

"Well, can you make more moves this way?"

"Yeah, all the time. My son in his room sleep?"

"Naw, he over Big Mama's house, been over there since yesterday. She been over there by herself lately. Taj drives her nerves but he keeps her spirit up."

While she spoke Mannish's eyes traced her curves.

Before long he couldn't resist her naked body's temptation any longer. He pushed her back on the bed and laid on top of her.

"Lemme' get your spirit up." he told her, kissing her lips. He pressed his tongue into her mouth. Cherise could taste the Hawaiian Punch he drank on the way over. He let his tongue travel down along the contour of her neck until it found a nipple.

"Ahhh!" she exhaled.

He kissed her on her stomach and goose bumps covered her flesh. His face disappeared between her legs. She orgasmed immediately with a flick of his tongue. She trembled from the implosion.

"Nigga… you… you… you… still… ain't… said… where you... been… aaahhh… Maaanniiisshh!"

He penetrated her. She hadn't noticed him pull his pants down.

"You scanless." she exclaimed.

"What? Take it back or i'ma stop." he thrusted with intensity.

"A good scanless, you a good scanless baby."

He gave her some more power strokes.

"I'm sor… sor… soreee.e.e.e. You feel soo good, fuck me daddy, fuck me daddy."

He laid the dick like he was supposed to. He pulled her down to the foot of the bed. She turned around and put her feet on the floor and spread them apart making a pyramid with her ass in the air and elbows on the bed in her provocative 6:15 position. He navigated his dick through her voluptuous ass cheeks to penetrate her pussy from the back and rode her like the stallion she was. He released his load and collapsed on the floor breathless.

She took him into her mouth and indulged in his sweetness mixed with her sweetness. Cherise laid on the floor next to her addiction. And put her head on his chest.

"Mannish, you know I love you right?"

"Yeah."

He felt a conversation brewing, something insignificant.

"I want you to go on a helicopter ride with me. You know you owe me for when you missed my cousin Susie's wedding."

He avoided giving an answer. "Oh yeah, how was that, was it cool?"

"It was off the hook. They had Jaheim sing for them. You know it was in Calabasas right? The whole place was decorated with the same color theme as the bride's dress and the groom's tux and that was peach and white. The ceremony was outside in the back in a big grassy area with a waterfall…"

He zoned out.

I don't give a fuck about none a that. I need to get up outta here. Naw, I ain't gonna leave. Maybe I should just put my dick in her mouth.

"…and after we danced, all kind of waiters started rolling tables of food out…"

"Baby?" Mannish interrupted in a low tone.
"Huh?"
"Shut the fuck up."
"Nigga fuck you."
"Not like that, but fa' real…" then his attention was diverted. "Ay who is that with all that fuckin' music outside!" he yelled, as he peeked out the window.

A dark blue Chevy Tahoe sat in front of the house rumbling the block. Mannish looked at Cherise heading in the kitchen punching digits on her cellphone.

"You expecting company?" he asked her.
"Boy no!"
"Well I'm bout to go put a hole in this fool's thoughts for thinking he could post up in front of this house on some bullshit."

Mannish picked up his American Express pistol *never leave home without it*. He went out the back door, but when he reached the front the truck was gone.

Lucky nigga, making all that gotdamn noise. Who was he looking for anyway? Maybe he was on the wrong block.

"Yeah, so I'ma holla at you tomorrow." Cherise said, then pushed the end button as Mannish walked back into the house. She continued talking to no one, "Huh, girl what you say? Yeah I know, but look Mannish here so I'ma get back girl." Click.

Mannish eyed her suspiciously, he told her,

"Ay look, run me some bath water and light some more of them candles."

She did as he asked and when she was done, he sat his gun on the back of the toilet and locked the door. After about a half an hour Cherise tried to open the door but it was locked.

"Mannish!" she yelled through the door. "Why you lock the door?"

"Cause I'm busy."

He relaxed in the tub and reflected on things until he fell asleep. Cherise woke him up thirty minutes later by knocking on the door. He got out, dried off, put his gun on the nightstand and got into the bed butt naked beside her. When he did, she rolled over on top of him and put the tip of her nose to the tip of his.

"I have something to tell you, don't get mad okay?"

"What's up?"

"The dude in the truck was for me."

Before she even finished her sentence, she noticed the color deep in his eyes turn red.

"What!"

"We ain't fuckin'. He came to take me..."

Before she could finish he slung her 125 pound frame off of him and onto the floor, swept his gun off the night stand and landed on top of her.

"You trick ass bitch! You got niggas coming where my son live! While I'm up in this mutha fucka! My truck in the driveway and shit. Now a nigga I don't know, know where I be. You knew who it was this whole time you bitch?!" He grabbed her by the jaw and forced the barrel of the gun into her mouth. "How long you been fuckin' around?"

She couldn't answer even if she wanted to with a gun in her mouth. Tears wet her face. He jumped up and went to the closet to get dressed. She began to climb up on the bed.

He spun around pointing the gun at her. "Get back on the floor where you belong, snake ass bitch!"

"I ain't getting on no fuckin' floor in my house! I said I ain't fuck the nigga!" By now she was yelling and crying. "I just met him! He Vallawn's friend! He was gonna take me out! You don't take me out! You don't even come around but when you feel like it and you fuck me even less!"

"That's my pussy! I hit it when I feel like I wanna hit it!"

"Okay keep thinking that."

"What that mean?"

"Hmmm."

"Fuck this!"

He dressed and left. He flipped through his music collection in the driveway. The stock sound system had an mp3 player that held thousands of songs. He found a song to fit his mood and turned it up. He let the four 15 inch JL audio

W7's pump "A Bitch Is A Bitch." by Ice Cube. He set off all the car alarms down the block.

He let the whole song play before he left. Then he went home and pressed play on the dvd remote. He watched Heat until he dozed off. He was awakened in the morning by a phone call. It was Big Mama.

"What's up Momma?"

"Sittin' hea tryna wake up yuh lazy boy, den I'm gon' make sum breffiss. You know Ty goin' ta court today. Sum public defenduh called me dis mo'nin' said Ty be in court 1:30."

"I'ma be over there. I'ma eat with yall."

"Alright." Click.

"Boy if yuh dont get yo lazy butt up I'ma...no, I know what, yuh ain't gonna watch none a dem cartoons latuh."

Big Mama shook Taj. He didn't move but giggled under the covers. "I'ma get my belt." Big Mama said. When she returned Taj was gone. "Where da hell..."

She opened the closet door. No Taj. Big Mama was too old to bend down to look under the bed and Taj knew it.

He laid under the bed with his little hand over his mouth to muffle his giggles. He slung a shoe out the bedroom door into the hallway. Big Mama turned around realizing he was in the hall. When she got to the hall and saw the shoe, she thought, *Oh you wanna play huh?*

He'd snuck from under the bed and into the

closet while her back was turned. Then he came out of the closet with a sheet over his head.

"Booo, booo I am the ghost of Taj. You must let him watch cartoons whenever he wants or I'll haunt you forever."

Then he snarled in his best ghost impression he'd learned from watching Scooby Doo. Big Mama knocked him to the floor with a pillow.

"Da ghost betta get in da tub."

"You know ghosts like pancakes right Big Mama?"

Soon as she opened the refrigerator the phone rang.

Dis betta not be Mable I swear dis woman miserable. I gots crazy churrins too. She ack like she da only one. I swear if dis her...

"Hello."

"Gladys?"

"Hey Mable, I know'd it twas you."

"You know dat no good son a mine back in jail again?"

"I know yuh told me yestuhday an' da day befo' Mable."

"Girl he done sold sum drugs ta da po'lece an' when da man pulled out his badge, da chile buss da po'leceman in da head. Dey talkin' bout sum 25 ta life, Chile I dont know whut I'm gonna do."

"Well Mable, yuh know I aint no stranguh ta none a dat.Ty got court today fa' dat stuff whut happen last week. He been laid up in dat firmry dey got in da jail til da otha day. An' I gots ta get redta go. I talk ta yuh latuh." Click, without a goodbye.

Big Mama got out some pork sausages.

I know Mannish gon' say sumthin' bout dis pork.

Come home from jail an' caint eat dis an' caint eat dat. I been eatin' 'erthang on pig from da roota ta da toota since I was shorta dan da pig. I aint neva seent nobody fall ova from eatin' no pork. She chuckled to herself. I tell yuh, deese kids today, dey need ta be worried bout whut dey doin' 'erday dats killin' 'em.

"Can I watch cartoons now Big Mama?"

"Come eat first. How yuh want yuh eggs?"

"Scrambled."

While Big Mama was whipping up the eggs, Mannish walked in.

"Momma, I told you to always lock your door."

"My do' is fine da way it is. I aint stole nothin' from nobody an' aint gots nothin' ta steal."

"But still."

"Still whut? Iffen a fool come in hea tryna stick me up, he'll just be practicin'. Go wash yuh hans an' come eat."

CHAPTER NINE

Big Mama handed Mannish the directions to the court. He looked on the paper for what courtroom because he damn sure knew where the building was, with all the trouble he's been in all his life. It was a slow day and the court house was pretty empty which raised Mannish's anxiety level. He had always made it a point to never go around the justice system intentionally. It's usually so much movement in the courthouse that he figured he could dip in, chill in the back with Big Mama until Ty's case was heard and then dip out.

They stepped in Courtroom 101 and only five people were in the audience.

Mannish noticed the court secretary. She was a black female, about 33 yrs old, about 5'5" in height. Her hair was cut in a short conservative style. She smiled. Mannish smiled. He led Big Mama and Taj down the back row of seats to the corner.

About ten minutes had passed when the bailiff said, "All rise. Presiding the Honorable Judge Joseph Ryder."

The Judge walked in and took a seat on his throne. He shuffled through some papers on his desk, surveyed the courtroom and called the first case. Another bailiff came from a rear door that led into the jury booth with a light skinned teenager with curly hair in a blue jumpsuit. He looked like he hadn't done much. Maybe he would get released today.

The Judge spoke. "Calvin Warner."

A white man in a grey suit, blue shirt and burgundy tie stood up and said, "Present Your Honor with counsel Public Defender John Handover."

The Judge continued, "Calvin Warner, you have been charged with four counts of murder in the first degree. Two counts of attempted murder. Four counts of firing a weapon in city limits. Two counts of firing a weapon into an inhabited vehicle. One count of evading the police. One count of resisting arrest. One count of assaulting an officer."

"Guilty!" The boy blurted out.

"Ah, Your Honor." The prosecutor said. "I filed a motion for Calvin Warner to be tried as an adult. It should be in your files."

The Judge flipped through some papers in the file.

"Oh yes, here it is. I agree, the severity of the case does warrant the request. I will let the case be transferred to a higher court."

Mannish sat in the audience and watched the little dude's life just get taken away. Mannish didn't know the details of the case but he figured if the boy was ready to plead guilty, they probably had him pretty good, maybe even had the weapon. Somebody probably told the boy that the most Juvenile Court could do was hold him until he was 25 yrs. old. So he knew it, the Judge knew it and the prosecutor definitely knew it. In Superior Court they would hold him his entire natural life.

Next on the docket was a big, tall youngster, 16 yrs. old.

He looked like he was 21 yrs. old with his full beard and rough features. He got caught with two twenty dollar crack rocks. They gave him probation. Let the games begin. Unlike the first kid who they knew they couldn't afford to let back out on the street, this kid hadn't got caught big enough, so they would give him some more rope to hang himself.

They figure he isn't going to change so they would just keep light tabs on him. Even cut him loose from probation early.

So after being under supervision for a while, the freedom would make him feel like he could do his thing again. The one time he slips up the courts are going to sit him down for a minute and his minute could last ten years. That's why they're called "One Time" because they could jerk off on the job and slip up a thousand times and it doesn't hurt noone, but all you have to do is slip one time.

The third case on the list was Ty.

"Tyshon Johnson."

The bailiff walked him in. He walked in and scanned the room. His eyes landed on Big Mama. She dropped a tear.

Ty mouthed, "Don't cry."

"Present Your Honor, with counsel Public Defender John Handover."

Mannish noticed it was the same guy for all three of the young defendants. He didn't even see another Public Defender around. He thought. *He must be handling everybody's case back there. He didn't even try to argue to keep Calvin's case in Juvenile Court. First thing I gotta do is get Ty a real lawyer.*

"You are charged with attempted murder and causing great bodily injury to a one Derrick Smitty. How do you plea?" The judge asked.

"Ah, Your Honor, for this case I filed a motion for it to be transferred to Superior Court."

Oh hell naw!

"Your Honor!" Mannish hollered out jumping to his feet. "I don't think you can grant that motion yet."

"And who might you be?"

"I am family of the defendant."

"And why can't I grant this motion? Please,

humor me young man." The Judge said condescendingly.

"Because Tyshon doesn't have his attorney present to argue in his defense."

"And who do you think Mr. Handover is?"

"A Pubic Pretend... I mean a Public Defender."

"He's Tyshon Johnson's Public Defender."

"We have a family attorney. We were only informed this morning about the hearing by the Pubic Pret... I mean Public Defender, which was very unprofessional. It was too short of a notice for the lawyer to make it. He can be here tomorrow if you will permit a continuance for a day."

"Very well, this case is continued for tomorrow morning at 8:30am."

The Judge banged the gavel and went into his back room. Right away Mannish started working his cellphone. His first call was to Jay.

"Speak on it." Jay answered.

"What up homie, who that lawyer that got your lil brother off that case last year?"

"I don't know, moms got the info though."

"Ay I need that ASAP. I'm talking bout ASA right now."

"Ay what's goin' on?"

"Just get me the number. Hit me right back." Click.

Mannish looked around as he thought of who else he could call when his eyes landed on the secretary. She was walking down the hall.

"Ay, Ma, lemme' ask you something. You gotta

know some good lawyers."

"Huh? I thought you had a family attorney."

"Yeah well that was bullshit, so now I gotta find one with a quickness, you gotta know one that can get my nephew out of this shit."

"Why would I want to help him? He sounds like a danger to society. Some jail time might do him some good, rehabilitate him from that destructive behavior."

"What the fuck you talking about?! He ain't even been arraigned yet and you got him guilty already! You punk ass bitch, the system got you brainwashed! My bad, I thought you was a sistah." Mannish about faced and headed toward the exit.

After Miss Secretary picked up her face off of the ground she said, "Hey hold up. You're right, I'm sorry.

I shouldn't pre-judge him like that. There's an attorney named Paul Downing. He's never lost a case in Joseph Ryder's court." Then in a low whisper, she leaned in and said, "He and the Judge are friends but he's expensive."

"You got a number?"

"Yeah, I have his card in my desk."

She jetted back in the courtroom. She came back out with the card and handed it to Mannish.

"Good looking out." he said then exited the building.

Big Mama and Taj were in the front getting

hot dogs with bacon wrapped around them from the man with the cart. Mannish dialed the number on the card.

"Hello, Paul Downing's office. This is Sherry."

"Is Mr. Downing in?"

"No he's in court. What is the nature of your call?"

"I need to hire him as representation for a juvenile named Tyshon Johnson due in court tomorrow morning at 8:30."

"Ah sir, that's very short notice, we don't normally..."

"Listen! This is a very serious situation. I was referred to him and I was told that he was good at what he does and I would hope that included client consideration. Tell him to call me ASAP. We're due in court in the morning at 8:30. Do you see my number on your caller ID?"

"Yes." she answered.

"Good and tell him money ain't a thang."

"Okay sir I'll relay the message." Click.

They were at Big Mama's house when Jay called back to give Mannish the number to the lawyer, but before Jay had called, Paul Downing had already called. They had a quick conversation about the details of the case and had an agreement to meet in court in the morning and an agreement for an exchange of $10,000. Mannish told Big Mama he was going home and left.

She let Taj watch cartoons in the bedroom

while she watched her soap operas in the living room on the 19 inch TV sitting on top of the floor model that hasn't worked since she used to watch Diff'rent Strokes on it. Big Mama leaned back in her old recliner and kicked her feet up. She thought about the days when she used to laugh with her husband at the sitcoms on that same floor model sitting in the same recliner.

Oh da' good ole days. We struggled but we was happy. I remembuh catchin' da' bus home from work 'er evenin' an' den still havin' ta walk a mile ta da' house. I remembuh one day I was pissed off because my husband had lost all da' rent money da' night befo' at some gamblin' shack on da' eastside. He had even done loss his weddin' ring. It 'twas Mable dat told me bout it. Mable knew because her man, or as da' kids say nowadays, her baby daddy, cause dey had plenty kids but neva got married, was dere dat night. I figured Mable was tellin' me sos we could break up so dat Mable could have my husband. Dats da' main reason I didnt kick his ass out da' house. Dat an' when I confronted him bout it, he admitted it. Da' next night Paw Paw came home wit da' ring, da' rent money an' a warrant fa his arrest fa robbin' a supuh market. Damn fool. He did a lil time an' was back home in juss a lil time. Whut I wouldn't give ta have my man right now.

CHAPTER TEN

Big Mama, Mannish, Taj and Shawna met Paul Downing in the court building at 8:00am. Mannish gave him $10,000 wrapped in a rubber band and the lawyer gave his word that he would handle everything.

When the hearing was over it was determined that the case would stay in Juvenile Court. When the court day was over they transported Ty back to his temporary housing. The first person that stepped up to Ty when he walked in was his homie from the neighborhood, Champ.

The charge Champ faced was a fender bender that turned into a kidnap for ransom.

"What up Ty, what they talkin' bout?"

"Nothing really, the lawyer said he needed some time to review the case and talk to the victim, that's Derrick's punk ass. But he did stop them mutha fuckas from tryna send me to get tried as a adult though. You know I was scared as a mutha fucka, bout ta drop guacamole in my draws. But what's been crackin' up in here today? Yesterday while I was gone you got one of your teeth knocked out."

"Ah nigga fuck you, where that nigga at now?"

"In the infirmary, but I put 'im there when I found out what happened and I did it with one hand. You talkin' bout where he at now like you put 'im there or something."

"I didn't need you to do shit! I was just waitin' for the right time."

Ty laughed. "You my nigga, I know how you get down from when that fool tried to rush me when I first came up in here and you choked him out."

"You betta recognize, but peep I got some pictures in the mail today. My sister hooked me up. It's a bunch of bitches from around the way. I got pussy shots and everything."

~COUNT TIME~

Count time blasted over the loud speakers. Everyone headed for their cells. The cells were more like rooms, wall to wall rooms with white doors with blue numbers on them. The unit was two floors with the dayroom in the center and TVs hanging from the ceiling down to eight feet from the floor. Everyone was assigned blue plastic chairs to use in the cell or dayroom. Ty and his cellmate, Champ, laid down to rest on their beds for a while. Ty stared at the ceiling with his one good hand behind his head. He thought about his Momma and how she was all messed up on the same stuff he sold. She had been smoking as long as he knew. It pissed him off thinking about all the dope she must smoke.

Shit, I'm out here competing for fiends and strugglin' on the block. She could be spending that money with me, instead of them niggas on El Segundo by her apartment.

"Ay Ty, you said your G-Moms came to court today too?" Champ asked.

"Yeah, but you know I stay wit G-Moms, she like my real momma."

"That's cool. I wish I could see my grandmother again, even if it was to come see me in court. She been dead for a few years now. I miss G-Moms fa' real homie. I used to go over her house every weekend and she used to make me go to church and shit, Jehovah's Witnesses at that and I used to never wanna go, you feel me? But now I'd go anywhere wit her. That was my girl."

Ty didn't answer, he just thought to himself.

Yeah I am lucky to have Big Mama. If it wasn't for her, aint no telling where I'd be. Probably in a foster home somewhere.

A week passed and Ty was back in court. It was immediately evident the lawyer had been handling his business because the case was dismissed.

Ty later found out that the lawyer had spoken with Derrick's Public Defender. Derrick was charged with the same thing so they both were looking at the same amount of time. So it was in the best interest of both of them not to pursue prosecution as victims. Knowing that in turn the State would pick up the case, the attorney exercised his friendship card to make sure that didn't happen. The charges remained dropped.

Ty returned to the jail to await the update on the computer for his release. Some of the boys were glad to hear that he was leaving because they didn't like him and some of the boys hated to hear that he was leaving because they didn't like him. He had that swagger.

"Champ, I gotta get back to the land. You got lil Ron and Ivan in here wit you now. Plus you ain't gonna be here but a couple months anyway right?"

"Yeah you go do yo thang, you said you gonna put me down when I touch down, act like you know, nigga."

"Let's go blow some greenery before they call me."

"Come on, I'ma roll a fatty, send my nigga outta here on cloud 9. You gonna think them cheap ass jail house shoes is moon boots keeping your ass to the ground. You clean the toilet out while I roll the shit up."

The plumbing system for the toilets in jail institutions worked on a suction system. If all the water was cleared out you could hear the suction sucking in anything in the atmosphere within close proximity, in this case, weed smoke.

"Naw fool, you handle the toilet. I'ma roll the shit up." Ty said.

As usual when they got high they started rapping.

Ty-killa rappin' off the head
When I stick yuh up don't move
Cough and yuh dead
12 gauge blast so it's like
off witcha head
Put yuh mind on the street
I'm locked down, but my mind on the street
Gotta get back to my nine on the street...
Champ cut in.
Hold up this Champ posted up like a food stamp
Stick and move in other words I fuck and vamp
Who knows what Champ'll do besides act up
Make niggas feel like, they got hit by a Mack truck
When they act tough
And when they get back up, they run for back up
Few months got a plan wit my nigga
Running the streets like I'm the Man wit my nigga
And gonna do what it take
like takin' out fools who fake

We tryna get the cake like a fat kid
Fact is the knife is under my mattress...
"Ay! You a fool fa' that Champ."
"I'm just sayin' though. At least I keep it real."

~CHOW TIME~

Came over the speaker and all the inmates lined up against the wall to file into the chow hall. Ty caught the eyes of a young troublemaker from across town. Ty's response to the evil look was "Nigga, you got a problem?!"

"Yeah, you goin' home huh? Who you tell on?"

Ty about faced without a word and went back to his room. Realizing his arm hadn't recuperated yet, he grabbed a sock, unlocked his locker and put the lock in the sock. He went back into the dayroom and before the troublemaker could say something else slick out of his mouth, he caught the locked sock with the top of his head. When he fell to the floor it startled his four other young Conrads who had been standing around waiting to see how he was going to bust Ty out. It took a few seconds but they jumped on Ty and Champ. A couple of allies from around the way, Lil Ron and Ivan, jumped in to help Ty and Champ. Ty kicked one of the Conrads in the mouth. His lips burst open like a hollow point exiting a tomato and three teeth fell to the ground. Lil Ron got the living shit beat out of him by two of the Conrads. The Correctional Officers intervened while Champ was kicking his opponent a new asshole. Everybody went to the box (solitary confinement) while the matter was investigated.

The next day Ty was released and Mannish was there to pick him up. "What's up Mannish." Ty yelled over the loud music. "INFINITI truck huh, when you cop this big dog? This mutha fucka off the hook."

Mannish turned the music down. "Fuck the truck lil nigga! What the fuck happened that day you got shot? What the fuck was you thinking fool? Everybody was at the house chillin'. You almost gave Big Mama a heart attack, almost got yourself killed and almost got a gang of time!" By now Mannish was fuming, and trying to restrain himself. "What was that shit about?" He spoke through clenched teeth.

"That nigga shot me cause I was his whooping ass."

"Rewind to why you was whooping his ass."

"Oh, well, you see what had happened was…" sigh. he paused a few seconds. "Aight look, the week before all that shit happened I found nine ounces in the attic. I knew it had to be you who stashed it there and I took it. Not to steal it but to sell it and give you the money to show you that I was bout this. I got the money for six already.

One of my boys had the money for one that

I was gonna pick up later that day. Derrick had two ounces for a week and he was playin' wit my... I mean your money. We was arguin' about it and he told me to get it like Tyson got his, so I punched him and punished him and he bust the heat."

So many thoughts raced through Mannish's mind.

First thing, I was careless for leaving that dope at Big Mama's house. For real, I forgot about it. That means it's kinda my fault. I'm supposed to be his role model cause he my sister's boy. But I'm portraying an image to him that the street life and the dope game is all good. This boy almost lost his life in more than one way.

Mannish was feeling guilty as hell but he still needed to straighten Ty out.

He barked, "Nigga you stole my shit, who said I wanted it sold!"

Ty thought, *either you was gonna sell it or smoke it,* but kept his thoughts to himself.

"This shit ain't no kid game, this a real life grown man game yuh young ass is tryna play out here. You can fuckin' get swallowed up by either the system or the Grim Reaper.

"You see your ass already in the system but you probably think it's behind the shooting, but it's behind the dope, the dope started it like most everything else."

"Mannish, my bad for stealing, but all that other shit, you can kill that noise. I still got the money and I can get the rest. I'm tryna get on. I'm out here, been out here on these streets. Big Mama watch her TV shows and she in bed by six. What you think I been doin' all these years when she told me go outside and play? What you think I did? I know all them alleys and rooftops. I know everybody in the hood and everything that's crackin'. I'm comfortable out there. I just slipped on some dum dum, I knew he had a gun too. I was just trippin', but I learned from that."

Mannish shook his head. "You ain't listenin."

"Nah, you ain't listenin'!" Ty shot back.

No one said another word. The CD changed. Somewhere in the middle of the song Jadakiss said if he get popped he ain't goin' into shock. He was gettin' acquainted wit the niggas in general pop. Ty felt that.

They parked in front of Big Mama's house.

"You need to pay attention to what you doin' before you drive your grandmother to the grave. You lucky she got old and can't get in yuh ass like she used to do me. Anyway go in the house, I'm outta here."

When Ty walked in the door, Big Mama was sitting in her chair and his Momma Shawna was sitting on the couch.

"Ty sit down." Shawna said.

Ty rolled his eyes up in his head with a sigh. *Here we go.*

"Boy I know you didnt juss roll yo eyes at yuh

Momma!" Yelled Big Mama. "Sit yo narrow behind down.

You done gone crazy! I thought sittin' in dat jail woulda learned yuh sumthin. But yuh go ta actin' a fool on yuh way out."

Shawna said, "What's wrong with you Ty?" It was barely audible, conscious that her position was extremely compromised. A disciplinarian crackhead is an oxymoron. Not even expecting an answer she asked again. "Ty what's wrong with you?"

"Nothin', I guess I just let my friends get me in trouble."

He said that just to pacify them.

"Well I guess yuh needs sum new friends befo' yuh let 'em get yuh inta sumthin' worsa." Big Mama continued.

"Since yuh friends is trouble aint no need in yuh goin' outside fa da next few months. Yuh needs ta heal up anyways. Gon' ta yuh room."

Ty went to his room without protest.

"Shawna, das yo chile, you see he needs sum guidance an' Lord knows I caint be runnin' in behind dat boy. I done give yuh da' numba ta dem folks, das leadin' yuh ta da' water, but I caint make yuh drink it. Da' Bible tell yuh he makes yuh lie down in da' green pastures an' leads yuh besides da still waters, but yuh gosta drink it fa yuhself baby."

CHAPTER ELEVEN

Shawna excused herself to avoid the inevitable lecture and went outside. She saw Mannish's truck down the street.

I thought he was gone, he can take me home.

He had just gotten out and was approaching two guys on the sidewalk.

Shawna called out "Mannish!"

He looked back and saw that Shawna was calling him and stepping off the porch. He turned his attention back to the two guys.

"What's up Mannish." they said at the same time, looking at his truck.

"Ain't seen you in a minute. See you still on top of thangs, put your boys down wit somethin'. We need to get some income comin' in, feel me." the one named Crimey said.

They called him Crimey because he was down for whatever and would never get caught no matter the situation. Even if his crime partner got caught he would be back in the hood ready for another lick. Half of the dudes from the hood that were in jail were his crime partners. Anytime a homie would get caught and see another homie in jail, one would say, "Jo-Jo was my crimey." The other would be like, "Jo-Jo was my crimey too! That nigga is lucky."

There was never any speculation about him working with the police or anything like that. He was just slick as a can of oil and had more moves than a can of worms. He just never translated it into seriously getting paid.

"Yeah real shit, we need to get some chips, niggas got bills." said Andre'.

"You fools don't wanna do nothin' but hang out and beat mutha fuckas up. I been tellin' y'all for years, you gonna either bang or ball. Y'all from the hood, we all from the hood. But are you gonna get money or gang bang?" Mannish commented seriously.

"Mannish, I want some money." Andre' said.

"Yeah, that's what your mouth say. I'll holla at you when I want somebody beat up." Mannish told 'em.

Crimey cut in, "Yeah Andre' could temple a mutha fucka for you."

Andre' looked at him like *fool shut up. You talk too much.*

"Temple a mutha fucka, what's that?" Mannish asked, not understanding.

Crimey kept talking. "You know this fool been doin' that karate shit at that school on Slauson since he was ass high to a midget. His skills for whoopin' a nigga ass ain't natural. See my shit is natural. My daddy was a nigga beata." Jo Jo held his fists up. "God gave me these. But anyway this nigga know how to poke a nigga on the side of his head in his temple and dead him on the spot…"

Trying to cut him off, Andre' said, "This fool is off the hook, always talkin' crazy and shit."

Crimey said, "Mannish you know that dopefiend named Cook?"

Mannish replied, "Yeah I heard they found him dead but they couldn't figure out what hap…" he stopped short, realizing that Crimey was telling the truth. "Ay boy you got hands like that? Or fingers I should say."

"Yeah Man I know a lot of stuff but don't nobody really know what I know. This fool ain't even supposed to know. He just happened to be there that day I hit that dopefiend."

They looked up and Shawna was coming down the street.

"Where you going?" Mannish asked her.

"I was coming to ask you if you could take me home, can you?"

"Yeah come on, I could make a stop while I'm over that way."

Mannish told the guys he'd holler at them later and left to take Shawna home. He headed to Hawthorne, turned onto Yukon and 126th Street and parked in front of a dope spot that Shawna was very familiar with. It was right around the corner from her apartment. Mannish promised her that he'd be right back and got out. Shawna stayed in the truck. Mannish hit a button on his chirp phone and said something into it. Someone peeked out the window and opened the door before he got to it.

"What's up Big Dog." Will said.

"Ay, I just stopped by cause I was passing thru. You finish wit that? If you ain't I ain't trippin'. Just checking to see if you playin' the game or playin' wit the game."

"Naw, neva that. You know me, I stay ready. It ain't all gone but I could break you off what I owe you right now. You got anotha half a thang on you?"

"Naw, but I could bring it back..."

"OH NOOOOO!!! PLEASE DON'T FUCK ME!!!" came a scream from the back room.

"What the fuck is that?" Mannish inquired.

"Oh, the lil homies is fuckin' wit a basehead."

Will and Mannish stepped into the back room to see what was going on. One of the young boys kicked the basehead in his ass.

"Ain't nobody tryna fuck yo stupid ass. Now take all yo fuckin' clothes off punk!"

When he was stripped completely nude he was ordered into the bathtub. Mannish just watched silently and wondered what they were going to do to this dude.

"Hey let's pour some boiling water on his ass." said the one with the cornrolls in the Shaq high school throwback jersey.

Chuck said, "Are you stupid?"

"Aight, let's make 'im drink some bleach." Throwback suggested.

"Nigga shut up!" Chuck said and went into

the kitchen to find something, anything to humiliate the crackhead.

He came back with two bottles of honey and handed one to Throwback. They proceeded to splatter honey all over the naked man. It almost seemed like some sick freak shit until Chuck burst open a five pound bag of flour on him.

"Now put your fuckin' clothes back on!"

"Can I take a shower first?"

"Hell naw, now put your shit back on before I think of somethin' else to do to your punk ass!"

He got dressed, they handed him a fifty dollar rock and put him out the house. Mannish was glad to see the crackhead was going out the back door. He didn't want his sister to see her husband looking like shit right then. When Travis left, Mannish inquired on who the dude was like he didn't already know.

"Ah just some crackhead the young homies be gettin' rec(recreation) on. They be fuckin' wit 'im just cause. He been comin' thru for a minute. A while back he got some credit but never paid it back so they whooped him. It evolved into whenever he'd ask for credit they would just whoop him first, then let 'im have it for free. Sometimes they'll be bored and he'll come thru tryna buy somethin' but they'll work 'im over for the hell of it. You know befo' you started ballin' you probably used to do them baseheads dirty too. Every hood got a smoker that's fun to trip wit."

"Yeah." Mannish answered, his mind clearly somewhere else. On how he was going to get that clown away from his sister. "Yeah, ah, check this out. Gimme' the eight stacks you owe me and I'ma run that half back for you in about two hours."

Will gave him the money.

When Mannish got in the truck he touch the screen of the monitor to turn the volume up and woke the neighborhood up with Pac lamenting how he hustled through the years and shed so many tears. He turned the corner and came out on El Segundo then made a right on Doty.

When he stopped in front of the apartment he said, "Shawna, you know life is better than this and you ain't got to live in this raggedy ass spot or do the bullshit you doing. When me and Kaitlynn was kids we used to follow you around everywhere. Would you want us to be following your ass now? And I ain't even bout to mention dude you fuckin' wit. You actin' like you gave up. Anybody would think you had it real fucked up growing up.

I mean I know we was poor and it's a lot a shit we didn't have, but it was cool cause everybody we knew was broke too, so if anything it made us want to grow up and get out here and get something. And you got a kid too. But you actin' like you don't. Fuckin' with that bitch ass nigga! I mean, is cum thicker than blood?"

Suprising the shit out of Mannish, she said, "I guess it be like that sometimes."

"What! Aight whatever. I got shit to do."

Mannish left and took the 105 Fwy east to the

110 Fwy south to the 91 Fwy east, exited Bloomfield, turned on Artesia. In twenty five minutes he was pulling into the security parking of his safe house in Cerritos. He sat in the apartment quiet for fifteen minutes to get his thoughts together. He had learned a long time ago from an old timer to sit in silence for fifteen minutes before he did anything. And just for the fact that he was getting ready to transport some drugs it was appropriate. Many guys have slipped and ended up locked away for a long time because they didn't take fifteen minutes out to collect their thoughts, plus he was plotting. He made a phone call to Jay. Twenty minutes later Mannish was pulling out of the building with two kilos. Thirty five minutes of medium traffic later he was in front of the dope spot alerting Will on his phone that he was outside. The door opened and Mannish ran in with the drugs under his coat.

"You right on time. This crackhead broad Dee Dee just bought my last couple ounces, rock for rock. She said she had some Hollywood producer in a hotel room on geek. She tworkin' him."

"Peep game Big Willy Will, I brung two whole kilos for you. You only have to pay for the other half of one but the other one ain't free. When I tell you what I want, don't ask no questions, just say aight or naw, feel me?"

"Yeah shoot."

"That fool that was here earlier?"

"Yeah, T."

"Yeah T, the next time he come thru here. I

want you to make him disappear. No dead body in the alley. No outta town and come back in six months, feel me? I'm talking to you cause I know you a business man and you gonna keep it real wit me. So holla back."

"What he do to y... my bad."

Mannish put his hand up. "It's cool if you can't handle it. It's still all good, but I'ma take these two birds…" Mannish said, picking up the two kilos off the table. "…and I'ma bring your half back later."

"Hold up. It ain't none of the above. You can put them thangs back down on the table. Dude don't be spendin' no real money anyway. I'ma..."

"I don't even want to know." Mannish interrupted, laying the cocaine back on the table. "So we have an agreement'?"

"Yeah we good Dog."

"Aight, I'm outro."

Mannish got in his vehicle and hit a couple of corners and pulled up in front of Shawna's apartment bumping his music loud enough to make everybody look out their windows. Shawna came downstairs and Mannish handed her $200.

"It's all good Shawna, I aint mad at you. Put some food in your refrigerator aight, I gotta go."

Mannish knew she would just give it to Travis for drugs. He wanted the job done ASAP.

CHAPTER TWELVE

Mannish had just crossed Martin Luther King Blvd.when he saw a familiar Dodge Magnum headed in the opposite direction. He immediately busted a U-turn and pulled alongside it at the red light.

Aiyana let the window down. "Hi Daddy."

"Where you goin'?"

"I'm going to get Big Mama, we're going to the supermarket."

"Where my lil man at?"

"In the back sleeping. You know he can't handle no car ride. What do you want to eat tonight?" she asked, subtly persuading him to be at home.

"I don't know, just do yuh thang. Ay, get me about ten boxes of baking soda and some sandwich bags."

"What! You must be crazy. People are not going to be looking at me crazy. The cashier will probably call the DEA on me. Big Mama isn't stupid you know. I'm not helping you in any way. Plus I want you to stop messing with that stuff anyway." she thought for a second then said, "You don't have any of that stuff at home do you?"

"Naw, and you right, I was trippin'. I'll send somebody else to get it."

By now the stoplight had changed to green. Car horns were beginning to blow as traffic began to build up.

"I'm holding up traffic Honey." Aiyana said.

"Fuck them, this is my city."

"See that's what's wrong with you. Bye Baby." she stepped on the gas pedal.

He watched her pull off, then laid his seat back and flipped his phone open. He scrolled down his call list and pushed the button on the side. A voice came back.

"Speak on it."

"Ay you got them two ounces from Big Will spot?" Mannish asked.

"Yeah, but I gave the crackhead Dee Dee half ounce of it for going to buy it for me."

"Aight cool." Mannish said ignoring the horns blowing and the cars backed up behind him. "Oh yeah, go get some baking soda, about ten boxes and some bags. Some niggas want they shit hard." Click.

Mannish threw the phone into the back seat and pulled his legit phone out of his jacket pocket and speed dialed Aiyana.

"Hi Baby, I'm always happy when you call me. The picture of you that pops up is sooo adorable." she said innocently.

Mannish smiled. "Well, you know, what can I say." he said, sounding like JJ Evans on Good Times.

"What's up Babe?" she asked.

"Oh, I just called to say I'm going to slow down on all that soon. I almost got enough to do what I need to do. Just a little while longer okay?"

"Okay Baby, it's just that, you know I worry."

"I know. I'll see you later." Click.

I hate it when he does that. I didn't get to say I Love You.

Tires near curb, foot to brake, gear shift to park.

"Wake up Naj, we at Gramma's house." Aiyana said.

When they made it up on the porch Ty opened the door. "What's up Yana?" Ty said.

"Nothing Boy, how's your arm?"

"It's almost back right, I get the cast off in a couple a weeks, but it ain't stoppin' nothin'. I'm a Soulja."

"Soldiers are in the military. What you guys are doing out here is called genocide. Where Big Mama at?" she asked, walking past him and sitting on the couch. Before Ty could answer, Big Mama came out of the bathroom.

"Aiyana, yuh ready Baby?"

"Yes Ma'am, whenever you are."

They left the house and took a ride down to the new supermarket on Slauson to check out the advertised low prices and quality food. Big Mama bought some pork chops and some pork links. Then they went to Trader Joe's in West L.A. to pick up some all natural organic items.

"Chile, I remembuh when I first come ta Califonya $2 of stuff was too much ta carry. Me an' my husband come dis way when he hea' its mo' money a man can make. I come wit 'im, but I neva had a problem bein' po', cause I know'd all dat matta'd twas it's a lotta love in da' house.

"I loved my husband even when he messed up. I loved my chirrens cause dey aint ask ta come hea'. But I tell yuh I dont know whuts goin' on in dey head. All dey know bout is bling, bling. Dat same bling, bling gon' be da' death of 'em. An' dem damn drugs, If dey aint sellin' it, dey usin' it.

Ecstacy used ta be how my husband made me feel. Now dey done made it where you can take a pill an' fall in love. I dont mind dat my time on dis earth is runnin' short cause da' world done gone crazy."

"Big Mama, don't say that."

"Chile please, when you been 'round long as me an' done raised many kids an' other peoples kids as me, den yuh would know da' world don' gone ta hell. Only thang brang me peace is knowin' my Lord an' Savior be hea' soon. All my chirrens been baptised since dey was lil but I tell yuh somethin', only sin God say he wont forgive is worship of any god besides him. Dat's dem drugs an' dat dirty money an' dat bling, bling. Da' Pastor was juss talkin' bout dat, yuh hea' me? Baby get me five pounds a dem apples. I'm gon' make some pies dis Sunday."

After they finished shopping they went back to the house. Ty and Naj were sleep on the couch with a few empty plates. They had chicken bones and crumbs scattered on the coffee table. There was also an empty Kool Aid pitcher and a couple of empty glasses with red liquid remnants at the bottom and greasy fingerprints around the rim. The TV screen was blue and the DVD player was on. Aiyana pushed eject to see what they had been watching. When the disc tray slid open it was Ice Cube's "Are We Done Yet?" She giggled to herself knowing that if it had been Mannish laying there asleep the movie would've been Heat.

After all the food was put up, Aiyana woke them up realizing that it was already after 4pm and if she would've let Naj sleep any longer he would be up all night. Ty grabbed the cordless phone and went into his room. Aiyana hollered into the kitchen asking Big Mama if she needed her to do anything else before she left. She got no answer. Aiyana went into the kitchen and found Big Mama slumped over in a chair, trying to catch her breath and sweating profusely.

"Big Mama!!!"

I don't know what to do! Should I call 911? I should call 911!

She punched the three digits!

"911 please hold."

"Hey! No! Don't put me on hold! Hello! Hello! ARE YOU OUT OF YOUR FUCKING MIND?!"

She hung up and called again.

"911 please h..."

"Hell No I won't hold my mother's in trouble, she could be dying and I need help now!"

"Okay calm down, what is she doing right now?"

"She's on the floor. Her eyes are rolled in the back of her head." Aiyana put her face an inch from Big Mama's.

"Her breathing is shallow, she's holding her chest."

"I need you to remain calm, an ambulance is on the way."

The hysterical state Aiyana was in when she called Mannish and Kaitlynn made them hysterical. Everybody met up at the hospital. When the doctor came out to tell them that Big Mama had a mild heart attack but was in stable condition, Shawna and Paula were on the verge of a girl fight. Paula had been raised by Big Mama too, but ran away when she was 16 years old with her boyfriend who had gotten her pregnant and moved her into his mother's garage, which was the result of a half assed attempt at turning it into a single apartment. They ended up wearing out their welcome and went from motel to motel until she got her county assistance and Section 8. Paula had another child, her boyfriend was killed and she started stripping and strip club hoeing. She got into so much shit, her middle name should've been Drama. Anyway she was at the hospital with her two kids that were now eight and ten. The big brother Jacob and his white wife were there also. The doctor told the family that Big Mama needed some rest and couldn't have any visitors. But not to worry, they could return the next day.

Shawna and Paula looked at each other with disgust.

They blamed each other for their misfortunes in life.

When they were both 16 years old Shawna had a boyfriend named T-Mac that was 21 years old that talked her out of her virginity but after numerous tries could never get her to give him head.

One day he was driving down the street in his homeboy's lowrider and pulled up alongside Paula walking to the store. He gave her a ride. Before he dropped her off she had a mouth full of dick. For the next few months, Shawna being none the wiser, he would get pussy from and head from Paula whenever he wanted. Getting head turned into fucking. Paula ended up pregnant by him and due to that Shawna broke up with him and fought with Paula because of her betrayal and deceit. Shawna gave Big Mama a report so bad that she grounded Paula forever. Big Mama said she'd figure out how much freedom she'd let her have after the baby came. Big Mama also banned T-Mac from coming to the house. A week into her punishment Paula ran away with T-Mac and lived in his mother's garage. Her life's been hell on earth ever since.

She's 27 years old but looks 37. Right after she had the second baby, T-Mac got shot to death by the father of what he liked to call his Tender Roni. She was his Tender Roni but someone else's 15 year old daughter. The girl told the police on her father because she thought she was in love with T-Mac. But now that she's 23 and in love for real she realizes that T-Mac was an urban pedophile. Middle aged white dudes from the suburbs with receding hair lines that molest 7 year olds aren't the only pedophiles.

The wrong group of girls for friends coupled with the fact that Paula's body filled out due to bearing children, had men's attention everywhere she went. She inevitably ended up at the strip club, which lead to popping ecstasy, snorting coke and smoking weed. She used anything to nullify the pains of failure, to which she completely blames Shawna.

Shawna's experience of losing her boyfriend to Paula because of her inhibitions caused her to give her all without question to the subsequent relationships and although she pledges her unconditional love she realizes it is her ruin. Before T-Mac, the girls were inseparable like Siamese twins. They used to tell everybody they were fraternal twins. They even slept in the same bed until Shawna found out about Paula's deceitful escapades.

When Paula was eight she moved to California to go to school. Her mother (Big Mama's little sister Gloria) thought it was conducive to Paula getting a good job and being able to compete in the business world. Gloria intended to move herself later. Until that time she would send money monthly to take care of Paula. It started out as a good idea until the money got shorter and shorter until it stopped coming completely. Big Mama didn't fret. She took care of Paula as if she was her own child. Then Paula broke Big Mama's heart back to back to back to back. First by fornicating and at a young age, then Big Mama found out it was with Shawna's boyfriend, then that he was a 21 year old man and then that she got pregnant. That almost sent Big Mama into cardiac arrest. To top it off Paula ran away.

Paula even had the audacity to try to get Big Mama to babysit a couple of times in the beginning. But Big Mama wanted her to understand what it meant to lay in the bed that you made. Big Mama would help eventually because that's what her life was dedicated to, making sure her kids were alright but not to the point that they wouldn't be responsible for their actions or drive her to the crazy house.

As a rebellious response to Big Mama making her tough it out, Paula only came around with the kids on days like Thanksgiving and Christmas and whenever she came she looked like she was doing worse than the prior visit. To Paula it was all Shawna's fault.

Kaitlynn kept tabs on Paula although she kept her distance. Kaitlynn could always reach her if need be. It was Kaitlynn who called her and told her Big Mama was on the way to the hospital.

Paula said her good byes to all the family in the hospital and excused herself. She had things to do in preparation to go to the Pussy Popping contest at the First King strip club that night.

CHAPTER THIRTEEN

A rapper from New Orleans named Los Capone came by the club the week before promoting his new song, "I got five hun'ed dollars to the best P-popper." But he gave away much more than five hundred dollars. Last week a girl with a pretty face and a fat firm ass won the money. Paula's argument was because a guy she had just started sexing was there she didn't want to get too freaky. Paula didn't want him thinking she was a hoe, although she stripped at a strip club and fucked him the first night after he was introduced to her by his homeboy whom she had also fucked. This week he was gone out of town on a run. She would set it out and get that money.

Paula exited the hospital and made her way through the parking lot. She pushed the button of her remote alarm system. The dust covered Oldsmobile Cutlass Supreme beeped twice and the interior lights came on illuminating the dingy tan upholstery. The driver's window was busted out. Paula and the two kids climbed in. She inserted the key into the ignition and twisted. The engine turned over like it wanted to start then it stalled. She tried a few more times with no success. The battery drained in her attempts. In addition to whatever engine trouble she was having, her battery was dead. She was out there for an hour before she found a combination of somebody who was willing to take the time out to help her and had some jumper cables. After the guy hooked them up the car still wouldn't start. He raised the hood and checked a couple of things. He discovered she was out of gas. He was kind enough to get her some gas, jump her car and send her on her way but not without her number and an engagement to jump her bones.

She went straight to a little swapmeet on the eastside that stayed open late. She needed an outfit for the night. Her and her two kids walked into the swapmeet. The first booth they came to had bikes, skateboards and remote controlled cars and things like that.

"Oooh Momma!" said the eight year old. "I want..."

"Hold up, you ain't gettin' a damn thing."

The ten year old said, "But you said the next time we came to the swapmeet you would buy us some sneakers."

"Did you hear what I said. Alls I got enough for is to get what I came to get for work tonight."

"Ah Momma you got a job now?" the youngest one said, "You don't take your clothes off for money no more?"

"What?!" she replied at the candidness of her child. "Take my clothes off for money?" she repeated, lost for words and stricken with shame. "Baby, I'm a professional dancer."

The two kids looked at each other then back at their mother. The expression on their face was that they just learned something new, not that she didn't do what they already knew, but that taking your clothes off for money was called professional dancing.

"You lil mutha fuckas is nosey, God! Come on, I got a lot to do."

After she tried on a couple of outfits and left a scent behind, she decided on a red satin thong with lace on the side that gave it the impression of shorts, sexy ass shorts. It came with a matching red, bikini type top.

Paula stopped by her beautician's house to get her weave tightened up. The beautician wasn't a hair stylist that worked in a shop that happened to be at home. She was unlicensed and worked out of her kitchen, hooking up her hoochie friends and whoever they would bring by for a discount. Paula liked to think she was getting quality work for playa prices.

When she left the beauty shop (Not!) she took

the kids home. The apartment was a mess as usual, with dirty clothes piled in the corner of the living room. Clothes also hung off of the edge of the couch and one of the only two broken down chairs that was supposed to match the dinner table but really didn't. The ten year old moved his mother's filthy sweater from off of the Play Station 2 she got from a hook up in the mall and sat in front of the TV to play his game.

"It's 8 o'clock yall put yall night clothes on." Paula told her kids.

They searched through a trash bag full of clothes to find a pair of pajamas the least dirtiest. She fried some chicken and sat a bag of sliced bread on the table. As they feasted she soaked in the tub. She slid under the running water, orgasmed and almost fell asleep.

She caught herself when her hair touched the water.

Can't fuck up the hair do!

She dried off and slipped on some jeans and an imitation Baby Phat (Baby Fat) T-shirt. She put her necessities in her club bag. Two outfits plus the red satin hook up from the swapmeet, check. Two pairs of twenty dollar stilettos, check. If you like Liz Claiborne you'll love this, it's not imitation it's in a plan package so your not paying for the name but it's the same stuff, fake ass perfume, check. Baby oil and condoms, check. Two ecstasy pills and a blunt, check.

10 o'clock, time to roll.

As usual she threatened a vicious ass whooping if the kids answered the phone or the door. She got in the car and the mutha fucka wouldn't start. With little thought she ran to her neighbor's door. She knocked a little more impetuously than she intended to because she was anxious and in a rush. She was supposed to be in the club dressed and ready for work by 10 o'clock. Her last warning she was told was her last warning.

Someone peeked out of the curtain then the door flung open.

"God damnit Paula, don't be fuckin' bangin' on my door like you the fuckin' po'leece!" yelled a big, black and greasy man with no shirt on and a big belly. He was barefoot. The only thing he had on was some filthy jeans.

"You almost made me flush my shit!"

He had two twenty dollar rocks in his hand.

"You know I be doin' big thangs up in here." he said.

"Nigga please, but anyway I need a jump like right now. I'll give you five dollars."

"Give it here."

She gave it to him and he moseyed on over to his pickup truck that looked strikingly similar to Fred G. Sanford's from the TV show Sanford & Son. The truck was so stuffed and filled with junk and it was so dark outside that he couldn't locate the cables.

"Damn you sho' is takin' long!" Paula complained.

"Shut up bitch, you see I ain't got no light. You keep talkin' shit you can take yo five back. I got plenty dope already."

"Whatever nigga, like I said, I got things to do. Next time you need to put 'em where you can find 'em."

"Next time you need to pass my house up with that bullshit! Oh here they are."

He pulled them out and gave her a jump. She sped through the streets to the club. She made the twenty minute trip in ten minutes. When she pulled into the parking lot there was no place to park. A promotional bus and truck wrapped with advertisement of the record label that said in big green letters 'I got five on it' was parked on Western Ave. The doors were open and the speakers were blasting the new single "I got five hun'ed dollars, five hun'ed dollars to the best pussy poppuh..."

People were running across the street from the other club. People that were just passing by pulled over to see what all the commotion was about. There were girls with some little hot pink coochie cutter shorts on and baby tee shirts that said 'I got 5 on it' in the street passing out posters, CD's and other promotional stuff. The bouncers of the club began telling people that they either had to come in the club or get somewhere. The rapper and his entourage headed into the club with everyone else in tow.

The club usually had a good crowd on Friday nights but with the hype from what had happened the week before plus all the attention they gathered outside, the club was beyond capacity. The good thing was that it was in the ghetto and the Fire Department couldn't care less. The pool tables were empty which was a first. The bartender had to get two of the girls to help her. Drinks were being ordered like crazy. The guys were getting their drink on and they were buying drinks for the girls to get them loose for when it was time to compete for the money. After an hour of the girls stripteasing and doing what the club was known for, Los Capone hopped up on the stage with the microphone in hand.

"Ay what's really good yall, I come all da' way from New Orleans ta see how da' girls pop it in L.A, cause in da' videos I ain't really seen nuttin'. But I got a homie from down here an' he tell me I gotta go to da' hood. Last week I come tru' here an' it was crazy man. It was so crazy I had to come back."

Then on queue the girl that won the prior week came out on stage. She had on some shredded Daisy Dukes, some clear plastic high heels and some metal stars covering her nipples like Janet Jackson had on at the Super Bowl half time show. She did a split and her shorts tore.

She rolled over on her back and tucked her

knees to her chest. She extended her feet towards the ceiling then they separated and arched down like the letter m. The audience could see her shorts had torn right up the crotch. She took the liberty to increase the tear. With perfect timing the DJ made R Kelly say, "It seems like you're ready."

Everybody's mouth dropped open at the sight of her pretty pussy lips. They watched her sink her middle finger in and pull it out glistening. And then the index finger, as the music played, "It seems like your ready to go all the way…" her two fingers lubricated her pussy lips in a sensual massage. Her hips began to wine. Her hands switched. The hand with the succulent pussy juice went into her mouth. Then she rolled over and came up on all fours, backed up to the nearest guy sitting at the edge of the stage and sat her pussy on his nose.

The rapper said, "Whew! It's gettin' hot in here." The crowd was going bananas. "Yall ready ta get it P-Poppin' up in here?"

The music kicked in loud and the speakers rumbled the house, all the girls started shaking their ass where ever they were.

The rapper began. "I got five hun'ed dollars, five hun'ed dollars to the best Pussy Poppuh. I could get these hoes poppin', five hun'ed dollars…" The song was hype and had the crowd pumped. At the end of the first verse the music went down. "All da' hoes that's bout they bizness get up here and stand across the back of the stage."

The music kicked back up and one by one the girls got loose, each one looser than the last. Paula's turn came up and she put it on thick. She bounced her fat butt, shook it like a saltshaker and a Polaroid picture. She did a handstand and popped her coochie upside down. She did a back spin and came out of it with the bottom half of her two piece outfit in her hands like the breakdancers did with their shoes.

The guys roared.

"That bitch is off the hook!" someone yelled.

She stood and jiggled her naked ass for the crowd which probably would've been nice had it not been so flabby and covered with stretch marks, making her ass look like a balled up road map.

A voice yelled, "Ay, which way to the freeway?"

Laughter erupted. But there was no denying she was putting it down.

She thought to herself, *They think it's a game.*

She went to the back of the stage and grabbed a Corona bottle, twisted the top off and took a swig. Just when people started to think, *This bitch is a lush, she needed a drink in the middle of her performance*, she sat the bottle down in the middle of the floor, then walked to the front of the stage, looked back once to judge the distance and did a somersault that landed in slow motion in a split on the bottle. Everyone was flabbergasted as they watched the bottle disappear. The niggas in the club lost their mind.

Somebody yelled, "I know you can take all this horse dick then!"

A couple of girls looked in his direction like, "Stop lying." One of them put the tip of her finger in her mouth as the look on her face changed to something like, *you are lying, aren't you?*

Paula was now on her back with half the bottle hanging out bubbling.

"HER PUSSY IS DRINKIN' IT!!"

Once she had done the somersault the rapper lost focus. Now the beat was just playing. He was a spectator along with the rest of the crowd. No need in judging this contest or seeing any other contestants. Paula was crowned the Queen Pussy Popper. Between the contest money and the money that had gotten thrown on the stage she walked away with $1500 in cash.

On the way home she thought, *I need a new car cause this mutha fucka be gettin' on my nerves. Tomorrow I'ma go to the dealership and get me a Navigator or somethin' like that.* She was feeling herself. Winning can do that to you. *Naw, cause mutha fuckas be jealous.* Knowing for real, her credit wasn't good enough to put $10,000 down on a Navigator let alone $1,000. *Yeah mutha fuckas be jealous, I think I'ma get something smaller. Stay lowkey and shit.* She parked in front of her project building. She pulled the plastic and the two bricks off of the floor in the back and covered her driver window with the plastic then held it in place by putting the bricks on the roof. She hit the alarm and the car churped. She went inside the apartment and all the lights were on.

I'ma beat the hell out them damn kids bout my lights!

She barged into the kid's room yelling, intending on waking them up but they weren't there. She checked her room, nothing. The bathroom, nothing. Back in the living room on the coffee table was an envelope. She picked it up. It was from the Sheriff's Department. The letter said the kids were taken due to neglect and for Paula to come to the nearest Sheriff's Station immediately.

There was a detective's card attached. Her hands began to tremble, her legs turned into jelly. She had to sit down. She sat there for two hours immobile. She tried to imagine the different scenarios of what could have happened.

The first enigma was.

What made them come in the first place? How did they know the kids were here alone? Were the kids outside and got into something? Or did one of these scanless bitches around here call them and snitch me out? Yeah, but who? Lord knows everybody that know me, know I leave them by theyself all the time. Is they gonna drug test me? Damn! They gon' lock my ass up. What to do? First thing in the morning I gotta get some of that stuff to clean my system out. Damn! What am I gonna say to these people? Damn! It's always some shit. If it wasn't for bad luck I wouldn't have no luck at all. Fuck that, I'ma tell 'em they my damn kids and I had just went to get 'em something from the store. Shit, I take good damn care of my kids, they ain't hungry or nothing. I'ma just go in there and demand they give me my damn kids. I'ma look all of 'em in they face like they crazy.

Once Paula convinced herself of how she was going to handle the situation, she fell asleep right where she sat. She was up at 6am, the fright of the situation was back in full swing. She wanted to smoke some weed to calm her nerves but she was worried about being tested. By 7 o'clock she was smoking a blunt. Her rationale was that she was going to clean her system anyway and if it was going to clean out what she did last night then it would clean out what she smoked now. At 8 o'clock she was sitting in her car in front of the drug store on 94th street and San Pedro drinking the concoction they gave her.

She decided to go home and call the detective first to give the stuff time to go through her body. When she called, the officer she was asking for wasn't in. She told the female officer on the other end of the phone that she wanted her damn kids in a belligerent tone.

"Ma'am, please calm down. My name is Officer McKnight and I can fill you in on everything you need to know but you have to come down to the station with a valid California ID and the children's birth certificates proving you're the parent."

"What the fuck you mean prove? I ain't gotta prove diddly squat. I'm the one carried they asses nine months. I'm the one busting my ass to provide. Prove these nuts!"

"Ma'am, I understand this must be an inconvenience for you, but please understand, I don't know who you are."

"You damn right! So why yall all up in my house, in my bizness?"

"That attitude is not going to help the children at all Miss. The first thing we have to do with everyone is establish identity. So come see me. Ask for Officer McKnight with your ID Now what time should I be expecting you?"

"Soon as I dig up all these damn unnecessary papers yall want and get dressed."

Blam! Paula slammed the phone down in the officer's face. She was already dressed and the birth certificates were in a folder in the dresser drawer. She just needed time to think. She didn't have any friends that cared about her enough to go down to the station with her, so that wasn't an option. She just had to get her thoughts together. She never was a good calculator. She could sit there all month and not come up with anything.

She went to the kitchen cabinet and grabbed a bottle of Paul Mason Brandy, poured herself a half a glass and headed to the Sheriff's Station, which was actually just a couple of blocks down Imperial Highway. When she walked into the lobby and identified herself, she was arrested.

"Hold up, what the fuck you doin', why yall handcuffin' me?"

"You are under arrest..."

"What the fuck for?!"

"Anything you say can and will be used against you in a court of law..."

"I ain't did nothin'!"

"If you cannot afford an attorney, one will be appointed for you..."

"Bitch let me go!" Paula yelled, while struggling to get loose.

"Ma'am, stop resisting."

Tussling back and forth, Paula and the two Officers fell to the ground. A couple more officers intervened and subdued her. They hauled her to a holding cell. In all the excitement she didn't get booked in or even searched. The officers had her purse but her cell phone was attached to her belt. Paula called her homegirl. "Hey listen, they got me locked up in the Sheriff's Station on Imperial. They didn't even tell me why. Look, call down here and ask them what they got me for and what's my bail. You know my name right?"

"P-Nasty?"

"Bitch stop playin', it's Paula, Paula Johnson.

I'ma call you back in ten minutes." Click.

Two girls in the next cell over barked. "Hey bitch!"

Paula looked around not being able to see anything, ensconced by three walls and bars.

"Hey bitch!" They said again.

Paula sat quiet not knowing where it was coming from or where it was directed.

"You hear me you snake ass bitch!"

Then the other said in a menacing voice, "You hear my homegirl talkin' to you, ain't you from the projects?"

Paula thought to herself, *Whoever they talkin' to like that is trippin', and she from the projects too. If that was me I'd give them bitches an earful. Then they betta hope I didn't get action at 'em.*

"Don't they call you P-Nasty?"

"Yall talkin' to me? You bitches is smokin', yall don't know me! I'll eat you bitches fa' lunch! I ain't wit all that punkshit! You hoes could die slow!"

"Damn P, hold up, it's Jackie and Mona. We was just fuckin' witchu."

"Well don't be playin'!"

"We saw 'em bring you back here, what you was doing, squabbin' wit the po' leece out there or somethin'?"

"Yeah them janky mutha fuckas playin' games and shit!"

"What happened?"

"Bitch I'm still tryna figure it out. What yall doing up in here?"

"What, you ain't heard? Last night that stupid ass nigga Teardrop kilt a po'leece. He had a gun on him when they was pullin' his dumb ass over for expired tags and tinted windows. He kilt the po'leece and got in a high speed chase. His dumb ass brung 'em right to the projects and jumped out the car and ran up in the spot. Me and Mona and Poppa up in there, just finish cookin' up a key.

We was weighing and baggin' grams. He didn't tell us what he did. He was sweatin' and shit but we ain't know nothin'. He just went straight into the bathroom. Bout ten minutes later the front door just open up. We looked up and it's the mutha fuckin' manager and the po'leece.

I'ma kill that bitch! Girl it was dope all over the table. They got Poppa up in here somewhere. They go in the bathroom and this nigga been gone out the window. They went up in every apartment in the building..."

Paula now realized what happened. The girl kept talking, but Paula wasn't listening anymore.

I gotta get outta here. She hit send on her cell phone and it automatically redialed her homegirl's number.

"Hello"

"Hey this me Paula, what they say?"

"Oh, I was finna do it."

"You ain't called yet!"

"Nuh uh, I was finna... ooh (giggles) you nasty... (giggles) wait I'm on the phone... aaah mmm hmmm..."

Paula got the hint and hung up. She called another "homegirl."

"What's crackulating?" is how the girl answered.

"Ay this P, I need you to call down to..."

"I caint call nowhere. My phone restricted. I can only get incoming calls til I pay this bill."

"Damn! Aight." Click.

Mona was still talking. "...you feel me girl?"

Paula replied, "Yep where they got Teardrop at?"

"Girl they neva found his ass?"

The jailer came and took Paula to be stripsearched and booked. They had the new digital fingerprinting machine so she didn't need to worry about getting the black ink off of her hands with the itty bitty piece of paper towel they usually give you. The detectives told her that she was not being charged with abandonment or neglect, that was an issue the Children's Social Service would handle, nor was she being arrested for the weed in the ash tray. They held up a bag with about ten roaches in it. They told her that she was arrested because the children had access to it and that was child endangerment which was criminal and resisting arrest. They told her she would be cited out and given a court date.

Six hours later she was free and back home. She punched in the digits they gave her on her cellphone so she could talk to someone about getting her kid's back.

They told her the kids would be placed in temporary foster care until the issue was resolved. They informed her of the court date. That was all the information she would get. She drunk the rest of the brandy. The current turn of events affected her dramatically. She had never been to jail before. Having her freedom taken was a psychological disaster then to add to it her kids were taken. In ten years there had never been a time that she was away from her kids that she didn't control. The alcohol which usually numbed the pain and lessened the intensity of a situation only intensified it this time.

She couldn't shake the ominous feeling she was having.

The Paul Mason brandy had her beyond tipsy. She stumbled out to the car. She wanted to smoke some weed but she was out, so she headed to the weed spot. Barely keeping the car in one lane she made it to the weed spot on 102nd Street. They were out so she swerved her way to the Avalon Gardens projects on 88th Street. They had some regular weed. She had money so she wanted the good stuff. She knew they had good stuff on 47th and Broadway. People came from across town to get the sticky ickey from around the corner from Big Mama's house.

Whenever she had money she would pass 48th right up to get weed on 47th and not even drop in to check on Big Mama. This time being drunk she turned down 48th inadvertently.

When she realized she'd turned too soon, she was passing Big Mama's house. She stomped on the brakes and skidded a few feet. Burnt rubber permeated the air.

Ty, his homies and a few crackheads scattered. Ty was the first to take cover behind the nearest parked car. A couple of his homies ran up driveways. The crackheads ran down the street and kept running. The car just sat there. Ty didn't recognize it because Paula hadn't been over since she got it.

Ty noticed the driver's window was down. Paula stared up the block reminiscing on how she used to prance up and down it in another lifetime. Suddenly, there was a gun poking her in the side of the head.

"What's up cuzz!" Ty said, still not realizing it was Paula.

Startled she jumped back and looked. Wrong move!

He pulled the trigger.

CHAPTER FOURTEEN

A bullet crashed through the back window. Another came through the window and lodged in the dashboard. Aiyana smashed on the gas pedal and ran through the red light heading southbound on Western towards Jefferson.

There is no statement to describe her fright that wouldn't be an understatement. Not only for the fear of her life, but for the lives of Big Mama and Naj who were in the car with her. The Hemi motor came alive and did what it was made to do. The Grand Marquis tried to give chase in vain. After a half of a mile, it became evident that they wouldn't catch the Dodge Magnum. The tinted windows of the Grand Marquis went up and they made a right turn on 36th Street.

Aiyana called Mannish and told him what had happened.

She told him that she was headed to the Southwest Division Police Department on Martin Luther King Blvd. He told her not to go to the police station, that he would handle it. He told her to continue down Western, that he was at the swapmeet on Slauson. They could meet halfway and switch cars. She explained that she was terrified and wouldn't dare drive another block if it wasn't towards the police station. By now she was turning left on Martin Luther King Blvd. She pulled into the Ralph's parking lot and told him she would wait there. 10 minutes later when Mannish pulled into the parking lot, they came out of the Burger King. Naj climbed into Mannish's truck to play his PlayStation game.

Mannish drilled Aiyana on what the shooters looked like, what color the car was they were in, what model, what year, license plate, where they turned off at. He tried to compile as much information as possible, but all he could get was, "A black car, like a police car... the windows were tinted but they might have been white or Spanish guys, they turned off on 36th Street."

Big Mama cut in. "Boy whut da' hell wrong witcha, got peoples shootin' at dis girl an' me. Whut yuh done done? Dont nobody deserve ta die behind yuh foolishness. I just come out da' hospidal an' you tryna send me ta da' morchery."

"Momma I'm sorry all this happened. I don't know who did this or why. I ain't tryna send you to the mortuary but I'ma find out who did this and I'ma make 'em pay."

In his mind he was thinking, *Hector, oh yeah, you gonna pay.*

Big Mama's final word's to him were, "How yuh gon' fine 'em iffen they wudn't afta yuh. Listen, you stay from 'round me wit dat foolishness an' watch yuh dont get dis girl an' dat baby kilt. Now, Aiyana take me home!" Big Mama said this while climbing in the truck, obviously still energetic and feisty despite her age or having had a heart attack.

Aiyana was still shaken, and upset with Mannish for what ever he did in her car. But as usual she didn't show it. She kissed him, got in the truck and drove off. Mannish stood there looking at the car. The back hatch had four bullet holes in it. Inside the back was showered with shattered glass. A bullet penetrated the back seat. Mannish's heart stopped momentarily at the thought of what could've happened to his lil man Naj. He noticed the bullet in the dash.

Mannish drove the car to Florence Ave. and turned right. A few blocks up he turned into American Glass Shop. He knew they would hook him up. For years he had been getting his windows shot out and for years they had been replacing them. Next he went around the corner from Big Mama's house where the Rodriquez family had an upholstery shop. He dropped the Magnum off and they told him he could pick it up the next day. So he left it and walked down to Big Mama's house and just as he hoped, his truck was in the driveway. Aiyana was still there. When he got into the house he thanked God that

Big Mama was in the bed asleep. He consoled Aiyana and assured her that everything would be alright but that he had some runs to make and had to take her home.

After he dropped her off he swung around to The Spot.

Jay was being entertained by two strippers. One was of average height, light skinned with a long straight weave. She was stripped down to a pair of white thongs, white bra and a pair of white six inch heels. The other one was dark chocolate and wore a black miniskirt and only had on one shoe. She had Jay's dick in her mouth while he was laid back like a kingpin with a blunt in his mouth.

Mannish said, "Ay Mr. Ghetto ass Hugh Heffner, sorry to interrupt your lil ménage a trois, but bizness calls."

They stepped into the bedroom for privacy. Mannish filled him in on what had happened and that he suspected Hector.

"So what's the next move?" Jay asked.

Mannish replied, "We gonna put wings on his back but first we gotta get some new ammunition."

Jay smiled and reached under the bed and pulled out a gun case. He unzipped it and there laid a brand spanking new AK47. The light reflected off of the steel like a mirror.

The wood finish was a carpenter's dream. It looked too pretty to use, especially for what they're used for.

"Where'd you get this pretty mutha fucka from?"

"From this Canadian the homie Tray was in the Feds with. We was hanging in the hood a coupla days ago and he came thru. He had two of 'em in the car wit 'im.

That mutha is plugged wit all kinds a shit. Dude had a catalogue. Ay Man, he got everything, tha nigga got shit that's takin' 747's down. Naw, naw, he got shit that's knockin' tha sun out the sky nigga. And he don't mind double hustlin.'"

"Double hustling, what you, mean?"

"He'll take dope. He said he got people in Indiana. But he won't take nothin' less than a kilo. He said he gettin' $30,000 out there. Nigga you hear me! $30,000 and that's whole. I'm thinkin' bout makin' some birds fly out to Indiana!"

"Hold up Nigga, cool yuh heels before you be coolin' yuh heels in the fuckin' pen. Fuck that. He said he got folks out there. We ain't got shit out there. And we ain't trustin' no nigga from another country that some nigga in the hood introduced you to, especially, one that was in the fuckin Feds. But we do need them guns though.

So look, this what we gonna do. Tell yuh boy to call his man. We gonna give him a kilo, that should get us quite a few joints, enough to serve these fools Hector and his boys up real nice and make sure you make him do the transaction."

"Aight fa' sho', I got that. When you wanna do

it?"

"What you mean when? Right now! Call yuh boy and see what's up."

Jay looked at the door as if he had X-ray vision, looking through it at the girls in the next room.

"How bout we do it tomorrow?"

"Naw Nigga, how bout we do it now! Fuck them bitches, they on your time and you on mine. Call dude."

"Aight, aight Mannish damn, I was just sayin' though."

Mannish lowered his eyes in a, *you trying my patience* look. Jay lowered his head, unclipped his cell phone from his belt, scrolled through his call list and hit the chirp button.

"What's crackulatin' my nigga Jay?" came through the speaker.

"What's up dog, what's up wit your boy?"

"Who?"

"Wit them firecrackers."

"Oh, he straight, what's up?"

"Tell him to bring it fa' tha no less than what he was talkin' bout."

"Okay fa' sho', when?"

Jay looked at Mannish. Mannish put up a hand with five fingers spread out, and two fingers on the other hand symbolizing seven.

"Seven days." Jay said into the phone.

Pow! Mannish slapped him across his head. "Ouch! I mean seven hours."

Pow! "Ouch! I mean seven o'clock."

Tray said, "Seven o'clock, aight that's what's up. That's a couple hours from now. I'm bout to hit him on his cell right now and see what's up. I'll hit you back."

Mannish said, "Tell that nigga to tell the otha nigga it's for anotha nigga."

"Ay, don't tell him they for me."

"Huh? Okay that's cool, it don't matter what I tell 'im. I'ma hit you back."

Mannish laid on the bed, grabbed the remote and turned on the TV and the DVD player. He flipped through the scene selection. The shoot out scene from the movie Heat came on the screen. Jay took that as his queue and exited the room closing the door behind him.

Jay's phone beeped. "What up?"

"Ay Jay bring me a eighth of a key too, hard."

"Aight you got it." Click.

Jay gestured for the girls to follow him into the other bedroom. He had two hours and two pieces of pussy to kill. He popped in a CD that started off with an upbeat Ciara and winded down to slow tempo R Kelly. The girls climbed up onto the bed like two five and a half foot felines.

The light skinned one seductively slid the chocolate one out of what little bit of clothes she had left on. She positioned Chocolate and dove nose first into her vagina passionately, yet greedily devouring her sweetness as if it would run out.

Ecstatic by the literal tongue lashing, Chocolate exploded into her captor's mouth with a moan that made Mannish's dick hard way in the other room.

Jay slipped into the light skinned one from the back and dropped his dick in her pussy with aggression. Her cries of passion sounded throughout the apartment complex.

Mannish had to adjust his pants. Jay pulled her hair back as he slammed into her with thunderous strokes. "Ooooh... bre..ee..eak... mm... myyyy... baaaack... daa... deee...ee.."

Jay pulled out of her and pushed her all the way up until her coochie was up to Chocolate's face. She was so stimulated, soon as lips touched lips she drenched Chocolate's face with her feminine all natural syrup. While Chocolate lapped up the juices, Jay raised her legs in the air and dropped his dick into her pussy. The experience was way better than her most vivid bisexual fantasy.

The door opened and Mannish stepped in unable to control his libido any longer. He had listened to the explicit moan, groans and screams for thirty minutes and finally lost the frivolous fight against a man's nature. It had gotten the best of him. When he entered the room he felt like he had walked onto the set of a porno shoot. He stepped up on the bed and maneuvered himself between Light Skin's hands which laid flat on the wall. Her head was the perfect height. Instinctively, she pulled down Mannish's pants and boxers. His dick popped up and hit her in the nose so stiff and hard that it almost gave her two black eyes. She fought the sensation to pass out and took him into her mouth. The warm sensation gave him goose bumps. He threw his head back to the wall. His eyes rolled to the back of his head and his knees got weak. As R Kelly explained how he extended 4 play to 12, Mannish released his load and collapsed. After a few minutes, he regained his composure and his mind focused back on the eminent bizness of purchasing the weapons and using them.

Mannish took a shower and chilled out while Jay and the girls took turns showering. The girls got in a Nissan Armada and left. Mannish watched them out the window, then turned to Jay and said, "Jay, ain't that them bitches from Charlie's strip club?"

"Yeah."

"Didn't she used to have a Camaro convertible?"

"Yeah that's her."

"Lemme' find out you big trickin'."

"Lemme' ask you something Mannish. Aight, you got two niggas, and nigga number one is trickin' fa' sho', but nigga number two gets serviced too. Wouldn't you say he could be categorized with nigga number one in the participation and gratification of trickin'."

"Nigga shut up and call dude back!"

"I'm just sayin' though, I'm just sayin' though."

"Nigga just hit yuh boy back and see what the

fuck is up. It's been a hour already."

Jay sent an alert over the phone.

"Jay, what's up man." came back after only a few seconds.

"What's the deal?" Jay said.

"Yeah it's all good. He gonna meet me over at Magic Johnson's T.G.I. Fridays on La Tijera. Me and you gonna have to hook up before that, so I can get the thang from you. We got about an hour, so let's just head up there now. I'm already on the westside so it ain't nothin' for me. Bout how long is it gonna take you?"

"I'm on Adams and Crenshaw, so whatever driving time it takes, what, bout twenty minutes."

"Aight I'll be in the bar."

"Aight." Click.

Fifteen minutes later a brand new black Range Rover pulled in and crept through the parking lot of Magic Johnson's T.G.I. Fridays and pulled into a parking spot. The parking lot was busy as usual for a Friday evening.

The Lakers were playing and this sports bar was one of the most popular places to be during a Lakers game, if you're not at the Staple Center. Jay hopped out of his double R truck just as three fine women were passing by.

"Hello ladies."

"What's up Billy the Kid?" one of them replied.

A confused look flashed on Jay's face. This bitch is trippin'. He was about to say, "Who the fuck is Billy the..." But she interrupted him when she put her hand on the wood handle of his 9mm sticking out of his waistband then pulled his shirt down over it. She looked in the direction of a police car going down an isle on the other side of the parking lot.

"You see the boys over there? You betta watch yuhself Billy. You get caught wit that burner and by the time you get out, your Rove'll be played out like Jheri Curls.

"Good lookin' out ma, what's your name?"

"Just call me, Pullin' your Coattail."

"Gimme yuh number."

"Bye, bye Billy." she said already walking to catch up with her girlfriends. He watched her walk. Damn! Her white pants hugged her voluptuous butt like skin. She effortlessly moved it in a hypnotic manner. Her four inch heels put emphasis on the arch in her back, making her butt stick out just that much more. The restaurant door closing behind her broke him out of his trance. He then surveyed the parking lot for the police car. He located it and realized it was nearing his immediate area. About another minute and they would be passing by him. He grabbed the handbag with the kilo in it and went inside.

The place was jumping as it does regularly. Jay passed right by the people in the waiting area which looked like an hour wait and went into the bar area, dapping security guards in the process. He noticed Miss Pullin' your Coattail in the waiting area but pretended he didn't. He wanted her to see his face was a VIP pass and she did. When he got inside he couldn't reach the bar counter due to the crowd, the loud chatter was deafening.

He gestured to the bartender with his hand for a drink.

The bartender nodded and hooked him up with a French Connection (Cognac and Grand Marnier) and passed it between two gorgeous women discussing the current Presidential race.

"Excuse me ladies." The bartender said as he passed the glass. Jay downed it in one swallow. He put a fifty dollar bill in the glass.

"Can you put this on the counter for me?" he asked one of the women. She obliged.

When the bartender looked back in his direction he pointed at the two women and made the drinking gesture again. He headed back to the entrance of the club with a twenty dollar bill cupped in his hand. He shook hands with the security guard, leaned in close and told him to let Coattail and her buddies in. Jay turned around and bumped foreheads with Tray.

"Damn!" Jay shouted. "Only nigga's faces I want that close to me is dead Presidents nigga!" then raised the bag for Tray to take. Tray didn't see it.

Tray yelled, "Let's go outside. I can't hear nothin' you sayin' it's too loud up in here." then led the way.

They crossed paths with Coattail and friends

on their way in. Jay got lost in her pretty face for a moment. Time slowed down. He wished he could read her mind. Her soft hand touched his, ever briefly. They passed. She disappeared into the crowd. He went outside feeling something inside his hand. A piece of paper, a closer look revealed a name and number. *Valerie.* Jay looked up and noticed a red Corvette blocking his truck.

"Who the fuck got me blocked in?"

"Don't trip homie that's me, I couldn't find no parking spot."

As Jay glanced around he said, "It's too many muthafuckas around here to do what we gotta do, feel me?"

"Yeah you right we could take it down the street to the gas station, but if you ain't tryna meet dude, I'ma need yo truck cause all that shit ain't gonna fit in what I'm in."

Jay thought a second. I got paper plates on it. "Yeah well it is what it is."

"That's him callin' me now."

Tray answered his phone and agreed with his dude on the gas station up the street. They switched car keys and Jay handed him the bag. Jay pulled the Corvette out of the Range Rover's way. Tray pulled the truck out. The Vette wheeled into the gas station across the street from the one the truck pulled into. Jay watched as the blue Chevy Tahoe with white pin stripes down the side drove in and backed up to the Rover. Tray got into the Tahoe with the bag. They sat and talked for about five minutes.

Then they both got out and transferred the big crate from truck to truck. The Tahoe left. Then the Range Rover left.

The Rover drove half a mile down the block and parked. The Corvette parked behind it. They opened the back door then the crate and inspected the weapons. The sight made Jay think about going to war with somebody, anybody on G.P. (General Principles).

"You came through for real with this my nigga." Jay told Tray.

"Nigga I got the hook up like Master P. More tricks than David Blain."

"Ay I'm gone. I gotta put this shit up. Ay, I almost forgot to get that money from you for them four and a half ounces, separate mines from yours."

"Next time I see you, I'ma flatten that."

"Next time tell me you ain't got the money nigga."

Jay barely inched two feet when a car ran into his fender so hard it caused his head to bust out the driver side window. Then several cars converged on him and screeched to a halt. Several agents jumped out and rushed at him. They were yelling freeze with guns pointing. They drug Jay out of the car, threw him to the ground and cuffed him. They put him in the back of a Monte Carlo while they searched his truck. They took out the case of guns and set them on the ground.

An officer found a kilo of soft and four and a half ounces under the back seat driver's side.

They told Jay he had enough guns and drugs to get him enough time to hold him until criminals were getting frozen and reprogrammed. He was taken to the MDC Federal Building downtown and placed in a cell over the weekend. His day in court was Monday. The Judge told him he was faced with charges of carrying a concealed weapon for the gun he had in his waistband, with charges of possession of cocaine, with charges of trafficking cocaine, with charges of distribution of cocaine and possession of a list of weapons that went all the way down two pages, there was trafficking and then the list of weapons again. The Judge said he was also charged with driving with no license. They charged him with wire fraud for conspiring over the phone. The only thing Jay was able to do was plead guilty or not guilty. He couldn't file any motions yet. No one had broken down any details of the case to him.

Jay was totally clueless. He went back to the custody of the holding facility. The ITS (Inmate Telephone System) was only operable by using a pin number, but he hadn't been issued one yet, so he couldn't make any phone calls.

Tuesday morning he was awakened by federal agents from ATF and DEA. It seemed the ATF agents were there to add to the intimidation factor because they did less prying for the shit load of guns than expected. Nothing like how the

DEA was sweating the four and half ounces of hard crack. They accused Jay of single handedly controlling the Los Angeles market for cocaine. They said that the way they play is that if his boy said he bought a kilo of cocaine a month for the last two years then he would be getting charged for 24 counts of sales of cocaine, and whatever the combined weight was. And they didn't even need to find any drugs as long as they had a snitch willing to testify. They told him that in his case they had drugs.

They had phone tap and they had a video of him handing the confidential informant the bag of drugs. They told him he was looking at biblical numbers. They told him that he had to live in the Old Testament to be able to do his time and make it out alive. Jay went back to his cell completely fucked up. It was three days before he was issued a pin number. Those three days were the longest three days in his life. It felt like three weeks. His first phone call was to The Spot, hoping Mannish would be there. After three rings someone picked up.

{You have a collect call from a federal prison. This call is from "Jay." Hang up to refuse, to accept press 5 to block all future calls press 77... Your call has been blocked.} Click.

"Damn!" Jay yelled!

Mannish hung the phone up and left the apartment, never to return. For the past week Mannish didn't know what had happened to Jay. He called the hospitals and the county coroner, in case Jay got jacked and killed. He called the police departments between The Spot and the sports bar. Maybe he got pulled over before he reached his destination. Mannish called the county jail. Everything came up empty. On Tuesday when there was still no word he had the apartment cleaned out and put everything in storage. Finally Friday he got a call from a federal prison.

"Damn!" Mannish yelled!

The collect call confirmed Mannish's fear. The Feds had a 98% conviction rate. That's because there's more rats in the federal system than ass on spring break. It was a situation that Mannish didn't want to deal with.

He pulled up to Johnnie's Pastrami's little parking lot and told two crackheads that were hanging out that he had left a half of an ounce in the apartment. That they could stay there for the next three weeks because he had just paid the rent the week before but he wasn't coming back. Before he could finish talking they were already on their way to The Spot. Mannish turned a few corners and got on the 10 Fwy East. He knew they would mess the place up and disarray any traces that two dope boys ever stayed there and probably get kicked out anyway. That was in the event the authorities came snooping around, they would be thrown off. He got caught in the evening traffic. An hour later he pulled into the security parking garage in Cerritos. The place was always peaceful every time he went there.

Why don't I come here more often?

He parlayed in the courtyard for a while enjoying the craftsmanship of the landscape and the serenity of the environment. A hundred butterflies danced around in his stomach when he noticed a man passing by that kept his gaze on him a little too long. His paranoia was up. The only thing he could think to do was follow him.

Rather follow than be followed.

The man stuck his key in an apartment ensconced in the back corner in a cubby hole. Mannish went around and went up to his apartment. He went to his stash and counted how much he had stacked in the last two months and how many bricks he had left. He counted with the convenience of a money machine but still after a couple hours fatigue set in and he dropped off to sleep. His head laid eight inches off the table on stacks and stacks of money like the most expensive pillow.

CHAPTER FIFTEEN

When Mannish woke up at 3 o'clock in the morning, he realized he had only counted a little over two hundred thousand dollars before he passed out. The intensity of the situation with Jay was mentally draining.

Sleep was always his defense mechanism. He had twenty two ten thousand dollar bundles in a bag on the floor and the table still had plenty of miscellaneous amounts of money rubber banded together. The sun was way up before he was done. The bag now had 33 stacks of money ($330,000) He had 30 bricks left, plus the 5 that Jay left at The Spot. Things turned serious when the numbers were done. He had action at reaching a million dollars in a couple of months. It would be enough to invest in real estate like he dreamed. He had to play everything right.

He made something to eat, laid back and dozed off on the couch thinking about his next move.

Before he left the apartment he made a call to the lawyer he had hired for Ty. Mannish asked the lawyer to get in touch with a good federal attorney and hire him to defend Jay. Mannish told him he'd pay him 10% for mediating.

The lawyer agreed. Mannish grabbed ten stacks of money and left. Later in the day he met with the lawyer at his office on Wilshire Blvd. and gave him a hundred thousand dollars.

"Make sure Jay don't want for nothing. Put $10,000 on his books. Make sure you keep me up on everything that's going on." he told the lawyer.

Mannish left Beverly Hills and went to Inglewood. He pulled into 310 Motors, a customizing shop, where ballers and entertainers got their vehicles hooked up. He had a brand new INFINITI FX flatbedded from the dealership for Aiyana in exchange for her Dodge Magnum. He had them put 22 inch Asanti rims on it, some TV's and video games for Naj. He had them put a 5% color, tint on the windows to match the burnt orange paint. They also added a couple sunroofs and some cameras in the rear bumper for live rearview images in the rear view mirror and a monitor in the dash. Mannish was impressed as usual with their work. It hadn't even been a week and they were finished already and had it sitting on display in the front gleaming in the sun. Mannish took it to Aiyana.

When she came outside and seen it on the grass with a big red bow on the hood it caught her off guard. She was expecting to get her Dodge Magnum back. Mannish always knew how to make things up to her.

One time I pulled up on Mannish in the drive thru at Weinershnitzel and caught him getting head from a female that didn't even look that cute. He seemed more embarrassed that she wasn't pretty than the compromising position she was in. By the time I made it back home, Mannish had set up a surprise for me. He met me in the driveway and told me he was taking Naj to the park for a while and left. I was still visibly disappointed. Mannish not offering to help me take the groceries inside had me teetering on the verge of pisstivity.

The front door of the house opened. A shirtless dark skinned male exposing his toned chest and biceps walked towards me.

I watched with an emotion made up of fright, confusion and delight. My fright disappeared due to his disarming smile and the fact that he was only wearing biker shorts and a bow tie.

He flashed his sparkling white teeth and said, "Mannish told me to help you." Without waiting for a response he reached in and grabbed the bags and took them inside. When I walked inside the house, the bare chested guy's clone was standing in the doorway to my bedroom with his arms stretched out like he was holding up the threshold. As soon as the front door was closed, one of the guys pumped the stereo up. The first song that pumped out of the system was, "Pony" by Genu-

ine. The two strippers went into their routine. I resisted but they were relentless, sexy and seductive. They gained control, freaked me and lap danced me. They humped me, took my hand and rubbed their crotch with it. They gave me a good dose of their hottest club routine. Then one took it to the next level and flicked my nipple with his tongue. He raised my dress up and put his head between my legs and sucked my clit until I came.

Then they were gone.

She sat in the INFINITI and admired it. The live rearview fascinated her. Just that one feature had her most ecstatic.

She started the motor, told Naj to buckle up, kissed Mannish and left to go show it to her mother and sisters.

Mannish was proud of himself for overjoying Wifey once again. He went to Big Mama's house to check on Ty.

"Hey Momma what's up, how you feel?"

"Well I been havin' pains in my ears, oh, but it aint medical. It's dat damn nosey ass Mable. Think 'erbody bidness 'round hea hers ta dip her nose in. Den she think it's her duty ta call me an' worry me wit otha' folk bidness. She tell me dat da boy Ty went ta jail fa' shootin' aint da only person he done shot. She was gettin' ready ta say sumpthin' bout Paula but I cut her off."

"Where Ty at now?"

"He back dere in tha garage makin' a racket he wanna call music."

Mannish went into the backyard. He heard some music that sounded like karaoke. He tried to lift up the huge door but it didn't budge. He walked around to the side and found the door unlocked. He walked in and counted six heads. He surveyed the room and saw music equipment, speakers, keyboards, a mixing board and a few other components.

Ty and one of his friends held microphones.

"What's up Mannish, What's the bizness?"

"What, yall the Karaoke Gangstas?"

"Oh you gonna go on me like that? My lyrics is tight, you betta ask somebody."

"I ain't gotta ask nobody. I'm right here right now." Mannish said, leaning back on the wall with his arms crossed on his chest. Ty started pushing buttons and flipping switches looking kinda confused on what buttons did what.

Mannish said, "Let me get a freestyle accapella."

With no hesitation Ty said, "Aight." and opened his mind.

Uh, uh, yeah, yeah, uh... act shitty
and leave wit a flat kidney
ask 50, you can find me in da club
probably got a Mac wit me
and I will get ta sluggin' G
they call me T
instead of pound pound and huggin' me
niggas be reachin' fa' tha thug in me
I'm tha' one take tha crew I'm runnin' wit

startin' trouble wit
out-a-town let's bubble it
watch everybody come back on chrome
double dipped
pull up in tha truck ta Roscoes
bumpin' Kurrupt and Roscoe
jump out and tuck tha roscoe
in tha studio cooking up music
cooking up dope fa' tha summa
ta' come thru laid back in a humma
cucumba color
on tha cell phone with tha homie
tha cell's his home
homie I'm finna drop some money on yuh books
wit a snow bunny that looks
like I'm goin' funny on you crooks
I'll spit out 16 fa' yuh
I'll spit 16 16's fa' 16 niggas
or at 16 niggas
til that 16 turn ta 1 point 6.

"Okay okay you working with something, but was that off the head?"

"Come on Man, you insulting my intelligence and my skill."

"Aight Ty don't hit me, I was just asking. If it's like that then..."

"It's like that."

"Then when you write it should be even better."

"Depends on how I feel."

"Where'd yall get all this equipment shit from?"

"I got some of it from some fiends, but most of it we robbed this nigga on the eastside for."

Mannish looked at Ty and shook his head, realizing it was too late to try to keep him out of the game of the streets. He would have to keep a closer eye on him. Maybe even take him under his wing. His thoughts were interrupted by a knock on the door.

Ty yelled, "Who is that?"

"Tyshon, it's Paula." came back from the other side of the door.

"He aint here!" he yelled.

"Stop playin'" she said stepping through the door.

Paula saw Mannish and said, "What's up Mannish?" in a school girl crush kinda way.

They grew up together. He was her younger cousin but she would've fucked him had he ever gave her the inclination that he was with it. She did the second best thing though, she searched for a man with his qualities.

"What up Paula, what's wrong with your face? Why you got that big ass Band Aid on your cheek?"

"Oh this." she said, touching it with her hand. "Oh, my clumsy ass hair dresser burnt me with the hot curlers the other day."

"Did you kick her ass?"

"You know it!"

"So what brings you through this way though?"

"What? I can't just pop up at my Big Mama's house and check on her?"

"You can do what you wanna, like you been doing as long as I can remember, but why you come here right now is what I'm asking?"

"Oh see, you trippin', Big Mama just had a heart attack and I just wanna make sure she aight. What? Am I interrupting something? You could've just said that! I'm outta here!"

She spun on her heels and was gone, mumbling to herself.

Mutha fuckas be actin' like they shit don't stink.

Everybody looked at each other.

Mannish looked at Ty. "What the fuck is Paula's problem?"

Ty gave an expression as if to say "Who knows?"

"Anyway…" Mannish said, shaking Paula out of his thoughts. "Can all yall rap?" he said to Ty's friends.

"I do." One of the girls said.

"We get down too." Two of the boys said.

"Those two right there, they sing." Ty said pointing at the two girls sitting on the couch. Mannish spent an hour listening to what they all had to offer. Then when he was ready to go, he told Ty to step out to the front with him.

"Check game youngsta." Mannish said, once

they were seated in the truck. "I'ma fuck wit you, but you gonna do shit my way. All this dumb shit you doin' on the block is over, feel me? I got a lot of work but I ain't in no rush to move it. Slow is fa' sho'. You gotta start actin' like a man. Yuh Momma need you. You know since Travis ran off and Big Mama got Shawna into that drug program shit is going to be different with her."

"Yeah all that's cool but I'm tryna be in shit like this. INFINITI trucks that don't nobody else got. Rims that don't move when you drivin' and shit.. I'm tryna rock platinum chains with frost bite. I'm just sayin' though, lemme' get my fifteen minutes of fame in five three minute videos."

"All that shit ain't important."

"Niggas that got shit, like to tell a nigga with nothin' that shit ain't important."

"Calm down lil nigga. All that's gonna come, but you gotta remember what comes first. You gotta take care of what you had before the money."

"I ain't got shit."

"You fool, you got Big Mama in there, who took care of your ass when yo Momma couldn't. But yo Momma still brung you into this world. You coulda been part of a bloody mess soaked in a tampon. Plus your Uncle..." Mannish said with a smile. "...worked his magic and got you out of jail. That's all family and that all come first."

"You right."

"Speaking of family, what the fuck is up wit

Paula?"

Ty dropped his head. It was a hypothetical question but Ty's response said he had the answer. Mannish leaned back in his seat. After a few seconds Ty mumbled something.

"Huh, what you say?" Mannish asked.

"I shot her." Ty said a little bit clearer.

Mannish jumped up. "Huh!"

"I shot her. I just grazed her though. I thought she was them bitch ass niggas that came through earlier that day. It was the way she rolled up, she was askin' fa' the heat to blow."

"When was that?"

"The night before Big Mama came home from the hospital. She extortin' me now so she won't tell Big Mama. She probably wanted $100 just now."

"Why you ain't tell me?"

"Ay Man I wasn't tellin' nobody. I was scared to death, I almost killed her. Big Mama would come outta retirement to kick my ass and plus, Man I ain't tryna stress her out. Big Mama might die or some shit and I ain't tryna see that. I just be tryna do me."

"Well look. I'ma get at Paula. You got her number?"

"Naw."

"That's aight, I'll get it from Kaitlynn. I got some traps to check. I'll probably slide through tomorrow."

Mannish pulled off, dialed Kaitlynn and got

Paula's number. Paula picked up on the first ring.

"Don't waste your time or mine. If you ain't talkin' bout no money you got the wrong number."

"Paula, this is Mannish. Where you at?"

She was shocked to hear his voice on the other end of the phone. For one, he had never called her before. And for two, she had just mouthed off at him not thinking she would see him anytime soon.

After a few seconds of silence Mannish said, "Paula, you there?"

"Yeah, what's up Man?"

"Where you at?"

"I'm at home in the projects." she told him, figuring he wouldn't want to come there, because it sounded like he was trying to see her for some reason.

"Which ones?" he asked.

She was wrong.

"Imperial Courts." she answered.

"What apartment?"

"Why?"

"Oh, yuh cousin can't come visit? It's like that?"

"Stop playin' you ain't been tryna come visit."

"Aight fuck it then, I'll just keep it. Ty had told me to drop you off a couple hundred dollars but fuck it."

"216."

"Huh?"

"I live in number 216."

"Oh, now you wanna tell somebody where you live. That's aight I changed my mind."

"Boy, stop playin'. You comin'?"

"Yeah I'm bout to make a run then I'll be there in about a hour."

An hour later Paula looked out the window when she heard 2Pac hollering to be buried a G. Mannish parked, hopped out of the truck and adjusted his Biz-e-Bee Apparel sweatshirt.

Paula yelled, "Up here!"

When Mannish strode into the house he noticed Paula still had on the Band Aid. He observed two thugs sitting on the couch playing Madden 2005 on a Sony PlayStation 2. He also noticed that they weren't engrossed in the game but were more like just wasting time, unlike the fanatics most players are.

Paula said, "So what's up?"

Mannish said, "Nothin'." with his eyes trained on the dudes on the couch. Paula extended her hand, palm upward. Mannish gave no reaction. She figured maybe he didn't want to pull the money out in front of strangers.

"Let's go in here." she said, heading into the bedroom. When they got into the room she closed the door. "Okay break bread like Jesus did with the 12 disciples."

"Hold up, cause I ain't Jesus, and you sho' ain't no disciple. And I don't appreciate you havin' these grimey ass niggas over here when you knew

I was comin' over."

"This my mutha fuckin house! Besides I didn't know if you was gonna trip cause I cussed yo ass out earlier or what."

"Oh, so they over here for me?"

"No, not like that. I just didn't tell them to leave when you said you was comin.'"

"Second of all, where you get off extortin' ya lil family member?"

"That nigga shot me!" she yelled back.

"You didn't get shot! The bullet grazed you." he said, snatching the Band Aid off of her cheek.

"So what you sayin', you ain't gonna give me nothin'?"

"Naw, I ain't sayin…"

"I need that money! I'm tryna ta get my stuff together! Them people took my kids and they want me to jump thru all kinds of hoops and shit, classes and shit. They talkin' bout I gotta move to a two bedroom."

"Why you ain't tell nobody?"

"Ain't nobody ever been there for me before!"

"You the one that separated yourself from everybody else."

"Well that bitch Shawna got all yall hatin' me!"

"What the fuck are you talkin' about? Shawna don't say shit about you! Look, I ain't even bout to go there with you." Mannish stuck his hand into his pocket. "I'm gonna give you this one time lump sum. Don't ask Ty for shit else."

Her eyes got big. But before he got it out of

his pocket he heard the distinctive sound of the INFINITI car alarm. He ran into the living room to look out the window. He saw shattered glass on the concrete from his passenger window and a silhouette of someone moving around in the driver's seat. He turned to exit the apartment and handle his bizness. But just then he was sucker punched with a strong right fist to the jaw that dropped him to the floor. He caught a foot to the stomach. A hand reached down and attempted to snatch his platinum chain off of his neck. It didn't break.

"Come up out all yo shit pussy!" a voice barked.

Mannish's vision cleared and focused on the two dudes standing over him. Both of them had a pistol pointed at him. He broke into a quick crawl and dove behind the couch and pulled his 9mm out of the small of his back. A burst of shots went through the couch narrowly missing him. He ran for the bedroom door with his gun in his left hand shooting back under his right arm. They fired again riddling the walls. One of them ran behind him shooting with his gun outstretched leading the way. Just inside the doorway Mannish tripped over Paula's body. She had gotten shot through the wall. Two more shots rang out from Mannish's gun. He heard a quick cry then silence from one of the would-be robbers. The other robber ran out the building. Mannish ran down the stairs behind him.

The would-be thief that was in the truck evidently couldn't bypass the sophisticated alarm system. He was probably scared off by the gunshots. Mannish pushed the button on his remote and started the engine as he ran to it. He put the key in the ignition and unlocked the steering wheel. The radio clicked on. 2Pac yelled as if on queue,

"Cowards couldn't stop me..." Mannish busted a U-turn to head out of the west side of the projects, the opposite way of the Sheriff's Station. Before he could turn the corner he heard more shots. His back window dropped into a million pieces. His music pumped into the street with clarity. "I can't deny it, I'm a straight ridah, you don't want to fuck wit me..."

He rounded the corner and smashed on the gas.

CHAPTER SIXTEEN

Mannish took the back streets to Cherise's house. He pulled the truck into the backyard. He needed to get it off of the streets as soon as possible with all the broken windows.

Cherise opened the back door. "Damn, what happened?"

"I don't know. I was parked in the wrong place at the wrong time. When I came back to it, it was like this. I'll get it fixed later but right now I need the keys to your Cadillac truck."

"Naw Mannish, I'm not giving you my truck. I'ma be stuck here."

"Don't act stupid. I bought that truck. I got things to do. Gimme' the fuckin' keys Cherise!"

She gave him the keys reluctantly. When he left she went back into the house.

"Dexter you can come out now, wit yo scary ass." Cherise said.

A 140 lbs. 5'7" pretty boy with curly hair and a light, bright, damn near white skin complexion came out of the closet wearing only a tank top, boxers and socks.

He said, "Whatever. You can call me what you want, but I ain't the only one who was gonna have problems if he caught me up in here. Why you didn't tell me he was coming anyway?"

"Nigga I didn't know. He come through when he feel like it. But he ain't been by in a while though."

"Cause he got anotha woman, that's why! He don't give a fuck about you and you be sittin' up here tellin' me I can't move in cause of this nigga. He just took your truck and left you stranded and shit."

"Nigga shut up! He getting money, being a man. You ain't doing nothing, you broke."

"I hope that nigga get caught!"

"He taking care of his son and me. You keep talkin' like that and this'll be the last time you beat these ass cheeks." she said, grabbing his boxers from the front along with a hand full of his dick. "Damn that's what I like and it ain't even hard." Cherise said, as she wiggled out of her thong and climbed onto the bed pulling him behind her.

"Come on hit this fat ass and stop hating."

She came down on her elbows in a doggystyle position, arched her back and looked back at him over her shoulders. She spread her legs. Her skirt rode up her hips and sat bunched up around her waist. Her big brown round ass commanded his full attention. She pulled a pillow close and laid her head down on it as if to say, *Fuck me now baby*. Her pussy peeked out from the back. His dick hardened and raised up like it was a cannon preparing to fire at the enemy. He inserted his thumb into her wetness and rubbed it up and down her lips to lubricate his entry. Then he navigated the head of his dick through the opening and pushed in two inches. She cooed. He pushed another two inches in, she inhaled. He withdrew halfway, her body tingled. Then he slammed all nine inches of his dick into her. She clinched the sheets. He pulled all the way out to the tip then slammed back into her. Repeatedly, his pelvis smacked into her ass. Then they fell into a rhythm. It sounded like someone was applauding. With every pump they slid closer and closer to the headboard, until her head was knocking on it.

"Boy, you gonna give me a concussion!" She put her hand up on the wall to brace herself.

He was long stroking her so much to the point where he would come all the way out and then drop it back in so deep that his balls were slapping her clit.

Sweat was burning his eyes. He let his dick sit deep inside of her while he wiped his face with his undershirt. When he began stroking again he changed up his rhythm and started grinding, slowly rotating his hips, exploring every corner of her pussy. She felt his dick enlarge and get hard as a steel pipe. She knew he was about to cum. She jerked forward on his upstroke. His dick came out.

"Lay on your back Dexter." she said.

He did as he was told. She straddled him and lowered herself so his dickhead gently slid through her lips. He cultivated the feeling. Goose bumps arose on his skin. She sat down completely devouring him with her vagina.

On the outside it appeared they weren't moving. She was flexing her inner muscles massaging his dick into an ejaculation. And ejaculate he did. He showered her walls with cream and the two of them dosed off.

About thirty minutes later they awoke and got cleaned up. Then she told him to take her to Vallawn's house to pick up Taj. When they left they had to walk down the block and around the corner to where he parked his 1987 Honda Accord. The paint was faded across the roof, hood and trunk.

When they were in front of Vallawn's building, Cherise chirped her on the Boost phone. She admired a brand new Navigator on 26 inch wheels with paper plates on it parked out front.

"Ay, I'm outside. Tell Taj to come out." Cherise said to Vallawn over the twoway.

Vallawn looked out the window then answered back. "Come in for a minute."

When Cherise got inside Q-Tip had his head stuck behind the 65 inch plasma television on the wall.

"I don't see what you talking about." he said,

after coming from behind it. He was just as surprised to see Cherise as she was to see him. A good surprise. Cherise was wondering what was going on.

"Maybe I was tripping." Vallawn said.

"Trippin' about what?" Cherise asked.

"Some way to hook up the satellite, the Wii game, the X Box, the internet, the DVD and stuff a certain way, I don't know. But since we all here and the kids are taking a nap, I want yall to taste something. You two have a seat. I just got a new blender."

She pulled a can of frozen pink lemonade out of the freezer, some whipped cream out of the refrigerator and some Bombay Gin out of the cabinet. While she worked on her concoction Cherise ran outside and told Dexter to leave. When she came back in the drinks were ready.

"It's called Pink Panties, tell me if you like it." Vallawn said.

"Ooh, It's strong." Cherise said.

"This a girl drink." Q-Tip said.

"Fool, just taste it before you say something."

He tasted it, frowned up his face then drank the rest down. "That shit is strong though."

"You want some more?"

"Yeah, gimme' some mo.'"

"Down yours Cherise, so I could make another batch." Vallawn said.

"Damn bitch, what you tryna do, get me drunk?"

"Nah, maybe that one was a little strong. Let me hook up some more right quick."

Q-Tip said, "Yeah that one got me warmed up, dick hard and everything." as he leaned back dipping his hand into his pants like Al Bundy.

"You said that like you trying to get some or something." said Vallawn.

"Well you know, I am in the presence of two fine bi... I mean lovely ladies."

"Boy, if Mannish knew you was talking like that..." Cherise said.

"I ain't scared of that nigga, naw, fa' real though I am. I respect his gangsta. It ain't like that though. I ain't tryna push up on you Cherise. It's just, you know, we in here. Ain't nobody gotta know nothing about nothing."

"You wanna fuck me Q-Tip?" Cherise said teasingly.

"Come on, don't play."

"Want me to suck yo dick Q-Tip?"

His dick got harder and poked out of the top of his pants. He fidgeted in his seat, put his hands on the back of the couch, then put them down by his side, then folded his arms across his chest.

He said, "See that's that alcohol talking."

"Nigga please, see you just fucked yours off. I gotta use the bathroom."

Cherise stood and headed upstairs to the bathroom.

He watched and marveled at how far her ass pushed her skirt from the back of her legs.

Vallawn told him, "Pussy ain't free nigga, especially up in here. You need to do like Snoop Dogg say and drop it like it's hhhooott."

She put her hand up on her hip. "I'm serious, you know I'm serious. Slide a credit card down a bitch ass cheeks or something."

"I'ma tell you what. I'm bout to go in the bathroom with Cherise and if she trip I'ma give you a thousand dollars for some of your pussy. But if she fucks me you owe me some ass later in the game for free, aight?"

"Aight." Vallawn agreed, thinking to herself, *anyway it goes is a win*. "Let me tell her something first."

"You smoking crack, fuck naw."

He picked up one of the glasses Vallawn had poured and drank it halfway down. Q-Tip went upstairs and strode into the bathroom full of confidence like he was at home and it was his wife in there taking a wiz. He shut the door behind himself.

Vallawn sat on the couch, picked up the remote and enjoyed her drink. She caught an episode of Martin on cable. Martin's character Kung Fu Joe was getting his ass whooped. Then a scene with Roscoe at Shanana's door swindling her for some money had Vallawn cracking up. She drank and laughed not realizing that Q-Tip and Cherise had been in the bathroom for 20 minutes until the show went off. Vallawn was entertaining the thought of crashing their party or joining in, when they came out trying to look innocent.

Well, Cherise tried to look innocent. Q-Tip's face expressed his state of mind. He had won the bet. He had fucked Cherise and like a Playa, he had fucked for free and would fuck Vallawn soon. Vallawn read his face and smirked with mischief in her eyes. She brought her attention back to Cherise.

"Bitch stop trying to look like Mother Theresa with your hot coochie ass." Vallawn said.

Cherise broke out in laughter. "You sent him in there!"

"I didn't send him anywhere."

"Bitch you know you wanted me to fuck him, and yo ass wanna fuck him too."

Before anybody else could say anything Cherise's phone squawked.

"Cherise!" It was Mannish's voice. "Cherise, where you at?"

She hurried to answer. She picked up the phone and pushed the button to talk but there was a loud tone. That happens when both ends try to talk at the same time. She released the button.

"Cherise!" came through the speaker again. She tried the button again. Two beeps sounded to let her know it was okay to talk. She put her finger to her lips looking at Q-Tip to indicate for him to be quiet.

"I'm over Vallawn's house."

"Why you didn't tell me you was leavin'?"

"You at the house?" She thought of saying my

house because he's never there but thought better of it.

"Yeah, what you doin'?"

"I'm trippin' off Vallawn tryna make some Pink Panties."

She looked at Vallawn and shrugged her shoulders.

"How you get over there?"

One lie deserves another.

"She came and got me."

"Aight, well I'm gonna come get you."

"You don't have to. She can bring me."

"I'm already on my way."

She dropped the phone and started pushing Q-Tip.

"You gotta go."

"Where he at?"

"I don't know. Just hurry up before he see your truck."

"I ain't going nowhere. I could say I'm here for Vallawn."

"Bullshit! We ain't even gonna try that." Cherise yelled.

"Gimme' some head first, then I'll leave."

"Nigga fuck you! What I tell you in the bathroom? I don't do that."

"You can't tell me Mannish don't make you suck his dick."

"You ain't him plus I said I don't suck dick."

"Yeah okay." he said with a lot of air in his words as he flopped down on the couch.

Under any other circumstances Vallawn would've went in the room and got the gun. But this was intriguing her.

"Nigga don't sit down!" Cherise yelled.

"Gimme' a reason to stand up like to take my pants off."

"Look nigga if you don't leave and he come find you here, I'm going make up a lie that's gonna make him kill you right here where the fuck you sitting."

"And I'ma tell him what your pussy lips look like. And how you shake and cry when you cum."

"Damn Q-Tip! I ain't got no time to be sucking yo dick plus you just came so it's gonna take forever."

"I tell you what, just put my nuts in your mouth and hum your favorite song."

She gave in and did as he demanded. After about a minute she said, "Aight dude, you gonna have to go."

He agreed and slipped his pants back up, grabbed the door handle and left.

The girls went out on the balcony to make sure he was completely gone before Mannish hit the corner. They watched Q-Tip's taillights disappear around the corner.

Cherise and Vallawn stayed out in the night air reflecting on what just happened. Cherise wanted to slap the shit out of Vallawn for not intervening. She looked over at her.

"Anyway, why you didn't help me? I woulda

helped you."

Vallawn couldn't resist. She took the opportunity to recite a line from the movie Friday.

"What about the time he tried to rape me in Smoke backyard?"

Cherise fell right in with her. "Oh, that was different."

They saw headlights hit the corner but they heard the music first. A burnt orange INFINITI FX on big wheels slowed then stopped in front of the complex.

They couldn't see inside but chances were it was Mannish.

The window came down and the music poured out.

It was Keysha Cole singing, "If he ain't treatin' you the way he should then let it go." The song had a good sound to it but Cherise couldn't help but think he was telling her something, telling the neighborhood something. The music went down.

Mannish yelled, "Come on!"

"Come up and get your son, he sleep." she yelled back.

The music went back up. He hopped out of the truck and left it running in the middle of the street. The dome lights lit up the interior. His leprechaun green velour sweat suit swayed in fluid motion at his every movement up the staircase. Vallawn acknowledged him when he looked up with a head nod. Cherise went inside to open the door.

"What's up stranger?" Vallawn said from the balcony.

"It's a strange world girl. I see the same strangers everyday. People have kids with strangers."

The door opened. Mannish got Taj and they left. As they rolled down Rosecrans to Crenshaw, Cherise sat with her arms folded staring at Mannish. He noticed but ignored her. There was too much on his mind and too many things to deal with. The air conditioner blew a whiff past his nose. He looked at her.

"You been drinking?"

"You know I love you right?"

"Yeah but I said, have you been drinking?"

"Why don't you ever come home?"

The alcohol started talking. "Day in day out I be waiting on you." she said, getting louder. "Why don't you ever come home?" she said even louder. "Cause you be over that bitch house!"

"First of all, stop yelling!"

In a lower voice she said, "When you gonna sleep wit me? You know we only had sex once in the last two months? And I ain't messing wit nobody else. Can you say that?"

"Cherise?"

"What?"

"Shut the fuck up. I ain't tryna hear all that right now. I got a lot going on. Both my vehicles got shot up. My boy Jay got popped and by the Feds at that. You know Big Mama ain't doin' so good and she even worse now cause the police called her and told her Paula was dead. They called my cell phone cause that was the last number that called her house. Ty had my phone when they called and after he told them that he called her earlier that day and what relation he was to her, they talked to Big Momma and told her she was found dead in her apartment. The last time I talked to her she told me that the Children's Social Service people had took her kids. Plus I got shit to deal with, with these mutha fuckas in the valley. Damn!"

He beat his fist on the steering wheel. She cringed and sunk down deep in her seat. And for the first time she noticed how comfortable it was in her seat. She admired the dashboard, looked up at the two sunroofs.

"Who's truck is this?"

"Mine."

"Didn't you just buy that truck that's at my house with the windows shot out?"

"Yeah."

"Where my truck at?"

"Damn 21 questions, yo shit at yo house!"

"I know you didn't let somebody else drive my truck!"

"Naw." he answered but his mind was somewhere else.

He ran a red light on Rosecrans and Van Ness and almost caused an accident. He snapped out of it, reached for the remote and flipped through Aiyana's CDs in the changer.

Fantasia's Baby Mama came up on the display. The song came on and hyped Cherise up.

"B-A-B-Y M-A-M-A." she sung along, annoying the shit out of him.

"Ay, who sing that?"

"Fantasia."

"Okay let her do what she do and you do what you do, but singing ain't it."

"Fuck you Mannish." She pouted. He pulled into the driveway behind her Cadillac truck and carried Taj in the house.

"Mannish can you hold me tonight, I forgot what it feels like to have a man in my bed." she said, while he tucked Taj in his bed.

"I can't, got shit to do but I'll holla if I make it back to L.A. tonight."

Before he left he went into the backyard to cover his windows to prevent cats and bugs and morning dew from getting inside his truck. Then he took Crenshaw to the 105 Fwy East to the 110 Fwy South to the 91 Fwy East to the city of Cerritos.

He stretched out on the couch and used the remote control to navigate to his favorite scene in his favorite movie. He fell asleep, the TV started watching him.

He repositioned himself several times but he never got up. His defense mechanism was in full effect. He was worried about too many new things on top of his usual hectic lifestyle. At some point the beep of his cell phone telling him he had messages woke him up. When he looked at the screen it said he had 14 messages.

Damn 14 messages! I didn't hear the phone ring once.

He looked at the time. It was 3 o'clock in the afternoon.

He thought back. It must've been about 12 o'clock last night when I went to sleep. I needed that lil rest. I feel really rested. He glanced at the date on his phone, his eyes shot back to the date. Then at the date on his watch.

Hold up!

He went and looked at the calendar.

What the hell...3 days! It's Saturday, Damn! I slept 3 days?

He went and flopped back down on the couch to listen to his messages.

{you have 14 messages. Press 5 to listen to your...}

beep. {first message} "Baby this is Aiyana. Where are you? You know I have to go to work and you have both vehicles."

beep. He pressed 4. {message sent at 5am Thursday}

beep. He pressed 7. {message erased, next message}

beep. "Baby It's 5:30. If you're not here in five minutes I'm going to call in sick."

beep. {message erased, next message} "Everything's okay I called in. Call me, let me know you're alright."

beep {message erased, next message} "Ay Man, this Ty. I know you wondering what a nigga doing up this early in the morning. It's because the police just left, some homicide detectives and shit. They wanted to know if we knew any of Paula's friends that had a white INFINITI SUV. I told 'em naw. Big Mama wondering what's going on, me too. Man, why they asking bout yo truck? Now I'm wondering why they call yo phone that day. Ain't like I'm in yo bizness but this family shit, holla."

beep {message erased, next message} "Mannish come get in the bed wit me. I don't even wanna get up today. My head hurt I think I got a hangover. Yuh son already got picked up by the school bus, we got the house all day, you can have it anyway you want..."

beep {message erased, next message} "This is Aiyana, your son got suspended from school. They said that he and his friends put a banana in the tailpipe of the Principal's car. I knew I shouldn't have let him watch Beverly Hills Cop last night. Kaitlynn had to go get him. Can you at least bring me one of the trucks? You never know when an emergency might come up. Are you alright?"

beep {message erased, next message} "This is Paul Downing, just calling to inform you that Jay had a court appearance this morning. It wasn't really anything, just procedural. The prosecutor hasn't turned over any discovery but everything is still in the preliminary stages. Uh, hold on...

yeah, okay tell him to come in Sherry. Okay hey Mantrell we'll talk later. Bye."

beep {message saved, next message} "Fuck you Mannish! You had me waiting on yuh ass all day. I'm about to go to the club with Vallawn. I'ma drop off Taj at Big Mama's house."

beep {message erased, next message} "Ay Man, this Ty, Cherise dropped off Taj talkin' bout goin' out, but she lookin' like one of them video bitches. I'm just sayin' though. She due for your foot in her ass."

beep {message erased, next message} "If you want me to call in sick again let me know. Me and your son are worried. Call us."

beep {message erased, next message} "Hello this is Golden INFINITI, calling to make sure that you have found a quality vehicle in Infin..."

beep {message erased, next message} "Man holla at me, a nigga tryna get paid. We gonna do this shit or what? You gotta come thru anyway cause Big Mama said get yo butt over here. She still trippin' bout them police that came over here a couple days ago."

beep {message erased, next message} "Ay Mannish this is Vallawn. I know you wondering how I got your number and why I'm calling. I've had your number for a while now. I got it outta Cherise's phone one day a long time ago!" He was shocked for real. With her fine ass. He thought. "Look Mannish, I don't like talking to machines. Just call me at 310-672-1234 bye."

beep {message saved, next message.} "Hey this me again, I'ma be at home all day, just come by when you get a chance." Vallawn said.

beep {message erased, you have no more messages.}

He took a shower and stretched out on the bed asshole naked. He thought about what he would do over the next 48hrs. He laid there for an hour before he was content, with a few things in perspective. He strode into the living room with his dick swinging, sat and watched his DVD for a couple minutes. This time he tried to figure out where the bank robbers went wrong at. He amused himself with his objective. He had watched the scene a thousand times and always just enjoyed the killing of the police and the cars left riddled and smoking. He enjoyed how Val Kilmer didn't hesitate a second to shoot when he saw the Feds. But this time he was deliberating on how they could've avoided that. He deliberated in the nude.

By the time he was ready to get dressed and head out it was going on 6 o'clock in the evening. He opened the bedroom window to get a feel of the climate. It was kinda chilly. He perused his closet for something appropriate.

He chose to dress in Coogi down to the socks. He took five bundles out of his Avirex jacket and threw them into a duffle bag in the closet. He grabbed two bricks, put them in a backpack and was out.

CHAPTER SEVENTEEN

Mannish's first stop was Vallawn's house. When she heard the loud music playing the same song he was playing the last time he came over she looked out the window and saw the FX stop in front.

She ran outside to greet him. "What's up Mannish?"

"What's up, who in the house with you?"

"It's just me and my daughter Shani."

"You got a credit card right?"

"Yeah."

"I need you to rent a car for me for a couple of days if you don't mind. Get your daughter and come on. We'll talk about what you called me for on the way."

"Okay I'll be right back."

He stopped her and said, "Ay, take this backpack, hold it for me til we get back. Put it up somewhere."

She came back with her daughter, purse, two

sandwiches and a bag of chips. They drove towards the airport where there were plenty of rental car agencies to choose from.

"So what's up, what's the bizness?" he said.

"You."

He laughed that modest laugh. "Me, what about me?"

"Hold up." she said. "Shani, you gonna eat this sandwich?"

"No I'm not hungry Vallawn."

"Good, more for me." Vallawn turned the game on, handed her the controller and put the headphones on her ears.

"Look Mannish I ain't finna play no games or beat around the bush. Cherise fucked Q-Tip over my house that night you came to pick her up."

He felt like she just hit his brain with a jolt of electricity, like someone poured ice water over his head.

"And some other nigga she fucking too dropped her off over my house."

"Her and Taj?"

"No, I had Taj alI that day."

He instantly reflected on everything Cherise ever did that didn't seem right. Every lie he ever caught her in. He thought about her telling him she wasn't messing around.

She had lied just to be lying.

Vallawn was still talking but Mannish didn't hear a thing she was saying. He was weighing his options and course of action. Then all that came to a halt and it all landed on the question of why was Vallawn telling him this anyway.

"Why you telling me though? She's your friend. That means you ain't shit either."

"Yeah, you could say it like that. But that's shallow and I say that because there really ain't no reason for her to play you like that and she been doing this even back before you started brushing her off. I guess you sensed something. That's when I got your number. I'm just saying you take good care of her. She don't have to work, never did in the 7 years y'all been together, even while you were locked up. You know like I know, like everybody knows, there's a shortage of men out here. We out number y'all like ten to one. Each man can have five women and it'll still be women with no man. But a woman has no excuse to have more than one man, unless she's trying to piece a man together. You know, one for financial reasons, one that can fuck the pussy right and you know like that. But you got everything a woman needs in a man, and believe me, I heard how you put the dick down. She's my friend but she's superficial. I've been thinking about this for awhile. I don't give her no money, I don't fuck her. Me and her don't have any kids together. How can she hold me in a higher esteem than you? She can't. I can't trust her too much. There just aren't opportunities for her to do me wrong like that. I know your value as a man, a hustler and a gangster."

She took his hand and placed it under her skirt between her legs so he could feel the moisture. He swerved into the next lane and played it off like he meant to change lanes. He thanked God there wasn't a car in that lane at that time.

"This pussy doesn't need to be touched by nobody but you. You and me."

She noticed he had pitched a tent in his Coogi sweatpants. She looked in the back behind her seat to see Shani still preoccupied with the game. She gently patted him.

"This ain't about me giving you some pussy. I'm talking about taking her place. The place she was in when it was all good."

By this time they were parked in Alamo's car rental parking lot.

"That's all I'm going to say about that. What kind of car do you want Mannish?"

"I don't care as long as it's comfortable and it ain't red or white. Those cars stand out and get the most tickets."

Twenty minutes later Vallawn pulled up to Mannish in a dark green Dodge Caravan.

"A van huh?" Mannish commented.

"In case things happen fast. I might wanna go up to Mulholland Dr. and enjoy the view while I enjoy you."

"Follow me to Big Mama's house." Mannish

said.

"Lead the way."

When they pulled up, Ty was waiting on the porch. Vallawn got into the FX with Mannish and Ty got into the driver's seat of the van. Mannish drove off and Ty followed. When they got back to Vallawn's house they all went inside. Mannish noticed Ty adjusted his pants before he sat down on the couch.

"What you got on you, a strap?"

"Yep, you know it."

"Let me see it."

"I don't let nobody hold my weapon."

"You lil nigga that don't apply to me, stupid." Mannish said, reaching down and taking the gun out of Ty's pants. It was a brand new Smith and Wesson, blue steel .45 automatic with a wooden handle.

"Where'd you get this from?"

"This dude came thru the block the other day with a couple of 'em. I got this one for a hundred bucks.

Mannish's antennas went up.

"A White boy?" Mannish asked.

"Yep."

"You gave him cash?"

"Yep, I gave him all I had too. First he wanted three hundred but I talked him down. For real anyway once I had it in my hand he wasn't gettin' it back."

"What else was he talking about?" Mannish asked, flipping the gun onto the couch.

"Nothin' really, he said he had more, different kinds too. I wasn't trippin' off none a that once I seen this."

"Did he say he'd take dope?"

"Yeah, yeah he did say that. You wanna get some. Hell yeah that's a good idea! I bet I can get a gang a shit for a chicken or a half of one!"

"That fool is the police." Mannish said.

Ty looked confused.

"Oh, the police goin' hard in the hood huh? You talkin' bout like them fools from Rampart, stealin' shit from the evidence room and sellin' it back on the street? Training Day shit huh!"

"Naw, they setting people up. That's the fool who set my boy Jay up."

Ty looked at the gun like it just turned into a hand full of shit. Vallawn played her position and waited until they were done talking. Then she went into the room and came out with the backpack and handed it to Mannish.

He asked her if she had anything to eat. Vallawn went into the kitchen. Pots, pans and spoons and knives started making that sound chefs make.

Mannish sat next to Ty, gave him directions and instructions on what to do with the two kilos in the backpack and how much to expect. He told him when he was done to meet him at his house.

Mannish ate and spent another hour and a half talking with Vallawn before he went home. When he got there Ty was already there. He was stretched out on the couch watching a movie and eating a Chili Cheese Fatburger and some Chili Cheese Fries from Fatburgers. Ty's hands were full, lips were greasy and his mouth was full. He gave Mannish a nod letting him know everything had gone smooth. Mannish scooped up the backpack containing the $30,000 and went into the bedroom where Naj was asleep, tucked under Aiyana who was reading a new released novel by Zane. She set the book down and eased out of the bed so as not to wake Naj. She wrapped her arms around Mannish's neck and held him tight. Her face wet with tears. She held him for five minutes quietly. He held her around her waist. Her feet didn't touch the floor. She was only 5'2". When she loosened her grasp, maybe more from her arms being fatigued then satisfied affection, he let her down. She looked him in his eyes.

"Don't do us like that again, please. I don't even care where you've been, I'm just glad that you're alright."

She got up on her tippy toes, put her hands on the side of his face and kissed his lips, his nose and his forehead.

She looked him in the face a little longer, then went and got back in the bed. He went and put the backpack in the back of the closet. Then he picked out a grey and white Biz-e-Bee Apparel sweatsuit made of terrycloth and some fresh white air force ones to wear the next day. When he turned around Aiyana was sound asleep. He grabbed a white L.A. Dodgers fitted cap and went into the living room. Ty was eating a Chili Cheese Dog. Mannish set his clothes down and went out the back door and into the garage. He had to stand on a table to reach the top of the cabinet. He got a guncase off of it. He unzipped it and removed the AK47 Jay had left at The Spot. He went and got Naj's pellet gun that was leaning up against the wall in the corner of the garage. Mannish took both guns over to his Snap On tool cabinet and went to work.

In fifteen minutes he had successfully removed the scope from the pellet gun and fastened it to the AK47. He put it back in the guncase, went down the driveway and put it in the van. He then went into the house to retrieve his clothes and Ty. They got in the van and left.

When they stopped in front of Big Mama's house Mannish told Ty. "Tell Big Mama I'll come see her tomorrow."

He handed Ty $500 in twenties wrapped in a rubberband.

"Good lookin' out Man."

"Fa' sho."

"Man, I got a lot more clientele lined up. I'm

ready to do this."

"All money ain't good money."

"It all spends the same."

"See that's where you got it fucked up at. It be like that sometimes, and sometimes you don't get to spend it. Slow up speedy. You gonna be alright. And stay away from that white boy."

"Shit, you ain't gotta tell me twice!"

Mannish headed back over to Vallawn's house. He called and told her he'd be over there in ten minutes and to unlock the door. He liked the way she was catering to him. It reminded him of what was good about new pussy.

When a new female is trying to lock you in, she's so sweet.

Whatever you want, you got that. If you want her to suck your dick upside down, you got that. Initially, Mannish had planned on fucking her all night but he decided to drag her on and make her wait for the sex. He had to be strong. He had to get his libidinous desire under control, but every move she made pumped blood into his dick.

He kept telling himself *Mind over matter, don't fuck her.*

Mind over matter, don't fuck her.

When they went to sleep they were in a spoon position. If she was paralyzed from the neck down, she still would've felt the wood in her back. He woke up in the morning to a blow job sooo succulent and slow. He raised his head to look and saw her head slide up and down on his glistening rod. Her hair hung down wild and long as she moaned like she was being fucked just as slow and intensely. When her head raised up, he could see her beautiful, dark caramel breasts hang full and firm. His head dropped back down on the pillow. His eyes rolled into the top of his head. His legs got tight and stiffened up. His feet raised up off of the bed. His head got light as if he was going to lose consciousness. Every muscle in his body spasmed. He erupted in her mouth. Chill bumps covered his flesh. More spasms preceded a dead calm. His dick laid limp on his belly. Drops of cum settled in his navel with a thread trail to the tip of his dick.

Vallawn laid her head on one of his thighs and caressed the other. She heard heavy breathing, he was back to sleep with a smile. This was a moment in time she wished she could live in forever. The phone rang and interrupted her groove like a scratched record. She bounced out of the bed to go catch the phone in the living room.

Her bounce woke him up. He got to see her naked body and fat voluptuous butt jiggle out of the room. This was one of those moments he wished would last longer than they usually did. He laid there thinking about what he had planned, which was to catch Hector slipping and completely off guard because it was Mother's Day. Hector would most likely stop by his mother's house unprepared for war.

Ain't no rules in war.

Mannish got out of the bed to take a shower. He was more than happy to be awakened in the fashion he was and he was glad she did it early so that he could get up and get out, post up and get the jump on Hector. When Mannish stepped out of the bathroom dressed, Vallawn was still on the phone. She motioned for him to wait. She ended the phone call then asked if he wanted breakfast.

He told her he'd probably get something from McDonalds.

"Can you take me to drop my daughter off at my mother's house?"

"What do you mean drop you off, Where your car at?"

"It's at the dealer. They're doing my transmission and brakes. I'll get it back tomorrow. Why do you think I was at home all day yesterday?"

"Damn, I got something I'm tryna do."

"Well go ahead then, handle your bizness." she said and pouted her lips.

She looked like a cute little kid disappointed because she was told she couldn't have any ice cream.

"Come on, damn, where you gotta go?" Mannish said.

She smiled and ran into the room.

She hollered back. "She lives off of Arlington."

He stepped out onto the balcony and pondered how he would work around the inconvenience. The only thing that made it so hectic was that he didn't know what time Hector would show up at his mother's house.

The whole time he drove he thought *Why didn't I just tell this bitch no?* When he parked in front of Vallawn's mom's house he said, "Why don't you just stay here?"

"You must be kidding. Me and my Momma don't get along like that. Wait a minute." She ran up the walkway with Shani and was back in less than a minute. "I'm witchu."

"Naw, no you ain't. Why don't you go over Cherise's house?"

"That's halfway back to my house."

"Yeah only halfway."

"What you gonna do, drop me off on the corner of Cherise's block?"

"Yeah, up the street or something."

"Let me call her. But I'ma tell you something. I ain't trying to be no sneaky bitch. If I go over there I'ma tell her I sucked your dick."

"Why would you do that?"

"Cause I did."

"Get the fuck in the van!"

He drove off thinking *Why didn't I just tell this bitch no?*

Lost in thought, he was near his destination sooner than he realized. He was in the Hancock Park area. He had to circle a few blocks a few times to remember. It had been a long time since Hector used to sell dope there with his Uncle (Papi Scarface) before Papi quit the game and left everything to Hector. Mannish spotted a church.

He remembered the church was right up the street from the house. He drove down the street.

There's the house.

A palm tree sat in front between the sidewalk and the curb. A lemon tree sat in the yard just as he remembered. He went down the block and turned around. He parked next to the church. The house was a hundred yards up. He sat and listened to the choir inside singing in praise to God.

Vallawn said, "Here I am hanging with you on Mother's Day. Um, not a good gift for Taj's mom huh? What were you planning on giving her or doing for her?" Before he could answer, if he was even going to, she asked another question. "How long we gonna sit here?"

"Listen, I don't want to hear your voice right now. I told you I had something to do. Now just chill out and shut the fuck up!"

Dejected by his statement and frightened by the tone of his voice she took his advice, reclined her seat and turned the radio on station 94.7 The Wave to hear some smooth jazz. Mannish looked at her with a less than friendly look then turned it off. He looked at his watch. 9:45am. He heard the church house sound off with handclapping.

He thought about the possibility of the church letting out and church goers being up and down the street mingling and going to their cars when Hector pulled up. He ran different scenarios of things that could go wrong. Then he started thinking that he could actually be there all day waiting. How did he know if Hector's mother even still lived there? He was trying to figure out a way to find out if she still lived there when a green candy flake Dodge Ram truck with 26 inch rims pulled into the driveway.

Mannish's face lit up. Vallawn could tell something caught his attention. Mannish scrambled to the back of the van and grabbed the gun case, snatched out the AK equipped with the scope and got back in the driver's seat.

He propped the barrel up on the side view mirror. He adjusted his seat and kicked his knee up to rest the gun on. Vallawn stared at him bewildered. Astonished and alarmed, she panicked.

"What are you doing?!"

"Shut up!" he said in an octave higher than a whisper.

Hector stepped out of the truck and began to straighten out his clothes. He had lost a lot of weight, probably due to his unfortunate hospitalization from the gunshot wound Mannish had inflicted on him. Mannish had Hector in his sights. He put the cross on Hector's heart and braced himself for the kick of the assault rifle.

He thought to himself. *A lil off center.*

Hector's body turned. The shot was no good. He lowered his knee an inch to put the cross on Hector's head.

"Mannish this isn't funny!" Vallawn said.

"I ain't here to amuse you." he said through clenched teeth.

She shouted, "Why you bring me to..."

Before she could finish her sentence, Mannish slapped the rest of the words out of her mouth. She leaped into the back seat as far away from Mannish as she could and balled up in a knot. He looked back to readjust and Hector was gone. Mannish let out a little sigh, but inside he was burning up. Forty five minutes passed and Hector was still inside the house. Church let out and as if that is what Hector was waiting for, he came out of the house. Church folk were in the line of fire, standing around the van and in front of the house. Hector's truck pulled out the driveway and rolled down the street slowly.

Mannish felt taunted. All the way back, Mannish didn't speak to Vallawn. Instead he pumped the radio all the way up to the distortionized max. He wasn't listening to it. He was zoned out. A billboard caught his attention and reminded him of what's normally done on Mother's Day when you're not contemplating murder. He made a stop at Macy's and bought Big Mama a goose down comforter, some pillows and some slippers. He stopped at the Conroy's Flower Shop and looked around at all the different kinds of flowers. The only thing he recognized was the Roses and Tulips. Oh and over there against the wall, Carnations. Mannish had to admit to himself he didn't know anything about flowers.

"Ay, look man." Mannish said to the man behind the counter. "How much for all these flowers up in here?"

The man looked at Mannish, condescendingly assessed his street attire and said, "Everything is labeled. If you have a problem reading the price tags, I can tell you the amount once you choose what you want. The lower prices are over there." he said, pointing to an area near the front. Mannish didn't turn an inch. His eyes were locked in on the dude behind the counter.

Did this fool just diss me? This nigga just dissed me!!!

He thought about slapping him like a bitch. Then he thought. *Fuck this spot, I aint bout to give this fool none of my money.*

But Mannish couldn't think right off hand where another flower spot was, considering he never bought flowers before. So he said, "Fuck it!" He realized it wasn't about the fool behind the counter, it was about the mother's in his life.

"Look faggot, I want every flower you got in this mutha fucka!"

"Hey who you calling a fa... wait did you say every flower?" he giggled then said, "Well you're looking at quite a penny. Just the stuff in that area..." he said, waving his hand over to his left. "...is gonna cost you at least a thousand dollars Mr. Donald Trump or should I say Bill Cosby."

Mannish looked around and estimated the whole load should cost about five thousand give or take a thousand.

He pulled out a stack of money made up of smaller stacks of money. Each small stack was a thousand dollars.

He threw five of them on the counter. "That's five thousand." Then he threw another stack. "That's incase I'm off in calculating." He threw another stack. "That's

cause your faggot ass is gonna show me some respect."He threw down another stack. "That's cause you going close up shop and deliver them mutha fuckas right now. I want you to split it all up in three."

Flower Boy swept the stacks up off of the counter and stuffed them into his pocket while Mannish wrote down Big Mama's address then Aiyana's.

"Hit these two houses right now, the rest is for a funeral. I'ma call you and let you know when and where to take 'em."

Flower Boy made his necessary notes and looked up into Mannish's face.

"You sure are generous to be so mean. Mr. Meany Pants."

Mannish left. Vallawn hadn't moved an inch while Mannish was inside. When he got into the van she had an expression on her face like a timid child. The music was still on, still blaring static. He had just crossed Rodeo Blvd. when he noticed a big, burgundy, puffy, comfortable looking Lazyboy recliner in a store window. A couple of people were standing around it, while a person was sitting in it. Mannish saw the person sitting in it set something that looked like a phone in the side of it. He pulled over and went inside to investigate.

There was a cordless phone set in a compartment on the side. There was a port to plug the phone cord into but the chair also had Bluetooth wireless. The armrest on the other side flipped open from the top. It had sections for remote controls, magazines and drinks. There was a button that would make two halves of a dinner tray extend out of the arms and connect and disconnect automatically.

It had Bose midrange and tweeter speakers hidden in the headrest. There were video and audio jacks underneath to hook up to the television and audio components. There was remote controlled heating and different massage settings.

There were also six buttons that controlled sounds of things like waterfalls, rushing river water, crickets in the night air, wind blowing through tree leaves, soft waves and non threatening sounds of the jungle.

I need this mutha fucka in my pad. Mannish

thought.

He went and did the paperwork for the warranty and gave them the address to Big Mama's house. When he walked outside Vallawn had got into the driver's seat. He sat in the passenger's seat and laid it back.

"Take me on 48th to Big Mama's house." he told her.

She just sat with both of her hands high on the steering wheel. It seemed like she wanted to say something. He wasn't in a hurry but wondered what was going on in her mind. He looked at her. His expression said, What's up?

She put her forehead on the back of her hands which were still holding the steering wheel. He laid his head back and looked to the roof of the van. The word's crept into his ears like thieves with finesse.

"I forgive you."

"Huh?" He heard her but wanted to clarify it.

"I said I forgive you." she said a bit more affirmatively. His eyes went back to the ceiling.

She forgive me? What the fuck is this? Do I give a fuck? She fucked up my shit! I hope she aint waiting for no fuckin' response.

The engine started up and Vallawn pulled into traffic. They went to Big Mama's house. Ty was on the porch with one of his partners. He waved at Vallawn. She waved back. Mannish started to summons Ty over to the van to take the gun and put it up but changed his mind. Ty would think he had a new toy. Mannish pointed towards the back with his thumb and told Vallawn, "Hold that for me. Put it up."

"Okay." she answered.

He got out of the van and closed the door. Before he walked away he bent down and said to her through the window. "If you say anything to Cherise before I do, this'll be our last conversation."

"Okay okay!"

He turned to head up the walkway.

Gear in drive, foot on gas.

"Hey!" Mannish yelled.

She smashed on the brake. He bent back down and said, "Happy Mother's Day."

She smiled and nodded.

Foot off brake, lightly on gas.

When she got to the corner a white van with Conroy's Flowers painted in big letters rounded the corner. He pulled passed the house a little then backed into the driveway. He opened all the doors to the van wide. Flowers were pouring out everywhere. Mannish grabbed two arms full of flowers, Ty grabbed two arms full. Ty's partner grabbed two arms full and so did Flower Boy. They entered the house and found Big Mama in the Kitchen cooking up something that smelled scrumdiliumptious.

Everyone chimed, "Happy Mother's Day!" in unison.

Big Mama's eyes lit up with a pleasant surprise. The floral scent permeated the air instantaneously. Good food and flowers.

"Oooh thank you guys so much, dere is so many, so preddy. Dere's so many." Big Mama said, seemingly, trying to touch all of them one by one using both hands. Flower Boy came back in with some vases to place some flowers in. They began putting them in places she pointed.

Flower Boy came in with a big purple vase full of Azaleas. He came back in with another vase full of Magnolias. He came back with two vaseless bouquets. He made about twenty more trips in and out while Big Mama marveled at the multiple symbols of love and extreme measure taken to express it. After Flower Boy was done he patted his pocket and winked at Mannish on his way out the door. Ty and his boy saw the wink and looked at Mannish with a suspect look. Mannish lept to his feet and caught up with Flower Boy on the porch, Ty and his partner were right behind him.

"Nigga what the fuck is wrong witchu? Something in your eye you need me to stomp out for you?"

"Oh my, heavens no! I was just saying you did good. She loves them. Flowers bring happiness into a woman's world."

"Aight nigga, but if you ever see me again, keep both your fuckin' eyes open, cause if you blink I'ma punch them mutha fuckas closed!"

Flower Boy was in the van and down the street in 20 seconds literally.

When they returned in the house Big Mama said, "Was dat nice man burnin' rubbuh in front my house?"

"Naw, that was some other fool Big Mama."

"Ooh, da' place smells so good, like I'm in da' garden a Eden. I gotta go finish cookin'. An' I made arrangements for us ta go see Shawna today. I'ma take da' food sos we could have dinner togetha."

"Awe Momma, why you didn't tell me til now?" Mannish whined.

"Boy I ain't seent yuh in a month a Sundays. I told Ty ta tell ya ta come ova hea."

"I ain't got no car."

"Boy please, you gon' lie ta me like I ain't got no brain. You mo' fool dan da' white mouf mule. All dem pretty cars yuh got. You know why da' white mouf mule so fool?"

Ty and Mannish said at the same time, "Cause he jumped in the lake to get out the rain."

"An' what happened ta him?"

"He drowned his fool self."

Aiyana called Mannish. She was all emotional and crying. She thanked him for the flowers. She had never in her life seen one person receive so many flowers not even on TV. She agreed to join in on the trip to go see Shawna. While they waited for her and Naj to arrive Big Mama finished cooking. Ty showed Mannish how he had learned to work the recording equipment.

"You doing alright but I wouldn't bump that shit in my truck." Mannish kidded.

"Man, why you gotta diss me like that?"

"It ain't your lyrics, those are tight. It just sounds like garbage though."

Ty wanted to say, "Fuck you!" but didn't. Instead he said, "My shit it tight."

"Naw, it ain't, but keep working at it."

"Speakin' of yuh truck, what the police talkin' bout?"

"I don't know."

"You gotta know something. She had just came thru that day and you left behind her and a couple hours later she get hit. And yuh truck was seen burnin' rubber up outta there, come on Man. Then you bring me your phone right before the police called it. Tell me you ain't smoke Paula behind what I told you."

"It ain't like that."

"It seem just like that."

"Aight, I'ma tell you cause it ain't even like what you thinking. I went over there to pay her off and get her off yuh ass..."

"Ay Man, if the police asked a hun'ed guilty niggas, 95 of 'em would say that."

"Nigga shut up and listen cause I ain't gotta tell you."

"Aight but I was just sayin' though."

"I'm just sayin' shut up. I went over there to break her off for you and you was gonna pay me back, believe that. But when I went over there she had these two niggas over there and them fools tried to jack me and you already know it wasn't going down. We bussin' all up in the spot. I laid one dude and they musta put about ten holes in the wall. One of them bullets that went thru the wall behind me hit her. I ducked into the bedroom and fell over her dead body, eyes open and everything."

Before he could say anything else Naj pushed the door open.

"Hey Daddy!"

"What's up my lil man?" Mannish said, picking him up. "What yuh lil bad butt been doing?"

"Nothing, Momma said we going to see Auntie Shawna."

"Yeah, let's go back in the house and get ready to go."

CHAPTER EIGHTEEN

The ride took an hour and a half. When they pulled into the Center it didn't look like much. They parked and went inside the building which was a small modest brick structure. They entered double doors and approached the front desk. They were escorted to a visiting room that had about thirty tables with four chairs attached to each one. The tables were spread equal distance apart from wall to wall and arranged so they made up three aisles. There were about ten groups of people throughout the room conversing. They found themselves seats by the window that looked out into a courtyard where you could see units of sleeping quarters, bungalows and the cafeteria. All the buildings were aligned to encase the courtyard which was about a hundred square yards. Some of the buildings were two levels. Some of them were three levels.

After fifteen minutes Shawna came through the door. Her hair was pressed and bumped under in a mushroom style. She wore a Biz-e-Bee Apparel t-shirt and some nice jeans by Apple Bottom even though her apple bottom had been smoked off long ago. Her nails were done. Her toes were done and exposed through some leather sandals. Mannish made sure she had enough money in her pocket to do whatever she wanted as long as she promised not to get high with it. She started with Big Mama and gave everybody an endearing hug one by one. She noticed Ty's hug was nonchalant.

She sat down and asked Ty how he was.

He replied, "You know me, I hold it down."

Big Mama intervened saying, "Holdin' whut down boy? Holdin' yuh pants down unda' yuh butt like yuh gotta use da' bathroom. I hope whoever yuh marry can keep dem draws clean likes I do, since you be showin' 'em off down da street."

Aiyana asked, "Shawna how you doing?"

"I'm doing good. They feed us good. I gained a couple of pounds. Can you tell?"

"Nope." That came from Ty.

Big Mama said, "Chile you was ta da' negative. You gotta gain some mo' weight juss sos da' scale'll go ta zero."

Everybody laughed. Even Shawna had to laugh at that one. She knew she was just flesh and bones.

Big Mama said, "Speakin' a dat, I brung some food. It's in da' car. Mannish an' Ty gotta get it."

"Mama we can't eat in here." Shawna said.

"Well we'll eat it out dere in da' courtyard like dem otha folks is doin.'"

"That's only for the people who been here like three months or more. Everything is like restrictive in the beginning. They only let yall come today cause it's Mother's day and my son and mother is in the group."

"Aww baby I had wanted ta surprise yuh wit a good home cooked meal."

"Momma it's okay when yall get home yall can enjoy it for me."

Suddenly, Mannish asked Shawna where the restroom was. Shawna told him it was in the lobby area where they came in. He excused himself. Five minutes later Mannish came back in. The man that ran the place was with him. Shawna's heart jumped. She wondered what Mannish did wrong that fast. She knew the man was a hard ass that kicked people out the program for petty shit and refused to refund their money. The contract you sign says no refund for any reason in big bold letters.

Ole sheisty, greedy bastards.

"Ah, Shawna, it'll be fine this time if you and your family dine in the courtyard."

"Oh, thank you Mr. Rodgers. I appreciate it so much, thank you."

Big Mama, Aiyana and Shawna went outside to find a nice spot to lay blankets while Mannish, Ty and Naj went to the car to retrieve the food. Big Mama never played when it came to having enough. There were Tupperware containers, six pots and bowls of stuff. It was like she was feeding everybody in the place. It took the three boys four trips to bring it all. There were two home baked two layer cakes. One cake was strawberry with vanilla icing.

The other one was chocolate wrapped in chocolate icing.

Two pies, one apple, one sweet potato. As the tops were removed, Tupperware tops peeled off and Saran Wrap unwrapped the aroma infiltrated and dominated the atmosphere. They all pigged out and helped themselves to thirds and fourths. One by one they laid back rubbing their bellies looking up into the beautiful baby blue sky with it's patches of cumulus clouds with resemblances only limited to the bearers imagination.

Naj said he had to use the bathroom. What started off as a legitimate search for the restroom turned into an escapade when he went through some doors and ended up in the girl's housing area. He walked down the hall. It had doors on either side. As he walked down he noticed some were open. They were singles, just a room. Some had small refrigerators and microwaves. A girl came out of a room ahead of him wearing just panties and a bra.

She didn't see him. He watched her walk up the hallway and dip into another room. As he passed her door he heard the bing of the microwave. Naj went into the room and hid under the bed. He thought to himself he would practice his catlike evasive maneuver special powers.

When she came into the room he would sneak out undetected even if she closed the door.

He didn't have a watch but he figured at least four or five minutes had passed. He knew his family would start buggin' if he stayed gone any longer. He came from under the bed, glanced passed the microwave and stopped in his tracks. He thought about it for a few seconds, then he decided to do it. Initially he had planned on taking the frog home. When he first spotted it in the garden and grabbed it he thought his mother had seen him. He had hurried up and stuffed it in his pocket. She didn't say anything. Maybe she would check him on his way out.

He opened the microwave, inside it sat a white Styrofoam container. (the hamburgerstand take out kind you get when you order a big chili cheese fries.) He put the frog in it. It was about the size of a potato. He closed the top back. The frog was bumping and scratching trying to get out of the hot tray. Naj opened the window and went and poked his head out in the hallway, nobody. He stepped out, made it down the hall and out the door. Everybody was still stretched out letting the food digest. Naj sat down on the blanket.

"Boy, I was just getting ready to come looking for you."

Naj was just reaching for another piece of apple pie when a scream shrieked out of a window to the left. Everyone jumped up in an erect position and looked in the direction of the scream. Aiyana looked at Naj suspiciously.

He looked like the cat that swallowed the Canary. He tried to disguise his amusement but inside he was tickled to death.

CHAPTER NINETEEN

They made it back to the house in good time because the traffic was light. On the way back Cherise chirped Mannish's phone but he didn't respond. It made him remember this would be the first year he didn't give her something on a special day, especially Mother's Day since she had gotten pregnant in April seven years ago. The next month Mother's Day had landed on May 10. He took her to dinner and gave her a tennis bracelet. Even the times he was locked up he arranged to make sure she celebrated in fashion. One year she woke up to a brand new Ford Expedition sitting on the grass with a red bow on the hood. This year she wouldn't be getting shit. Not even a hard dick in her mouth. Not his anyway.

She better hope the dick she's been getting comes with gifts. By the time they got to Big Mama's house Cherise had sent a chirp alert to his phone seven times. Aiyana felt the phone vibrate in the seat. She was accustomed to him not answering the phone in her presence whether it was bizness or some other female vying for her man's time. She pushed a couple of buttons on the CD player. The CDs in the changer shuffled. Mary J started singing about how her man think she don't know what he's doing. Halfway through the song Mannish caught on to what she was saying. He looked at her with that Gary Coleman on Diff 'rent Strokes look. One eye closed, lips poked out.

"What you talkin' bout Willis?"

Aiyana busted out laughing. "The response of a guilty man."

CHAPTER TWENTY

Mannish dropped Big Mama and Ty off, then Aiyana and Naj, then chirped Cherise back.

"Why the fuck you keep blowing up my shit like that!" he barked at her.

"You had sex with my friend nigga huh! And then told her not to tell me. And the cold part about it is you gave her a gun. She lucky I didn't shove it up her ass. But I still had to kick her ass on GP. Yeah, that's why she in the hospital right now. You gonna do me like this, on Mother's Day at that?"

Mannish's mind was racing as he raced through traffic from lane to lane.

Cherise said, "You betta come get this big ass target out my backyard before it be ashes to ashes and dust to dust around this mutha fucka."

He tried to push the button to speak but she was ranting and raving.

He finally got through. "I'ma say this one time. You fuck wit my truck this'll be the last night you sleep in that house and the last time you drive a Cadillac truck."

"Nigga don't try to play me, you gonna take care of your son.

"He gonna be living wit Big Mama! What hospital she at?"

"Why? You wanna check on yuh bitch!"

"What hospital?"

"I don't know."

"What's her whole name?"

"Damn nigga! You really concerned huh?"

Just as she was getting ready to launch into another verbal tantrum she heard footsteps coming through the kitchen approaching her. She looked up as Mannish moved up close to her. She parted her lips to pop something fly out of her mouth.

Mannish calmly said, "You fuck Q-Tip?"

The look in her eyes and silence answered the question.

He slapped her unconscious. She fell between the couch and the coffee table. Mannish checked on Naj. He was sound asleep hugging onto his favorite teddy bear. His television was playing the *Big Daddy* movie starring Adam Sandler. Mannish scooped Taj up still wrapped in his comforter, carried him outside and laid him down in the back seat of the truck. While Mannish took him to Big Mama's house, he called the nearest hospital which was Daniel Freeman on Prairie in Inglewood. They had no one named Vallawn come in that day. He was on hold with the next hospital when his line beeped.

"What's the bizness?"

"Hey, this is Vallawn."

"Where you at?"

"On my way home."

"From where?"

No answer.

"Hello?"

"Hello." Vallawn answered.

"From where Vallawn?"

"From the hospital."

"What happened?"

"I sprained my wrist."

"How you do that?"

Silence.

He waited it out.

"Shooting." she said in a low voice after a few seconds.

"Huh?"

Silence.

"Shooting at Cherise." She said.

His next and expected question. "Why were you shooting at Cherise?"

"Cause she hit me."

"You told her you sucked my dick, she hit you, you shot at her and you sprained your wrist?"

"Yeah, kinda like that."

"What you mean kinda, that's what happened right?"

"Let me tell you face to face."

"I told you not to say shit and I told you if you did I wasn't fuckin' witchu."

"Let's just talk a minute for real. There's something I need to tell you, please."

"I'll think about it. Maybe tomorrow."

"How about right now?"

"I'm in the valley."

"Mannish, you're at the light on Florence and Crenshaw."

She startled him. He scanned everything in the vicinity quickly and spotted the rental van at the light facing the opposite direction flashing it's headlights. The light turned green. He crossed the intersection and pulled into the Shell Gas Station. Vallawn made a U turn (illegal as hell) in the middle of the intersection. She pulled in and parked next to the FX. She got out of the van and tried to open his door.

It was locked.

Trying to see through the tint she said, "Can you open the door?"

He let the window down two inches. "You didn't say all that. You just said face to face. I ain't fuckin' witchu, you talk too much."

"I ain't the one who talk too much. You need to check yuh boys you got in these streets."

"What the fuck you talkin' about?" he responded, unlocking the door.

She got in and sat facing him. He noticed that

her left wrist was wrapped up but his attention was on her elaborating on her last comment.

"One of your boys you be having selling dope for you told Cherise that he saw me and you in the van earlier in front of the furniture store. I couldn't deny it because she saw the van in my parking stall. She kept on saying we were fucking and had been fucking. I tried to downplay the situation by saying I sucked your dick while you were asleep and she hit me and..."

"Who told her they saw us?"

"I don't know. She wouldn't tell me."

He put the vehicle in gear and pulled out of the gas station in direction to Cherise's house.

When he stopped at Cherise's house Vallawn said. "What you gonna do, ask her who it was, Why you bring me?"

"Naw, I'm just gonna get my truck and take it to Big Mama's house cause Cherise might do something stupid. I need you to drive this car for me."

"What if she comes outside?"

"She sleep." he said as he got out.

The tail lights casted a red glare down the driveway as the white truck backed out. When it got into full view Vallawn said, "Damn!" because the truck was really nice.

He pulled up next to her.

Talking through his non existent passenger window he said, "On second thought, I better not take it over there."

The detectives investigating the murder were asking about the truck. He thought about taking it to Cerritos, but wasn't ready to risk showing anyone his safe spot.

"I'ma have to park it at your house til tomorrow."

Vallawn nodded, more than happy to oblige, hoping he would spent the night and even if he didn't he would still have to come back to pick up his truck.

Once the truck was parked and covered up at Vallawn's house, they went to get the van from the gas station.

As soon as Vallawn got out Mannish hollered, "I'll see you later." and was gone.

He undressed, showered and slid into bed with Aiyana. The floral scent was kicking throughout the house. She rolled over, dug her face into his chest and doze back off. The alarm clock that gets Aiyana up every morning didn't wake him. Aiyana got into her daily routine of getting herself and Naj ready for the day. Her profession was the most valuable yet severely unappreciated job of being a school teacher. She taught junior high school students at John Muir Junior High which was located right in the middle of the hood on 59th and Vermont. She was underpaid but Mannish always made sure she had what she needed and more than what she wanted. Without the element of having concern for the wages she could enjoy what she did. More times than not, she would find herself being a supplemental mom to neglected kids with potential, great potential. If only somebody would pay attention to them. The importance of her job intensified when she gave birth to a child of her own. It was a different time from when she and Mannish were growing up, where once you were taught the basics of reading and math nothing else was emphasized. Back then the parents put greater emphasis on prayer to get you through it all.

Aiyana helped her pupils understand the make up and dynamics and realistic effects of such driving forces as the government and religion.

She let them know who, how accessible and what the jobs were of the city council. She encouraged them to seek professions other than rap stars, sports stars or actors.

She taught them about the propaganda of the media and how it uses something called "sound bites" to influence the public in the wrong direction, by editing things to seem a certain way. They call them sound bites because they take bites of things people say and piece them together to make it sound how they want. She showed them facts that show that a lot of people they saw on TV bling blinging weren't even financially secure. She showed them the reality of percentages.

"The percentages aren't even as good as one person out of every school, but let's just say it was. What do you do if you're not the one? You have to have primary and secondary goals."

She looked at Naj and wondered if she contributed to him being so mischievous and crafty because it takes a certain amount of intelligence to be so.

"Kiss your daddy bye Naj."

Naj leaned down and kissed Mannish on the nose, then ran into his room to stash one of his toys in his pocket to show his friends. Aiyana stared at Mannish, sleeping like a baby and giggled to herself at how innocent he looked.

She marveled at the law of opposites attracting. She knew what he was into because of his arrests and the fact that they lived well off on his salary but he never had a job in his life. She kissed him on his lips. His face frowned from being disturbed, then smiled as if he acknowledged her although, he never opened his eyes. He rolled over and buried his body under the covers.

He's so cute. Aiyana thought to herself.

She and Naj stepped out and started their day. Mannish's day started at 11 o'clock. He awoke to the beep of the messages on his phone. He picked up his phone off the nightstand, pushed a button, punched in his passcode and put it on speakerphone.

{You have 4 new messages and 2 saved messages.}

beep {First new message} "Good morning

baby, this is Aiyana. I didn't see your truck or anything else outside, so I hope you didn't need my car, but for some reason I'm sure you'll be alright. Be careful, I love you bye."

beep. {message erased. next message} "Hello Mannish, this is Paul Downing I have some important information for you. Call me when you get this message."

beep {message sent at 9:45am}

beep {message erased, next message.} "Mannish, you didn't have to hit me. You treatin' me like one of them niggas out in the street."

beep {message erased, next message.} Mannish, dese peoples juss bring me dis big ole preddy chair. Dey tell me it do so much stuff but dey aint know how ta show me nuttin'. You gotsta come show me, an' I needs you ta go ta da funegal home wit me an' ova ta da graveyard in Inglewood. I spossed ta be dere by elebm, bye. Oh thank you fa' dis fancy chair."

beep {message erased}

He called Vallawn. "Ay, come get me wit a quickness. I'm in Lafeyette Square on Somerset and St. Charles. I gotta take Big Mama to handle some bizness for Paula's funeral."

"Okay here I come." She was just happy to be needed and elated that he didn't cut her off for telling Cherise about how she serviced him. Thirty minutes later she was in front of his house.

When he got in the car Vallawn said, "I like it in here. I never knew all this was back here, no wonder it's gated off on all those other streets. One way in and one way out. You doing your thang baIler. Can I be down with the R-O-C?"

"Just hurry up and take me to Big Mama's house."

She realized he was in a bit of a hurry so she just drove off quietly. When they walked into Big Mama's house it was 12:00 noon.

"Boy I told yuh I was spossed ta be dere at elebm." Big Mama said, "Hello Vallawn, where Cherise?"

"Uh, at home."

"At home? Well whut you doin' hea?"

"Dang Momma, she wit me for the day. She the one driving to take you where you gotta go." Mannish interrupted.

"It smell fishy but alright let's get ta goin', I'm aldredy late."

Everything went fine at the mortuary and the cemetery. They just needed Big Mama's approval on what they had to offer and the check for the services, which Mannish deposited the money in the bank to cover.

They took Big Mama back home then Mannish spent an hour hooking her chair up to everything and programming it to her liking. Then Vallawn took him to pick up his truck. He drove it to the glass shop. The Mexican's recognized him.

"Mi amigo, you mucho problemas huh? You likey pay money, you good costumer." one of the

Mexicans said.

"It ain't on purpose, believe me."

An hour later they had him as good as new. He hated to do it but he took it back to the dealer. Even with the rims and everything he put on it he took a loss of a few grand. They cut him a check that he took across the street to the Porsche dealer. He put a few stacks of money with the check and drove off in a black Cheyenne SUV, tinted windows, no rims, nothing fancy. He felt he needed to be low key for a while until he alleviated himself of a few problems. Dudes had been calling him to pick up money all day and needed to re-up but he had them on hold. They would be on hold all day the next day too because he and Ty would be tied up with the family. He went straight home from the Porsche dealer. When he walked into the house Aiyana was helping Naj with his homework and correcting her student's tests.

After five minutes of rummaging through the DVDs, Mannish hollered, "Where the hell is my *Heat* movie at?"

Naj and Aiyana looked at each other. "We don't know." they said in unison.

"It's in there somewhere." Aiyana added.

Five more minutes of clattering. "It ain't in here! Where the hell is my movie at?" he yelled.

"Baby, aren't you tired of watching that same ole movie?"

"No! Now where is it Aiyana?"

She shrugged her shoulders. He stomped out of the house and burned rubber down the street. He went down to the nearest Blockbuster. He asked the cashier to direct him to the section where they had Heat.

The cashier said, "Okay Ma'am." into the phone then hung up and told Mannish that they were out of that movie. Mannish went back home steaming.

"Naj, tell me what happened to my movie?"

"I don't know."

"I'ma throw your Shrek movie into the fireplace if you don't tell me."

Silence.

Mannish snatched the Shrek movie out of the movie rack.

"Mommy hid it! It's in her purse!" Naj yelled running and grabbing his DVD.

"Aiyana!!!"

CHAPTER TWENTY-ONE

Paula's mother Gloria, Big Mama's little sister, flew in for the funeral. It was held at Angeles Funeral Home on Crenshaw Blvd. The way everything was arranged was nice. Flower Boy had delivered. The casket was mahogany with chrome handles. Those who came to show their respect for Paula only filled the place to about 15% of the occupant capacity. There were a hand full of friends no one in the family knew, the owner of the strip club and a couple of dancers.

There was a small section of people from the Projects. Jackie and Mona were among the morners. Even Teardrop showed up, still on the run from the police. Mannish recognized another face among them. It was one of the fools he had a shootout with in Paula's apartment.

His heart jumped.
What should I do?
It was a crazy situation because Kaitlynn

and Big Mama were right next to Mannish and he didn't want to raise any suspicion. It just so happened Mannish had his gun on him, not particularly expecting That Nigga to be there, but knowing all Paula's friends were the grimey type. He watched That Nigga watch him furtively but acting like he was really paying attention to what the preacher was saying. It was just the way of That Nigga's crafty nature Mannish observed. It was the same way he was pretending to be into the video game that day at Paula's apartment.

Mannish thought. *He's probably the one that shot her. I never really cared who might have fired the fatal shot. I was just grateful to have gotten out of there alive. Even though she was dead, I was mad at her for creating the situation. Two of 'em were dead and they had no one on the planet to blame but themselves. What if it was That Nigga's gun that killed her? Should I avenge her death? Would it even be avenging since they were on the same team? What would she have done if they woulda killed me?*

While Mannish was thinking he got up and stood in the back. He masticated on different perspectives of the situation. He'd had a plethora of experiences just as serious as this one. Currently, he had so many things on his plate. One of his concerns was staying out the way of the police investigating Paula's murder, even though he still had unresolved issues with Hector that would command police attention. Speaking of the police he wondered who the hell the two white dudes were looking like Men in Black on the back row.

The preacher spoke about how Paula was with the Lord and how he had called her up. In response to all the crying and phony grieving and carrying on like Paula was Shirley Chilsom, the preacher said it was not a time to mourn but a time to rejoice because it was God's will. Mannish went outside to get away from all the B movie actors and to see if he was being paranoid or if those two guys in there were in fact officers.

Right on the front street about fifty yards up was a black Mercury. It looked like a detective's car. He went and peeked in through the tinted windows. There was a walkie talkie on the front seat and a clipboard on the back seat with some pictures on it he couldn't make out. But there were six photos on the top that resembled a six pack. The type the police used to show victims or anyone able to identify suspects. It's usually someone they suspect along with five other similar looking guys. That was enough to make him believe it was a police car and that the men inside were in fact the police. It was confirmed when he spotted a pair of handcuffs sticking out from underneath the passenger seat. The question now was what were they doing at the funeral? They were homicide detectives no doubt. Maybe they were just following up her death, seeing if something presented itself. They were probably still looking for the white truck. They probably didn't know about That Nigga inside. Mannish was on his way back to the building when That Nigga came outside and headed straight for him. Mannish unbuttoned his suitcoat and tucked his left hand in his right waist side.

Clutching his gun he thought. *Damn, outside the mortuary it's gonna go down? Well after I smoke this nigga they can take his ass inside.*

"Damn cuzz, if I didn't know betta I'd think you was bout to bust on me. But look cuzz, I already kissed and said bye to the rest of the family. I seen you wit 'em so I figure you family too." He extended his hand, Mannish shook it cautiously. "I just came to show my respect. She was the homegirl. Them white folks up in there got me on noid. All white folks look like the police to me, and I got warrants and shit so I'm gone."

He walked off to the parking lot and climbed into a blue Cutlass Supreme with a mural on the trunk of some gangstas G'd up with blue khaki suits on and blue Chuck Taylors, running into a police station, guns blazing. That Nigga hit a switch and the whole car jumped up off of the ground. He bounced out of the parking lot, threw up his hand in the form of the letter C out of his sunroof at some girls in a Volkswagon Jetta that he cut off to get into traffic.

That burned out ass nigga didn't even recognize me.

Mannish shook his head. He was glad he didn't have to pop That Nigga during Paula's funeral. He went back inside. Everything was wrapping up. They were getting ready to go to their cars to caravan in a procession to the cemetery. The family stood in the front a while and conversed with the others. Suddenly, Mannish noticed a yellow puddle forming around Naj's feet. Naj was staring at the black unmarked car.

"Naj! What the hell you doin' peeing on yourself?"

Naj was in a trance. "Daddy that's the car that was shooting at us that day."

"Boy, that's a police car. Aiyana come here, this boy peed on his self. Take him to the bathroom and clean him up right quick."

Aiyana hustled off with Naj.

CHAPTER TWENTY-TWO

Mannish had the Porsche truck pulled to the front when Aiyana and Naj come out from the bathroom. They got in and Mannish drove up to meet with the other vehicles in the procession. Someone came by and stuck a big yellow funeral sticker on the windshield and told them to turn their headlights on. After a couple of blocks Mannish saw that the officers that were there were accompanying them to the grave site. That completely altered his plans to go to the grave site. He took a detour, dipped through a few back streets and stopped at the Millenium Barber Shop. He got out and told Aiyana to go ahead and catch up with Kaitlynn and the others.

"I'll call you later. Tell Ty I said to just keep his eyes open." Mannish told her.

Aiyana reluctantly agreed and left. He went inside the barbershop and passed a few girls trying to throw a basketball in the hoop and he went out the back. Q-Tip was kneeled in a huddle of six guys gambling. Q-Tip was on the dice.

"Ha! I see eight, can I see nine? Ha! Come on nine sweet Nina Ross big hotel boss." Q-Tip looked up at one of his opponents. "You know how many times I fucked yuh bitch? Ha, nine times." he said throwing the dice.

Out of the blue, Q-Tip got snatched up by the back of his white tee. Instinctively, he gave Mannish an elbow under the chin as he stumbled back. Q-Tip reached into his pants for his weapon as he spun around, but before he could fully draw his piece and plant his feet, Mannish dove into him. They crashed to the ground. They struggled for possession of the gun. Everybody watched not knowing who to assist because true enough Q-Tip was their man and they hung on the daily, but Mannish supplied them packs through Q-Tip and made it so good that they always got it on consignment. In a quick motion Mannish gave him three furious blows to the face.

Q-Tip's body went limp. The hand holding the gun fell flat on the ground. Mannish grabbed the gun, sat on Q-Tip's stomach and looked down at him. Q-Tip laid helpless, breathing heavy and dreading what Mannish would do next.

"Why Q-Tip?"

"Man, I only told her I saw yall. She was the one saying you and Vallawn was fucking. I never said that!"

"Oh shit! That was you! You fucked my bitch and you telling my bizness? I was just bout to check you bout fuckin' with Cherise but you all up in my bizness tellin' her shit too? Awe, you gotta go. You violated the rules and got disqualified. You think about this on your way to hell."

Mannish put the gun under Q-Tip's chin and pulled the trigger.

Blam!

The top of Q-Tip's head blew out like a melon ran over by a car. Mannish reached into Q-Tip's pocket, pulled out his keys and pushed the button on the keyless entry alarm. A Navigator nearby chirped and the doors unlocked. He went to it, opened the door and went right to Q-Tip's stash spot. He knew where it would be because he's the one that hooked Q-Tip up with the Mexican Fernando to make spots for him. And plus when he dropped the Magnum off for them to fix the bullet holes they told him they put a stash in his homie's new truck. Mannish pulled a extra 9mm clip and a kilo of cocaine out of the stash.

Damn he ain't even broke the shit down yet. Ty gave this to the fool three days ago. And he just riding around with the shit.

Mannish looked up. All the guys were standing there trying to look hard, like he didn't just shock the shit out of them by blowing Q-Tip away.

"Ay!" Mannish said to the six guys, tossing the

kilo to whoever would catch it. One caught it. Mannish told him, "Aight, it's on you, since you out here looking like a thug's posterboy anyway, you collect all the money. Yall split that up. It's six of yall, so that's six ounces a piece and I'ma let yall get it at half price." he thought about that figure for a second, then said, "Almost, half price. Give me $300 a piece. So that's $1,800 from each of yall. Thugsta, be looking for a youngsta named Ty to come get that tomorrow. $1,800 times 6 is $10,800. Just make it $11,000."

Mannish threw Q-Tip's keys on the ground and then turned to leave, he quickly turned back.

"Ay, since you owe me 11 stacks, let me use your car til Ty bring it back tomorrow."

Thugsta threw his keys to Mannish. He caught them and raised his hand high in the air.

"You betta not have no bucket either. If you got a bucket I'm taking my shit back nigga."

He pushed the button. He heard the alarm chirp. He looked and seen the lights flashing on a new model Monte Carlo SS, midnight blue in color, on 22 inch Asanti rims.

"Okay my nigga." he said jumping in and pulling off.

But not before Thugsta ran up, opened the door, reached under the seat and retrieved a black Desert Eagle hand gun.

Mannish made a couple of runs, collected money from a few of his boys around town, then went to Big Mama's house. He knew the food would be off the hook. When he walked in everybody was in the livingroom.

The funeral had Shawna emotional. She was crying about how Travis had just up and disappeared on her. Big Mama was telling her that he was a no good piece of trash that ain't never done right. But none of that fazed her, she just sobbed more. That was her husband. They had taken vows to never depart. Vows that she took seriously and now he was gone. Kaitlynn told her that she needed to concentrate on finishing her program and staying drug free instead of worrying about that fool. Kaitlynn told her that when she finished her program she would help her get enrolled in school or a technical trade center.

Aiyana also agreed to help Shawna get on track however she could help.

"Tyshon!" Big Mama yelled on her way back into the kitchen.

"Yes." he answered stepping into the kitchen.

CHAPTER TWENTY-THREE

"Go wash yuh hands an' put these bowls an' plates on da' table."

He came back and set out steaming bowls of rice, black beans, corn, cabbage and a bowl of chicken gizzards. He set out platters. One had a ham. One had several Cornish hens laid on top of a bed of stuffing. Everybody sat around the table after Big Mama made them wash their hands of course.

She said grace. "Please lemme' stay 'round as long as possible cause dese chirrens juss dont know how ta ack. I dont know whut it is done change. It's all bout da' Benjamin's. Dey dont know nuttin bout whut on da' inside a person. Lord teach 'em, show 'em da' way ta see whut is in da' heart. Show 'em da' way dey could choose betta da' people whut dey deal wit. It's okay ta have nice things, we know cause only you make it possible. But 'erthang glitta aint gold. It's plentya wolf in plentya sheep clothes. Lord I dont know whut happened ta Gloria's baby, Paula but I know somebody was doing sumthin' dey had no bizness. Anyways she in a betta place cause she was down hea' runnin' 'round like a chicken wid it's head cut off. Thank you fa da' beautiful service an' dis healty food. It is tru yuh son Jesus Christ name we pray Amen."

Everyone said, "Amen." in unison.

It was like Amen was the bell. They all came out swinging. Mouths too busy chewing to speak. Big Mama never ceased to fulfill the ultimate satisfaction of the taste buds.

The first words in ten minutes were, "You know Gladys you sho' can cook just like Momma usedta, of coarse not as good as me, cause I learned what yall know plus mo'. Don't get me wrong Gladys you put lotsa people ta shame." Gloria said.

Kaitlynn, getting slightly offended at anybody insinuating that there was a better cook than her Momma, intervened and said, "Auntie, you know I graduate from college next week."

"Naw, baby I know'd you been goin' ta school quite a while. You finsta graduate Kaitlynn? I'm so proud of you. I wish Paula woulda stayed in school and did the right thangs. I wish I could blame this fast California fa' messin' her brain up, but I can't, cause dem girls back home done gone crazy too. Everytime somebody put something new in da' sto' dey just gotsta have it. Dem

Baby Fats and Pastries shoes and boots. What da' big deal be bout?" said Gloria.

"Auntie you gonna come to my graduation?" Kaitlynn asked.

"Yeah baby I'm here, why not."

"Okay and we can take some pictures for you to take back home to Uncle Clevis."

"I sho' wish my babies was sweet like you, not to say they ain't no good, but dey ain't. Maybe it gots something ta do wit all dis new technology stuff yalls got. So much goin' on it take yo attention away from yo family. When ever dey home whichen dey neva is, dey got dey face in a computer. Iffen dey ain't doin' homework or somethin' got ta do wit dey job, dey playing games or watching a show. It's so much going on like ta drive me crazy. Den dey even got's all dat stuff goin' on dey telephones, and you know what, ain't no such a thing as do witout. Yall kids today gon' get it iffen it kill yuh. When we was comin up our Momma said we gotsta do witout so much we thought it was our last name."

Big Mama said, "We didn't have dis A.I.D.S. running 'round, worst thing could happen ta yuh from messing 'round was gettin' pregnant. Nowadays yall got so much ta worry bout yall lucky when yuh just pregnant. An' mens knew how ta be mens an' take care a home. Womens in general didn't work. Yuh know, yuh had yuh nurses an' maids an' stuff of that sort but mostly da' womens jobs was ta raise da' chirrens, dey mens an' da' house cause none a dem three could take care a dey self."

Kaitlynn said, "Well I don't have anything but my half of apartment at school to take care of and after I graduate it's going to be the same way. No man, no kids."

"No baby you gotsta get you a man and some kids." Gloria said.

"Who says? I don't need the complications. My brothers and sister have kids. When I want to be around some children that share my blood I know where they live."

Big Mama cut Gloria off before she could say anything else. "We been goin' back an' fort bout dis for years Gloria. You aint boutsta change her mind in no one damn day."

"I've seen my brother..." Kaitlynn said, looking directly at Mannish. "...put women through too much hell. And I know he's a good man in his own little way, but um... I'm cool."

Kaitlynn wasn't done talking but she paused because she heard a noise on the porch. The door opened and Cherise walked in with an ominous look on her face. It betrayed her ill intentions. She ran up on Mannish drawing a knife from behind her back held high over her head.

She brought it down on Mannish. He was completely stunned and caught off guard. He raised his hand less calculated than needed. The knife pierced his shoulder as Cherise tumbled to the ground under the force of Ty tackling her. Mannish rushed to help subdue her and wrestle the knife out of her hand.

Big Mama was in the back ground hollering, "Girl you done loss yo damn mind! You in my house wit dat foolishness?"

The two took her outside. Mannish's mind was scouring the town thinking about a place to dump her body to rot undetected, for the dumb move she just tried. Shit, she almost got him good. His story could've been over. She was getting ready to catch hell now. She was putting up a struggle. The two managed to get her down the walkway to the Cadillac truck. Suddenly, her body went limp so they dropped her to the ground. She began to cry at a low whimper at first then it grew into a full ball.

"Why?! Why Mannish can't you love me? Why? I ain't good enough for you? Why? I had your child. I do everything you tell me to. But as always I sleep by myself while you layin' up wit some other bitch! You treat that bitch up there like she gold or somethin'! Am I nothin'?" By now the whole house was on the porch listening to Cherise bear her heart. "Don't you have enough pussy? Did you have to fuck my friend too?"

That comment impulsively made him look at Aiyana. Though he knew and Cherise knew it wasn't true technically. He also knew the shock wave of the comment was intense. Cherise's intent. No one would say anything right now but he had to mitigate the impact.

"I didn't fuck your fuckin' friend. Don't be out here in front of my family wit this bullshit!"

"She sucked your dick you bastard!"

"You betta stop yellin' out here and causing a fuckin' scene!"

The neighbors had already begun enjoying the show without paying for tickets.

Cherise stood continuing her ranting. "You know what, I hate you! And you know what else. Taj ain't your fuckin' son nigga!"

Mannish knew she was just trying to get under his skin. Taj looked just like him. He was more sure that Taj was his son than Naj and for sure Naj was his child. Without warning he slapped her down. She screamed then Kaitlynn screamed. Mannish looked up to the porch and everybody was huddled over Big Mama's body. She was sprawled out on the ground. Mannish ran up to see what was the matter. Big Mama was having another heart attack. Immediately, Kaitlynn whipped out her phone and dialed 911.

The call went through. "911 please hold."

"These muthafuckas put me on hold!"

"Fuck that, we can take her to the hospital ourselves." Mannish said.

"No, it'll be alright. They'll be here soon as I

tell them what's going on."

"Fuck them. I got a SS Monte Carlo sitting right here. We could be there in 2 point 2 seconds."

"You could have an accident or anythi... Hello, yes my mother's heart stopped or something, she needs help now."

"A unit is on the way Ma'am." The operator said.

The operator stayed on the line with her and helped her monitor Big Mama's breathing, pulse and such. In only a matter of minutes the siren of the ambulance could be heard blaring up the block and lighting up the neighborhood.

CHAPTER TWENTY-FOUR

Everyone sat in the waiting room inanimate, expressions expressionless or somber at best. No one had said much since the ambulance pulled away from the house. Mannish thrashed himself mentally for causing the commotion that ostensibly precipitated this situation.

I stressed her to the max.

While they waited in the waiting room Kaitlynn rationalized that Big Mama was susceptible due to being weakened by the last heart attack, the stress from Paula's funeral, dealing with children's services, Shawna and many other factors including Cherise's frenzy. The elevator opened up and Jacob stepped out with his wife and two mulatto kids in tow. Kaitlynn ran up to him and threw her arms around his neck.

"Jacob I'm glad you're here. It's so scary." Kaitlynn said, shedding tears. "We don't know what's going to happen. They said they'd keep us posted but we haven't talked to anyone in over an hour."

"Well what was the most recent statement or elaboration thereof made?"

Mannish interrupted, "Nigga you shoulda been there! What was the most recent statement or elaboration there of..." he mocked. "Nigga that was an hour ago, three hours after we got here. Don't let us interrupt what you was doin.'"

Jacob looked at Mannish for a second then turned his attention back to Kaitlynn and said, "What did they tell you?"

Kaitlynn cried. "They said that she was in critical condition and that they needed to operate. They were using all kinds of medical terminology which I understood none of. I should've taken up medicine instead pursuing the stupid technical field."

"What else did they say?"

"Nothing."

Mannish said, "Why you actin' all concerned now. Last time we was all up in here, where was you at, takin' violin lessons?"

Jacob took two steps forward. Mannish took two steps forward as well.

"What are you saying Mantrell?"

"I'm sayin' you turned your back on the family. When you got married you shoulda took yuh wife's last name bitch."

Jacob's wife Sarah responded. "Honey, why is he talking like that?"

"It's okay honey, please take the kids and see

if you can find a cafeteria and get some juice and sandwiches."

"You sure honey, will you be alright?"

Mannish blurted irresistibly, "What you gonna do if he ain't?"

Jacob said, "Honey please." with that she headed down the corridor. Then he looked at Mannish and said, "That's big talk. You sound like a bitter man. How can you fix your mouth to pass judgment on me when you been messing up since I can remember, and I'm older than you? It's no wonder Momma didn't have a heart attack years ago. You didn't even graduate from high school..."

"I might not have graduated, but I did learn how to knock mutha fuckas out with one punch."

"That's all you and your felonious cohorts do know how to do. Your violent behavior won't help any..."

"I've touched more money than you will ever see unless you get a job at the bank."

"Illegal money."

"It all spends the same."

"With no education you won't..."

"Nigga just cause I didn't graduate don't mean I don't know shit. You wanna have a conversation about trigonometry, quantum physics, nigga I could tell you how to make a nuclear weapon, uranium or plutonium enrichment. What's, next bruh. Yuh neighbors is probably missing you and the white bitch fa' bingo."

"Damn!" Kaitlynn hollered, "Why can't you two get along? So you chose different paths in life, so what! That doesn't make your blood any thinner. You're still family, we're family and this is a family crisis."

Just then the doctor came through the door. He broke down a few details of the surgery. He explained that Big Mama would be placed in the intensive care unit. That she was stable but no visitation would be allowed until the following day. When the doctor disappeared back to wherever doctors go, Mannish left the building, Ty right along with him. The last time Ty was at home alone and Big Mama was in the hospital he almost killed his cousin Paula. He would stick with his uncle this time. They jumped in the Monte Carlo and burned rubber. Gloria and Kaitlynn rode home with Aiyana. Mannish and Ty rode to Cerritos in silence. When they got inside Mannish's apartment Ty plopped down on the couch.

"Ay, is Heat the only DVD you got in this joint?" Ty asked Mannish.

"You tell me."

"It look like it."

"Okay then." Mannish went into the bedroom. Five minutes later he was asleep.

Ty went into the bedroom to see if there were any DVDs in there. He'd already seen Heat a thousand times. Ty liked the apartment. It was nice but basic. He could tell no one else stayed there. He thought to himself Mannish had his game tight to have a hide away so far. Ty left the neighborhood only rarely so he felt this was far and phenomenal. He looked in the closet and almost fell out.

He'd only seen that many bricks of cocaine on the news. He picked up four of them just to feel them in his clutch.

After his imagination ran wild with thoughts of ghetto fabulousness, he put them back and went to continue dreaming on the couch. He couldn't sleep so he watched the only movie there. Before it went off the TV was watching him sleep. The next morning they went and found a restaurant to eat breakfast. They stopped at the mall for a change of clothes and a fresh pair of shoes. Ty ran over to Sun Coast and copped a couple of DVDs. Dave Chapell's Season 2 and State Property 2. They went back to the apartment and Mannish retired to the bedroom and vacillated between sleeping and thinking. When the sun set he got up, took a shower, got dressed, grabbed three bricks, put 'em in a bag and threw 'em on the couch.

Ty looked in the bag and said, "You already got some people lined up for these?"

"Yeah."

"Well throw some more in there Man damn! You got all that shit. Let's get off that shit. I told you I already got niggas tryna fuck wit me fa' real. This ain't no bullshit. Niggas got bread they spendin' wit otha niggas. I need to do this. Look I'ma tell you like this, real shit, if you send me to take these to yuh boys they ain't gonna get it. My rep is on the line now. My folks gonna think I was just bumpin' my gums."

"Aight I'ma give you one."

"One! Man you playin' me. At least gimme three. I could take six but gimme three."

"Who you think you are, Al Capone?"

"First of all Al Capone didn't sell dope and I ain't say I could move no boatload. I'm talkin' bout that shit in there, What, it's about 50 of 'em. Gimme a month I'll down all of 'em. At the rate you goin' you ain't gonna have to hide 'em in the closet you gonna be able to wrap' em and stash 'em under the Christmas tree and it's only the beginning of the year right now."

Mannish couldn't help but laugh. "You funny."

"I'm serious, what you tryna do, get a possession charge?"

"Aight Ty look, I'ma give you three cause you making a little bit of sense, but I'm telling you be careful, it's more about being free than the money."

Ty looked him in the eyes sincerely. "I feel you."

They left headed back to L.A. Mannish drove in the carpool lane speed limit. He had six kilos in the trunk.

"Man, highway patrol got on at the last entrance and they merging over this way." Ty said, positioning himself where he could see them through the side view mirror.

The highway patrol maneuvered until they were two cars behind them. A break came in the yellow lines allowing cars to exit the carpool. Just as Mannish was about to veer over he noticed the Highway Patrol car's blinkers signaling they were about to do the same. Mannish stayed put. The police car never exited the carpool either.

Mannish and Ty sweated for several more miles looking for the next opportunity to exit. Right before the break the patrol car jumped out into the next lane. At the break the car behind their Monte Carlo exited and almost hit the patrol car causing them to swerve back into the carpool lane right behind Mannish and Ty. They sped up and stared at the driver of the car that almost cause an accident.

A beautiful female looked back nervously, put her hand up and mouthed, "I'm sorry."

The officers smiled and let her slide. Now they were right behind the Monte Carlo. Mannish and Ty shit on themselves when the lights on top of the car started flashing.

"Damn!"

"This a SS Mannish you can out run 'em."

"Damn!" was all that came out of Mannish's

mouth but his brain was multitasking, thinking *here we go again with the bullshit.* The chase is on no doubt. He scanned the traffic for his maneuverability and the distance of the next exit. He thought about avoiding at all cost having his nephew go down with him. He thought about the fact that he didn't even know who's name the car was in. He thought about all the spots he may have touched and left his fingerprints. He thought about what items he had in the car that could lead back to him if he had to bail out of the car. All these thoughts were processed through his brain in seconds.

Mannish changed lanes at least to appear he would pullover on the shoulder. He and Ty were petrified. The Highway Patrol car zoomed past them.

OOH SHIT!!!

Mannish parked in his driveway still listening to the messages left in the last 24hrs.

beep {next message} "This is Vallawn. Tell me what I can do. I thought we were cool when I saw you the other day. You just used me to take your mother on an errand? I'm not tripping about that but you're not returning my calls. That's not the way it's supposed to be, call me please."

beep {message erased, next message} "Yes this is Attorney Paul Downing. I called you the other day and asked that you call me to set up an appointment. This matter would be of great importance to you. So get with me as soon as possible. Bye bye."

Mannish looked at his watch realizing it was too late in the evening to call.

Damn! I gotta remember to call him in the morning.

beep {message saved. next message} "Hey Man, this is Shawna. I know it's late but knowing you I thought you might be up. I'm at Momma's house and I was just sitting here thinking and tripping on everything that's going on. You know with Paula getting killed, Momma being sick and Travis disappearing. You know I love him and would do anything to have him back. I don't know, I just wanted to talk to you. I'm glad you got Ty with you. Maybe I'll see yall tomorrow." Click.

{message saved. end of new messages. First saved

message} "This is Paul Downing just calling to inform you that Jay had a court appearance..." Click.

Mannish hung up. He walked past the Porsche and INFINITI and stepped up on the porch.

CHAPTER TWENTY-FIVE

Ty waited until Mannish got inside then he pulled off. He thought about the best route to take. He had to make three stops for Mannish and three stops to his own clients. He would head out to the farthest spot and work his way back. He took the 10 Fwy West to the 405 Fwy South and exited El Segundo Blvd. When he got in front of the house, Will was on the porch. He gestured for Ty to come up. Ty checked the chamber of his gun, stuck it in the small of his back and got out the car with a kilo in his coat. They went inside and he handed Will the brick.

"Tell Mannish I really needed two of these. I got another spot popping like a mutha scoota. Ay look, I'ma give you the chips for both of 'em right now. Get that back to me ASAP!" Will said, as he handed over the money.

Ty thought briefly about just giving him one out of the backpack right then. But naw, that would do nothing for his image. He had his own people he needed to deliver to.

"Aight I got you. We'll see what's up fa' tomorrow." Ty told him.

Ty made the two other drops for Mannish. Then he made his first delivery to his own people on Washington and Palm Grove. He rang the doorbell to the brick building.

"Who is it?"

"Ty!"

They opened the door and let him in.

"What's crackin'?" Ty said.

"We were getting ready to record some lyrics. You know we stay doing that."

"Yall might have to let a real nigga hop on that cause that track is knockin'."

"I thought you came to handle bizness."

"Two birds wit one stone Big Dawg, give me yuh money, I'ma give you the thang, then it's like what's next, feel me."

"The money is around the corner at the house."

Ty looked at him like fool you knew I was coming.

He read Ty's face and said, "I don't do that kinda bizness up in here."

"Okay I feel you but since we here and yall look like yall about ready, let me parallel park on the track. All I need is one take. I'm goin' off the dome."

The producer KB had never heard Ty rap before but due to his arrogance he gave his nod of approval. Ty stepped into the booth, put the head phones on and signaled to turn the music up. Capriciously, he started.

"Hustla, peep the life of a killa.....

"Hold up, I missed the 4. Lemme' start over. The tempo kinda slow so I could say more. Let's go."

He nodded his head for a few seconds then he came in on the 2.

Life and times a tha boy
I spit my life in rhymes still don't cuss in front a G-Moms
Snuck out tha house ta go bussin' on front lines
Leave 'em lyin' like fresh wax breakin' fingas necks and backs
Extortin' bizness men til they checks max
Lil nigga movin' shit like exlax
Watch fa' tha train cause I'm gettin' head sex on tha tracks
Watch fa' enemigos or end up dead next on tha tracks
Learn ta drive in somethin' stolen that I stole from tha fiend that stole it
Cold shit sometimes I'll give tha nigga a nickle ta roll it
It's Sunday night and everybody in tha house wit Big Mama
I'm down the street cuttin' up wit tha homies in my pajamas
apprehended by tha Police hollerin' up tha street fa' somebody ta get Momma
Tha homie on Miss Roberts roof posted up wit that 12 gauge that eat flesh like Dahmer.

"I lost count, was that 16?"

"Naw, it was fourteen but you good. I like that

you did that off of the top off your head." KB said.

"Right on. I write too. I got concept songs, stories and all kinds of shit."

Ty's client interrupted, "Umm, we do have bizness to handle."

Ty responded by heading to the door. "You right."

"Ay youngsta, what's your name?" asked KB.

"Ty tha K-I."

"Okay when you come back around I'll give you a copy of this song mixed and everything and maybe we can record something else."

"Yeah fa' sho' we can do that."

They left and got in their cars. Ty followed his boy around the corner. As they were going up the steps to the house he told Ty.

"Damn boy, you got new whips on big wheels, pushin' kilos. You wasn't just talkin' huh. I see yuh. Let's go inside."

He came out the back room with a bag containing $15,000. Ty looked inside, flipped through a few stacks.

"Everythang is everythang, looks like this may be tha start of a beautiful relationship."

The next stop didn't go smooth.

"You took too long, I spent, that shit." The dude said with a slow drawl and low, red eyes that expressed he was high on weed. "I went to the car lot yesterday and copped that Lexus Land Cruiser right there." he said, pointing out the window of his apartment. "I put 10 on it. I gotta give 'em $600 a month, sat it on them Spreewells.

That mutha fucka nice huh?"

Ty looked with blatant disdain. "Nigga you went and spent all the money on a car. You ain't even got cop money?

You stupid ass nigga! You tryna fuck up my rep wit my connect before I even get goin'? You lucky I got somebody else who want it!"

Ty turned to leave.

"Ay." Dude said.

"What?"

"I ain't stupid." he said, leaning back on an imaginary pole looking half sleep.

Ty continued out the building obviously pissed off.

When he looked up the first thing he saw was the Land Cruiser.

How tha fuck you gon' have a Land Cruiser and a Landlord?

He made the next exchange successfully. He looked into the bag sitting in the passenger seat at the one kilo left.

Mutha fuckin' dumb ass nigga spendin' my money on a car.

Ty called another person he'd had on hold since Mannish first broached the subject that day he dropped him off in that fly ass INFINITI truck.

"Mannish could do that without spendin' his cop money. And I'ma be like that."

He started rapping to himself while the phone rang.

I'll spend my cop money

but what I get wit tha cop money
gon' make my cop money grow
til I could cop me somethin' money green
and still have cop money
pay cops on the team
now that's cop money

Someone answered the phone.

"What up my nig?" Ty said.

"You already know." said the voice on the other end of the phone.

"Aight, I got that for you."

"Oh you do, okay okay what it do? Come thru."

"Aight."

Ty was on Slauson and Avalon and needed to get to 54th and Normandie. He tried to chart a route in his head that would result in less chance of running across a police car or worse, having one run across him. There wasn't a freeway that could get him from this point A to that point B. While he was still, thinking and driving down Slauson a police car busted a U turn and got behind him. His posture corrected itself from gangster leaning. Their lights flashed and they gave a quick chirp of the siren. He pulled over. The two officers approached the car from both sides cautiously, beaming their flashlights into his eyes. Before the policemen could utter a question Ty smashed on the gas and made the SS do what it do. He rounded the first corner before the police even got their gear in drive. Two blocks north he passed another squad car. They quickly made a U turn simultaneously activating their roll lights. He made a left on the first block and darted down 54th Street running every light without a flinch. He knew if he continued his lead on them he could maneuver on the oneway streets and short blocks that ran along the side the 110 freeway. At the last second before he crossed the overpass on 51st Street he turned the car into a hard right and a fish tail kicking up dust and gravel. He remembered there was an on ramp to the freeway on 51st. It would take him north and completely out the way from where he needed to go but it was looking like that mission was aborted anyway. He saw the police pass up the turn in his rearview mirror. Then he saw their lights back up and head his direction. He entered the freeway and opened the carburetor up to an efficiency of 10 miles a gallon. He saw a train of lights coming down the ramp. Ty watched his speedometer move like the second hand on a watch.

It moved from 5 til to 25 after with a quickness. Four miles up, he interchanged to the 10 Fwy West and got off on Crenshaw four more miles up. Not a police car was in sight. He hit a couple corners and pulled up on Mannish's grass, ran in the backyard and grabbed a car cover and covered the car. Then he called Mannish.

"I'm on your porch!"

Seconds later Mannish opened the door. Ty crossed threshold breathing heavy and anxious. He closed the door behind him.

"I just had to shake the Ones."

Mannish immediately peeked out the window to see if Ty had ditched them for real. He knew from experience that the phrase was usually a wish more times than an actuality. It looked as if the coast was clear. Ty plopped down on the couch. The backpack fell to the floor.

Ty pointed at it and said, "That's 90 stacks. Money for all six of 'em. It's a kick in there already paid for and I got somebody on hold for one tomorrow."

"Aight but what's up wit the police?"

"They was fuckin' wit me for nothin' at the wrong time and I got up on 'em. This was just a minute ago but I was way on the other side of town over by the neighborhood."

"You probably did something to make 'em fuck witchu so you could out run 'em in a SS."

"No disrespect but you crazy as fuck, wit a chicken in the passenger seat. Plus I already know I'm a high speed specialist. Who you think Mac Dre was talking about?

Ay, but fa' real though I might have to get me a SS. That's me right there."

"That's why niggas in the hood all be having the same kinda cars. One nigga'll get some shit. The homies see it everyday, might ride in it or drive it, now they want one. I bet that's what happened with tha Dodge Magnum."

"Man, you might be right. But I'm gon' get me a SS.

Speakin' of that, what's my cut? This ain't no non-profit organization I'm running."

"Take that key, that's yours. Tomorrow we'll straighten out dude for the one that's paid for."

"I didn't make it to the barbershop to pick up that money from Thugsta but I'll wrap everything up tomorrow."

Ty went over to the stereo, flipped through the CDs and put Cassidy into the player. Mannish disappeared back into the bedroom. Ty adjusted the sound high enough to enjoy but not loud enough to disturb anyone in the house.

He went to the hall closet and got a pillow and a blanket. He zoned out on the couch thinking about the money he was about to get his hands on. The music took him.

He repositioned to maximize his comfort. Cassidy said something about the law. Ty smiled, proud he had out ran the police with 90 grand and a kilo. His homeboys wouldn't understand it. They wouldn't even believe it.

Oh, they'll believe it when I come thru in my own shit wit my name in that black eye purple paint.

He drifted off to sleep with the rap album playing in his ear and the game heavy on his mind. He dreamed he was at a club where Cassidy was performing. What he was hearing in real life transferred into his dreams.

"And if you bastards doubt I'ma hustla, ask about me." Cassidy said.

Ty shouted up to the stage. "You betta ask

about me!"

The beat stopped. Cassidy hollered back. "What if I just ask you?"

Ty jumped up on stage in a white Dickie Khaki suit and fresh off white Chuck Taylors. He stepped up to Cassidy with the sickest imposterproof swagga, looked him in the face and started rapping into the microphone while Cassidy still held it.

Put that track back on and I'ma tell yuh,
T to the wiz-i
Rebellious and stay fliz-i
They jealous
I don't fake no funk or get careless
You just be talkin' bout it
Catch you at a light in my hood
You walkin' up out it
My foul clique do damage
But I'm tha worse one
Gotta make sure yuh dead
I'm postin' up til tha hearse come.

Ty grabbed the mic because he was hyped up and too
animated to stand in one place.
When I grab the mic rappers say yuh prayers
Like when church done
You get this first one fa' fun
But when tha verse done
You gon' need a nurse ta come.

A light flashed in the crowd, could've been a gunshot.

The lights came on. It sounded like it was raining outside, maybe not rain but definitely water running. Ty swung his head from left to right looking for the source of the noise but the light was blinding. Then he heard more noise, more water like a crashing wave. He snapped out of his sleep. His eyes popped open just in enough time to see Naj reaching up for the switch to cut the bathroom light off. It was the toilet. Naj was using the bathroom.

Ty rolled over and went into a dreamless sleep. The next morning he was awakened by Naj dripping a drop of water on his forehead every few seconds. Ty snatched him down by his jacket.

"What you doin'?"

Naj burst out laughing. "Nothing, the ceiling leaking."

"Oh yeah?" Ty looked around and saw a cup of water on the floor.

"What's this then, boy you know I'll put you in that cup." Ty told him while pinning him down and tickling him.

"Come on boy time to go." said Aiyana at the door.

Then they were gone.

Ty made himself a big bowl of cereal and put some cartoons on the TV and chilled out on the recliner. At eight o'clock Mannish walked in with a big bowl of cereal.

"Ty, get yo ass out my chair."

He complied and Mannish took a seat on his throne.

They enjoyed the antics of Bugs Bunny outsmarting Yosemite Sam.

"I called the hospital last night. They said Big Mama was cool but they wanted to watch her for a few more days. Kaitlynn and Aunt Gloria was up there. Punk ass Jacob was up there too with Sally Pure Bread." Mannish said.

"What's up wit Shawna?" Ty asked.

"You know you betta not let Big Mama hear you callin' yo Momma by her first name. But she wasn't there. I don't know, she left me a message the night we left the hospital after she got back to the house but I ain't talk to her. Why don't you call her and wake her up?"

"Naw, I'll talk to her later."

They watched the cartoons a little while longer. Then Mannish excused himself to shit, shave and shower. When he came back into the living room he threw another kilo, Ty caught it.

"That's for yuh boy that paid in advance."

"Aight, I ain't finna shower or change or nothin'. I'm finna move these two thangs and hit the mall, Then I'ma go home and take a bath."

"I gotta see this lawyer about something. I'ma hit you when I'm done so we can take Thugsta his car back and pick up my money."

Ty uncovered the Monte Carlo and left.

CHAPTER TWENTY-SIX

Mannish went to the Wilshire district to see the lawyer. The building was a towering structure. It looked like it was made of glass. There were forty foot palm trees extending into the heavens from the roof. Mannish found a parking spot in front of a meter, put two quarters in it and went into the enormous structure.

When he stepped into the office the lawyer's door was open. He motioned for Mannish to pass by Sherry and enter his office. Paul Downing pulled out a file so thick it landed on the desk with a loud thud.

"Mr. Johnson it seems like there aren't many things that you haven't been arrested for. Since the time you were twelve you've been having run ins with the police and..."

"And what? How bout why we talkin' bout me gettin' in trouble since I was a kid?"

"Please Mr. Johnson, I apologize if I've offended you but my intent was to say that you've got some detectives that feel you have gotten away with far too much dirt and received far too little time. They want you locked away if not for life then until you're too old to care about anything other than getting your Depends diapers changed.

Do you know a detective named Ramirez?"

"Detective Ramirez? No, but I guess he knows me right?"

"Yeah, okay do you remember a Detective named Middleton?"

"Yeah I remember that cocksucker. He busted me on my last case."

"Okay well I understand that case involved a murder, which was an officer, a DEA agent, Middleton's partner to be exact. It involved a conspiracy to distribute drugs and a few other charges."

The lawyer breezed through a couple of pages. "You were apprehended six months later, yada yada yada. They didn't have enough evidence, yada yada yada. You pleaded guilty to a lesser charge and got two years. Well Detective Middleton's dick never got soft. He would've preferred you got no time so he could bust you good, even if it meant planting something, entrapment, whatever. He kept tabs on your every move while you were in jail. He knows you were moving drugs inside but it wouldn't get you enough time so he made sure the C.O.s knew not to fool with you. Did it seem like you got away with things pretty smoothly on your last bid?"

"Yeah it did and I was moving more shit than fiber. Ain't that a bitch! They knew the whole time.

I thought I was just that good. So this fool is lurking around waiting for me to slip?"

"The file also says there were a couple of guys you were acquainted with in there, Mack and Keno. Well, anyway to answer your question, no they're not exactly waiting for you to slip. A year ago Middleton was in a shootout on the scene of a bank robbery attempt and was hit in the spine and subsequently paralyzed from the neck down. He's out of commission but he has briefed two pairs of detectives on the situation and these guys are your nightmare. It seems they've been on your ass something terrible but somehow you've done a good job of evading them. One pair adopted Middleton's attitude of entrapping you if they have to. The other pair are going to kill you first chance they get."

He pulled out two pictures.

"These two are partners, Ramirez and Hunter coincidentally named."

Mannish's heart almost busted out of his chest when he saw the photos of the two cops that were at Paula's funeral.

"From the look on your face I'll gather you've seen these two somewhere."

Still taken aback he answered, "Yeah."

"I should have some more photos in a week or so."

Paul noticed him thinking so he leaned back in his chair and looked through some papers while Mannish dealt with all the information.

After a few minutes he said, "There is more if

you think you can handle any more right now."

"Shit! I don't even know if I can for real."

"Jay is cooperating with the government and he's willing to testify."

"What! What the fuck you talking about? After I paid for getting that fool a lawyer and put money on his books!"

"Well it seems the situation is, he talked to them before you sent the money but after you refused to answer his calls. The gun connection is a paid snitch, some guy named Tray. It was a ploy to get you trapped up. They thought they could get you with the drugs and weapons but it didn't work out that way. So they did the next best thing and put heavy pressure on Jay."

"Damn! Damn! Damn! This shit is crazy. I need to go think about what I'm gonna do."

"Well the first thing you need to do is pay for my intelligence gathering. This was definitely extraordinary. It was just fortunate that I have friends in the right places."

"How much you want?"

"I want everything you got because you may not be alive too long to enjoy it."

Mannish's expression turned grim.

The lawyer said, "Okay bad joke. I was kidding, only kidding, unless you're going to let me have it. But no seriously it will be $50,000."

"$50,000!"

"Before you snap my neck, let me say that I presume you have lost interest in helping Jay."

"You fuckin' right!"

"After retaining the lawyer and depositing $3,000 into Jay's account which is the max allowable at one time where he is at this moment, there is a surplus of $47,000 which will cover it. The retainer should carry Jay's attorney to pre-trial. At which time he will request more money or he will discontinue representing him. Though I need to tell you due to his cooperating Jay won't need the attorney."

"Yeah I got you. I gotta go think."

Mannish left, got in touch with Ty and met him behind the barbershop. They pulled up at the same time. Everybody was hanging out in the back as usual. Mannish pulled up but didn't get out his car.

"I see you got away." Thugsta said.

"Who you talkin' to?" Mannish asked.

"One of yall!" he said looking over at Ty as he was exiting the Monte Carlo dressed in a white khaki suit.

Thugsta got his keys from Ty, pushed the keyless entry button for the trunk, dug in and got a screwdriver and a different set of paper plates from another dealership. "I was on the freeway last night when my car flew passed me doing a buck sixty. It's all good though." When he finished changing the rear plate he reached into his jacket pocket. "Here go yuh $11,000. Can we get two mo' like that?"

"Naw." Ty butted in. "But you can get two for

tha fourteen five. That's love cause you gettin' it on consignment. Niggas that's buyin' straight up is gettin' hit fa' fifteen."

Thugsta looked at Mannish, Mannish shrugged his shoulders like. *Hey, he said what he said.*

Ty said, "If you want it lemme know right now and I'll drop it off tomorrow and I'll be back Friday fa' tha 29 stacks."

"Aight lil homie, we can do that."

"My name ain't lil homie. It's Ty."

Ty got into the Porsche Cheyenne with Mannish and they left. Ty reclined his seat not even concerned with where they were going. Ty laid back and daydreamed about being the man for a while. When Ty snapped out of his trance they were a block away from the hospital.

They pulled in the parking lot, went to the front desk and received their visitor's stickers. Big Mama was resting and watching her soap operas when they walked in. Ty ran up, laid his head on her chest and stretched his arms about her.

"Big Mama you gonna be aight?"

"Yeah, dey say dey gon' send me home in a few days. So it look like I'm gon' be around sos you can drive me crazy some mo'."

Ty looked up with a smile on his face. "Okay I could work wit that."

He found a chair to sit in. Mannish stepped up and put her hand in his. "Momma I'm sorry for what happened, I know it was my fault. Letting my problems follow me. I know I've always been a problem to you."

"Ty." Big Mama said, "Go in da' waitin room' fo' a bit chile." Once the door was closed behind him Big Mama told Mannish to pull the chair up to the bedside. Her voice was low and a little bit weak. "Yuh know when we first moved out ta Califonya, me an' Paw Paw was happy. We had figured we made it out da' country an' da' city life was gon' make all our dreams come true. But when you become old like me you start ta realize dat you spent all yuh young days chasin' da' wind, like Solomon say in Ecclesiastes. It's all chasin' da' wind cause aint nuttin' new under da' sun. It's all vanity.

"You tryna be sombody. You tryna fill a empty spot. But if you keep God inside you aint nuttin' can top dat. It's so fast out hea' an' seem like it's gettin' fasta by da' minute. When we come out dis way it 'twas fasta dan whut we had known befo'. Yuh Paw was a strong handsome man an' I was da' prettiest lil thang an' I knew it cause wudnt nowhere I could go where da' men didnt try dey hand. But afta' we was hea' bout a year Paw started dressin' fancy. He wudnt wearin' da' clothes I sowed fa' him as much. He start lookin' like he was goin' ta church all da' time, just fancy you know, talkin' bout he had sum new friends dat was distinguished gentlemens. But no such a lie, I didn't believe it fa' a minute.

"Sos I got ta snoopin' an' come ta find out he was workin' on sum white woman whut had a lotta money. Boy, it hurt my heart so much I liked ta kill da' two of 'em. Iffen I had a gun I woulda. I went ta da' restaurant downtown where dey liked ta meet up. I tore inta da' boff of dey ass like da' devil. I was cussin' an' fussin' an' yellin' an' screamin'.

"Da' place was full an' if I tell you I acted a ass. I messed up everybody's day. It 'twas glass an' broke plates an' food every where. I cut up until da' police come hall me ta jail. Sumhow he end up gettin' dis woman ta pay fa' all da' damage an' bail me out. But I was stubborn, I wouldn't leave. I was thinking he musta sexed her up real nice ta pay up like she done.

"I just sat dere. But dey said look, just like when you screw up you gotsta get locked up. When yo bail get paid you gotsta get the hell outta hea'. When I walks outside he right dere wit a cab. So I makes 'im pay fa' da' cab but I dont let 'im ride wit me. I goes on ova ta dis man's house, dis man named Mack. He'd been tryna sweet talk me fa' da' longest time. But I neva paid him no mind, not til den anyway. I laid up wit him for a day an' a half tryna be sumthin' I wasn't, a whore. I started feelin' dirty. It wasn't right. It was wrong, I knew it was wrong so I went home an' soaked in da' tub. Dat night I told Paw whut I done. He forgave me an' made love ta me like neva befo."

She looked to the ceiling and distantly said, "Lord I loved dat man. I neva fooled around on him again an' neither did he. We promised ta neva bring it up an' ack like it didn't happen. A month later we come ta find out I was pregnant.

Cause a da' promise we just didn't question it.

"At least not open ta one anotha. But when you come out I knew you was dat man's son. Paw, if he eva know'd it, he neva showed it. Dat man end up gettin' kilt by da' police one night ova dere behind Crenshaw fa' doin' somthin' he had no bidness. Every time you get inta trouble, whut you been doin' since you was in kindergarden, I think about him an' everything whut happened. An' it may have affected da' way I was witcha."

Big Mama laid her head back down on the pillow and stared at the wall on the side. The room fell silent.

After a minute she said, "I needs ta rest myself son."

Mannish stepped out of the room and saw Ty sitting with Kaitlynn.

He said, "She sleep. Are you gonna just chill out and wait until she wakes up or come back later. Where's Shawna? Oh yeah, she had to go back to the program huh?"

Kaitlynn said, "She didn't go back to the program but she's not at home either. I haven't seen her since the other night. When I woke up she was gone. The people from the program even called. I told 'em Momma was in the hospital so they're not tripping."

Mannish said, "I'm gonna go find her, I'm outta here."

Ty was right on his heels. "She probably out there smokin' as usual." he said.

Mannish looked at him but didn't say anything. He thought to himself his sister really failed as a parent and for Ty's sake he hoped she wasn't smoking again. They drove to the neighborhood and pulled up on a group of crackheads.

"What's up Mannish, What's up Ty?"

"Any of yall seen Shawna?"

"Naw, we ain't seen her."

They got the same answer all over the neighborhood. They drove to the spot on El Segundo. Someone was peeking out the window when they walked up to the door.

"Ay, both of them coming." J-Stone said.

"You think he know?" Chuck asked.

"I don't know, I got the heat though in case he start trippin.'" replied J-Stone.

Before Mannish could knock on the door Chuck yelled, "What's up?" through it. Mannish took offense because they had always opened the door for him. But he checked his attitude because he had just popped up and they didn't owe him any money. Maybe he didn't need to go in anyway. He just had one question.

"Have Shawna been by here?"

"Naw."

He hated one word answers. But he and Ty left and pulled up to Big Mama's house and found Shawna sitting on the porch.

"Where the fuck you been?" Ty shouted.

She looked timid and answered him as if he was her father and she was the kid.

"I was with Bone."

Her answer disarmed them because they had heard Bone had stopped smoking and was working and doing good. They almost felt embarrassed.

"Well, you aight?" Mannnish asked her.

"Yeah, I'm okay."

Mannish and Shawna went inside the house. Ty stayed outside because he saw Mike and Swiss walking up the street.

"What's hapnin'!" Ty asked.

"What's hapnin' witchu stranger?" Mike answered with a question.

"Why you say it like that nigga?" was Ty's response.

"You ain't been hangin' wit us cause you tha man now."

"Kill game homie, I'ma always keep it real. What's tha problem wit me tryna get some real money and I'm wit my fam bam too?!"

"Naw, we just sayin'..."

"You just sayin' what?" Ty said, pulling an ounce of chronic out of his pocket. "Nigga let's go in tha garage and blow some a this sticky ickey."

They proceeded to the garage. Ty set the music up while Swiss rolled a couple of blunts. He told them how he blazed the booth on the westside the day before.

Mike said, "Oh yeah, Champ came through here the other day on a Pocket bike motorcycle. He had just jacked some fool for it. He was lookin' fa' you."

"Oh yeah, what he say?" Ty responded sounding excited that his boy was out of jail.

"Nothin', he was just kickin' it. I got his chirp number."

"Well chirp my nigga then!"

Mike sent an alert. A voice came back over the speakerphone. "Ain't nothin' but a gangsta party." Champ sung.

"Champ, what up, this Mike."

"I know homie, your name popped up. That's why I said..." he began singing again. "Ain't nothin' but a gangsta party."

"You stupid."

"I'm tha people's Champ!"

"I'm over here wit Ty."

"Ty baby, what tha bizness is?"

Mike held the button down wit the phone in the air.

Ty yelled from his comfortable spot on the couch. "You already know. Where you at?"

"I'm where you at. You at the house?"

"Yeah, in tha garage."

"I'm there, gimme a half hour."

After that everybody sat quiet and enjoyed the high that the sticky purple stuff had taken them to. Ty stood up and liberally blessed his homeboys with $500. He put another $500 in one pocket for Champ and went in the house to put up $11,000. His mother Shawna was in his room asleep. He crept to his dresser and pulled the drawer open slowly and quietly to avoid waking her. He knew she needed her rest plus he's the only one who needed to know where his stash was. He stuffed the roll into a couple of pairs of socks then folded them and stuffed them inside each other to look like the rest. Then he crept back out without a sound. On his way back out he saw Mannish on the phone yelling at Cherise to bring Taj over. Mannish hung up the phone and looked at his watch.

She said she'd be here in an hour.

He dozed off thinking about the uncertainty of his future. He wanted to spend some time with his son just incase he didn't make it. He was awakened by the horn blowing out in front of the house. He looked at his watch.

An hour and a half had passed. He stepped outside onto the porch and Vallawn was standing on the curb leaning against her Toyota Camry, arms folded.

"You can't return nobody call, Mannish?"

He was temporarily stunned. He looked at his watch again then looked back at Vallawn.

"What you do, bump your head or something? You don't just pop up at my Momma's house out of the blue. Get the fuck outta here! I'll holla at you later!"

"I don't care about you hollering, but are you really going to call me later?"

"What?"

"Mannish, one of us is overreacting. I ain't gonna say it's you. But it's been a few days since we've talked and you didn't return my call. I can be patient. I can wait if you're going to come through. But please stop talking to me like that."

Mannish stepped down to her and in a low tone he said. "Listen, I got some heavy shit to deal with and I don't know how it's gonna turn out. But I do know one thing for certain and two things for sure. If I lose focus I could end up dead."

She looked in his face with what seemed like genuine concern.

"Is there anything I can do?"

"No. But anyway Cherise is on her way over here to drop Taj off so..."

"So what? I ain't scared of her. I'm trying to see what's up with you, what you are going to do and if it has anything to do with me."

"First of all it ain't about if you scared or not. I ain't tryna have no shit in front of my Momma's house. So your going to have to put yuh foot on that accelerator and roll up out."

"Mannish by no means do I want to disrespect your mother's house. But tell me you're going to answer my call next time."

"No, cause you might call me in five minutes."

"You wouldn't answer my call if I called you in five minutes from now?"

"No, cause you woulda just left five minutes ago."

"Mannish!" she whined and pouted. "That's not right!"

He looked at his watch again.

She licked her lips. "I'll put it in my mouth."

He felt his little man armstrong jump up.

"Aight Vallawn call me tomorrow."

"Okay." she sang while she ran around to the driver's side of the car.

"Hey!" he said.

"Huh?"

"Don't eva eva eva eva come by here uninvited no mo."

"Okay, dang." She pulled off. Ty came down the driveway followed by his three partners.

"Ay Man, these my homies Champ, Swiss and Mike."

They all dapped Mannish and went up the block.

Cherise pulled up from the other direction. Taj jumped out of the truck and got his bike out from the back.

"Watch this daddy!" Taj said attempting to pop a wheelee on his bike.

"Lil man, you gotta pedal a little harder when you pull on the handlebars."

"Okay daddy."

He tried a couple more times then rode down the block to speak to Ty.

"Aight I'ma call you later to come get him or I'll drop him off, I don't know." Mannish said to Cherise.

Cherise turned her music up and left. Taj came flying by and went up the block. While Mannish was looking up the street at him he noticed a black Grand Marquis halfway up the block. He tried to zoom in and see if anybody was inside it. Just when he knew he saw some movement, the car pulled out and headed his direction full speed. He could hear the motor roar. He looked for Taj. He was on his way back. Mannish wished he was close enough so he could grab him and run into the house. The car rammed up on the curb and slid to a halt two inches from Mannish's legs. Two white gun-ho detectives jumped out with guns drawn. The passenger fired two shots missing Mannish narrowly as he ducked under the front of the car.

"Daddee!" Taj screamed.

"Run in the house!" Mannish yelled back.

Taj ran up on the porch, but he didn't go inside. He just stood by the door and stared. One of the cops kneeled down over Mannish using himself as a screen. He put the gun in Mannish's chest right at his heart.

"Hey! What tha fuck you doin?!" Ty yelled with his homies right at his side.

The other detective raised his hand and gun. "You guys hold it right there!"

"Fuck that! What yall doin' wit my uncle?!" Ty spat back.

"Alright, all four of you down on your knees. Now!"

Reluctantly they did. The detective kneeling over Mannish whispered to him.

"Your black ass is going to get a pass today.

Count your blessings, this is your second escape. You're lucky that my partner Hunter missed you the other day on Western and you took off in that fast ass Dodge Magnum. But the next time I catch your ass slipping I'm going to plug yuh."

The cops climbed back in their car, backed off the curb and pulled off. Taj ran down off the porch as Ty and his crew ran up.

Everybody asked, "You alright!"

"Yeah, it's cool." Mannish said then turned and went into the house, Taj in tow.

Ty wrapped up his conversation with Champ.

"Aight Ty I'ma find a apartment right quick. Either we gonna rent something or move some fiends out they shit. However we bout to do this, you know how much we gonna make off of choppin' a whole key down and sellin' all rocks. I'ma do what I gotta do, you just keep 'em comin'. I'ma holla at you in a minute."

Later on as Mannish, Ty and Taj relaxed in front of the TV Taj told Mannish about how much fun he had on the helicopter ride his mother took him on. He told him about all the things they flew over and that they landed on top of a building and went inside to have dinner.

"You know what Daddy. I think the helicopter man like my mommy."

Mannish just looked at Taj. That's when Kaitlynn, Gloria, Aiyana and Naj came in. Everybody retired to a piece of furniture in the living room. They discussed Big Mama's condition which was getting better by the days.

The next morning when Shawna still wasn't up at 10 o'clock and Ty was tired of waiting to have his room to himself to get dressed for the day, he went in and found she was gone and gone with his $11,000. He ran out on the porch and looked down the street as if he might see her standing in view. He cursed and fussed and called her a dopefiend and crackhead.

He was upset and so busy venting that he didn't notice the women in the house looking at him like, "Where'd you get $11,000 for her to steal."

The automatic next thought was Mannish!! Someone thought. *Oh, Big Mama hurry up and come home and give both these boys the bizness.*

Ty thought about where she said she was the day before. "…with Bone. He ran down the block to Bone's house and banged on the door. Bones' mother answered. "You got some damn problem, beatin' on my do' like you da po'lece?"

"Bone here?"

"No. He at work."

"When he get off?"

"At six o'clock, why?"

Without an answer Ty turned around and headed back home.

She yelled out, "I know Gladys raised you better than that Tyshon! Wait til I talk to her!"

CHAPTER TWENTY-SEVEN

Kaitlynn left the house headed to the campus to pick up a few things she'd left in her dorm. Ty was walking down the middle of the street and whistled bye to her when he saw her car pulling off. Kaitlynn stuck her hand out through the sunroof.

When she stepped into the courtyard of the college campus she realized it would be the last time she stepped on the campus, at least as a student. She went up to her room. She sat down on the couch and reminisced about all the times she stayed up all night at the desk typing away on her laptop to finish a paper due the next morning.

All the times the girls would come over for a slumber party.

They would talk about the boys on campus and do each other's hair, facials, and nails. She remembered she had to take her family picture down. Because invariably she would have to convince one of the girls that they didn't want to meet her brother Mannish, without talking about him negatively. Her roommate Meagan even went all out and got his number out of Kaitlynn's cell phone. When Meagan called, Mannish put her on hold and called Kaitlynn to ask her why she gave his number away. He knew Kaitlynn liked Aiyana too much to throw a monkey wrench in the relationship. When she told him she had nothing to do with it he clicked back over and told Meagan he didn't fuck with sneaky white bitches.

Kaitlynn went and said goodbye to a few people and got a congratulations from a lot of folks. She returned some overdue books to the library. She sat in her favorite spot in the corner by the last bookshelf where she'd spent countless hours studying. She had a view out the window of the eastside of the courtyard where she could see everyone going and coming from the gym. She remembered how she used to always make sure she was there at eight o'clock every Friday to watch the one guy that caught her attention in the entire school. He would always come out all sweaty and glistening with a basketball tucked under his arm headed over to his dormitory. No doubt to shower and get ready to top off his Friday evening with a date that she wished could be her. But she kept those thoughts in her mind. He didn't even know she existed.

Just as she was about to stand up the object

of her fascination stepped out of the gym, with more sweat dripping from his muscular body than usual. He was palming the ball effortlessly with his massive hands. He was conversing with somebody who was obviously as engulfed in the game as he was, made evident by his wet t-shirt.

Kaitlynn sat still in the window up three floors as if the slightest move would cause detection. She was so nervous. His friend gave him dap then spun off in the direction of his dorm. He just stood there like someone pushed pause on him. Then suddenly he looked directly into Kaitlynn's face. She wanted to duck down out of his view but she was frozen. With his eyes trained on her he pushed a button on his cellphone and put it up to his ear.

She watched him with the ambivalence of amazement and embarrassment, awe and confusion. He pointed to his phone and then to her. Her phone rang startling the shit out of her.

CHAPTER TWENTY-EIGHT

"Hello?" came out of her mouth timidly. It was barely audible.

"What's up?"

She looked back outside. Nothing, nobody. He had disappeared.

"Kaitlynn?" came through the phone again. "Kaitlynn?"

Her mind was single-tasking, floating on the reminiscence of the recent fantasy.

"Auntie?" Ty hollered into the phone.

"Yeah, I'm here."

"We at the mall right, and I'm just sayin' though, are you gonna trip? I mean we shoppin' fa' somethin' to wear to your graduation. I'm just sayin' though, I'm lookin' at these bangin' brown suede Chuck Taylors. I'm tryna wear 'em to the graduation."

Only half listening and comprehending none she answered.

"That's cool."

She walked out of the library and looked at

the gym.

Was I tripping?

She pulled on the door to peek into the gym. It was locked. She looked at her watch.

2pm Tuesday?

The gym has never opened on Tuesday since I've been at this school.

She got into her car and rode the before rush hour stress-free traffic on the freeway to the hospital. When she walked in Big Mama was eating Jell-O.

"Dis is da' only thang I can eat. Erythang else taste like babyfood. I aint neva even fed yall no babyfood. Iffen it wudnt from my breasts it 'twas rice and beans, sweet potatoes an' stuff like that. An' when money was tight I'd feed yuh French fry sandwiches. Tell me sumpthin' baby, is it still left ovas from da' dinner I cooked?"

"Truthfully Momma, that stuff sat on the table for a couple of days. So it all got thrown away."

"Looks like I'ma juss haveta go home an' fix me sumpthin' ta eat." Big Mama said trying to sit upright in the bed.

"Momma, you know the doctor ain't ready to release you yet."

"Ta hell wit da doctor. He go home 'eryday and eat sumpthin' nice."

"How about I go to Boston Market and get you some roasted chicken and mashed potatoes and gravy?"

"Okay." Big Mama said, giving in and laying

back on the bed.

"Okay I'll be right back." Kaitlynn went out the door.

Twenty minutes later Kaitlynn pulled into the parking lot but before she could get out the car Big Mama grabbed the door handle on the passenger side frightening Kaitlynn but it was locked.

"Chile! Open da' do' fo' sumbody see me!"

The lock popped up and Big Mama got in.

"What are you doing down here?" Kaitlynn asked.

"Chile take me home."

"I'm going to take you back in that hospit..."

"I'm yo Momma an' I said take me home! Not now but right now!"

Big Mama had a point so Kaitlynn pulled out the parking lot and headed home.

When they walked in the house Gloria said, "Hey honey, glad to see you is doin' fine enough to come home. I thought dey was gon' keep you longuh."

Big Mama looked at Kaitlynn like, "Don't you say nothin.'"

"Iffen I wouda know'd you was comin' home I woulda sho' fixed a meal."

"They didn't release her Auntie Gloria, she escaped."

"Ooh Gladys, you is a mess. But I'ma tell yuh bout yo Momma." she said looking at Kaitlynn.

"When she was about thirteen she was playin'

in the front yard wit da' boys from next do' and she did sum kinda fancy move and one a dem boys went down like a sac a potatoes and she came down on top a him like dey do on TV wit da' wrestlin'. But she mussa come down wrong cause she broke her collar bone. She hid it from our Momma for about three days. I usedta haveta help her get dressed. Den one day Momma noticed Gladys wadn't usin' her left hand at da' dinner table. At first she thought maybe she was feedin' da' dog unda da' table. But when momma told her to raise it, Gladys couldn't. Dats how she found out it was broke. Den she had ta fuss at da' girl ta make her come go ta da' doctor. Den a week later she managed ta get outta da' cast dey had done put on it.

"Sos Momma took her back and dey put on anotha one. Well she get up outta dat one too. She always been stubborn bout what doctors want." Then Gloria looked at her sister. "Gladys, you done got old now you got ta listen ta what sumbody say sumtime."

Big Mama obviously ignoring what Gloria said rubbed her belly and walked toward the kitchen.

"I think I'm gon' make me sum peach cobbla."

"Listen, you just sit down and rest yuhself. I'ma fix you a nice pie."

"Yeah Momma, that's the least you can do for me since you made me smuggle you out of the hospital."

Big Mama sat down in the recliner her son

got her for Mother's Day. She reclined it back and flipped the arm up. She pushed a button and the relaxing sound of water flowing through a stream came through the speakers embedded in the cushion behind her head. She closed her eyes. Gloria went into the kitchen. Big spoons and bowls started to make music, the music of an experienced hand at work.

"Well, see you guys later." Kaitlynn said, "I have a hair appointment, be back later."

When the Range Rover pulled off Big Mama got up in an attempt to put Gloria out of her kitchen. While the litigation about the rights to the kitchen ensued, the phone rang. Big Mama answered.

"Gladys?"

"Yeah Mable, dis is Gladys."

"I thought that was you in the car when yall passed by a little while ago. How you doin'?"

"I'm fine, but listen hea, I was juss bout ta..."

"Well I'm glad to hear you is doin' good cause I liked ta died when that amballams came screaming down the street."

"It's nice ta know you worry bout me. I'm gon' call you lat..."

"Yeah you know I calls everyday and one of the childrens'll tell me you was awright but I just can't sit easy til I hear it out yo mouth. That remind me, the unda cover po' leces was meddling wit yo son Mannish yestaday. I suppose he ain't did nothin' cause they ain't take him downtown.

You know if that was any of my no good childrens the po'leces woulda hauled they ass down to the station cause they be done did sumthin'. Let me tell you what my son did..."

"Mable I gotta get sum rest. I talk ta yuh lat..."

"Yeah chile, you needs ta just lay on down and relax. You can believe if I didn't have no kids to worry my nerves 24-7 I could get me some rest even though they grown they wouldn't know what to do if I was to up and die tomorrow. My daughter call me this mo'nin'. She need me to cook her a pot a gumbo. I tell her this gon' be the last time. She gotsta sit down and watch sos she can do it herself..." Click!

Big Mama hung up the phone and went to her room to lay down mumbling to herself. "I'm tired fa' real now. Mable gots sum lungs on her. Likedta give me a headache. Maybe I shouldna hung up on her, shoulda juss put da' phone down. Let her talk til she run outta words in da' english language."

Ty and Mannish came in the door laughing about a funny situation Ty was telling him about.

"Hey boys, yall keep it down Gladys in her room sleep." Gloria said.

"Big Mama home?" Ty asked in a quieter tone. That's cool. My ole scanless Momma ain't come back huh?"

"Sorry ta say but no."

Ty said, "But anyway look what we got you Auntie Gloria. I know you said you didn't want nothing new cause you already had in yo suitcase what you was gonna wear but we seen this old la... I mean older lady in the mall and she helped us pick out something. You gonna like it I promise you."

He gave her the bag. When she pulled the dress out of the bag her eyes lit up at the colors and designs. They knew she was happy with it.

Mannish said, "We gonna have to get Big Mama something tomorrow but it's cool cause the graduation don't start until about one o' clock or something."

Ty said he was going back down to Bone's house.

Mannish went to Ty's room and laid back on the bed. He was stressed and hadn't had time to think. He had street funk with the police and he had them trying to get him on criminal charges. But so far Jay was the only weak link that could sink him.

Mannish remembered he had seen Andre' walking in the direction of the liquor store a few minutes ago. He thought about what he could do for a few minutes. Then he got up, looked under Ty's mattress and just as he suspected Ty's pistol laid there. He grabbed it, made a phone call and went out the door. He drove around the corner and up the street. He spotted Andre'. He still hadn't got to the store yet. Mannish pulled to the curb.

"Damn Dre' I saw you headed to the store about a half an hour ago. You ain't made it yet?"

Mannish said to him.

"Ay, what's up Mannish. Naw I was fuckin' wit the homies around the corner for a minute."

"Hop in, lemme' holla at you."

Andre' obliged. They took a ride and turned a few corners.

"Dre' you gave anybody that temple demonstration lately?"

"Naw, Man I just been chillin'."

"Let me ask you something?"

"Yeah Man you can ask me anything, what's up."

"Would you do five years and kill somebody for $100,000?"

Without need for deliberation, he said, "Hell yeah!"

Then he said, "Ain't nobody getting no five years for no murda."

"I didn't say kill somebody and get five years for it. I simply said do five years and kill somebody..." He made sure to reiterate. "...for $100,000."

"Yeah I would."

"For sure?"

He looked and seriously nodded his head, "Fa' sho."

Mannish reached under the seat and came up with a pistol and handed it to Andre'.

"Damn this a nice joint right here." Andre' said looking at the piece.

Mannish dug in his pocket and produced a

roll of hundreds in the amount of $10,000 and handed it to him also. Andre' was flabbergasted.

"You givin' me all this shit?"

"Yeah and I want you to remember this number."

"Okay write it down."

"Naw, I don't want you to just have it on you like that. You gotta memorize it right now."

They rode around and went over the number until Mannish was sure he had it locked in his memory.

"Ay, you know Jay?" Mannish asked him.

"Yeah, yuh boy. He caught a case right? What about him?"

"I was just askin'."

Mannish dropped Andre off at the liquor store and made a call. Within three minutes the Feds ran down on Andre'. They had gotten a call thirty minutes prior. An anonymous caller said that they had spotted an America's Most Wanted suspect and told them he was in the general area around Big Mama's house. When they got another call saying a man was chasing people around with a gun they were already in the area. They immediately located the man described by the caller and apprehended him. Andre's gun charge was punishable by five years in the Feds.

For the good fortune of the Princess of the household on the eve of her graduation, everything for the rest of the day was chill.

CHAPTER TWENTY-NINE

Everybody was at the graduation with all smiles and good cheer. They made a bunch of noise and stood up when they called out Kaitlynn Johnson. She walked across the stage so proud, chest stuck out and head up high like a noble peacock.

Ty said, "Uh oh, hope she don't get the big head, she ain't gonna be able to fit in the limo. But then we could tie a basket to her feet and use her for a hot air balloon. Then we won't have to worry about gettin' searched at the airport."

"Boy cut it out." Big Mama said nudging him in his side.

After the ceremony Kaitlynn said goodbye to some friends that it was very possible this would be the last time seeing. And some that she would no doubt remain acquainted with for years to come. She introduced some of her friends to her family.

"...And this is my nephew Ty." Kaitlynn told one of her friends.

Ty said, "What's up lil Momma, you know I was clapping for you when they called your name, and I didn't even know that Kaitlynn knew you. I just know that I want to know you." he said licking his lips.

"Boy, how old are you?" she asked him, with hand on her hip.

He frowned up his face at her. It was obvious he had some bad words for her. But just then he regained his composure, smiled and brushed his fingers across his chin. He looked down at his brown khaki suit then checked his brown suede Chuck Taylors for the slightest smidgen of dirt.

Then he said, "Check this out Babygirl. I'm Da Truth a.k.a. Ty Boogi, the next big thing so you betta come on in on the ride up cause I ain't gonna recognize you when you wavin' up at me later in the game."

"Is that right?"

"I'm just sayin' though. I know if this school ain't taught you nothin' else you should've learned to take advantage of opportunity wit yo pretty ass."

"Boy!" Big Mama said loudly.

Then he said, "Kaitlynn can give you my hook up when you get yuhself together." and strolled off to a nearby snack stand.

"He's an arrogant little something." the girlfriend said.

Kaitlynn said, "Don't let him bother you."

"I like him though, with his young, cute, thuggish self."

Kaitlynn felt a tap on her shoulder. She turned around and her heart tried to jump out of her chest as she looked at her object of fascination eye to eye.

"Congratulations on your degree."

She wanted to say, "Thank you and congratulations to you too." but the words wouldn't come out. She was speechless. Beads of sweat appeared on her nose.

"Kaitlynn, right?" he filled the silence.

"Uh, yeah, yeah, Kaitlynn."

Everyone marveled, they never seen her like this before. She was dumbfounded.

"I'm Daniel. I just wanted to speak because this is it. I won't be seeing you anymore, that is unless we exchange information."

"Yeah Daniel... I mean... um... take me... I mean umm take my number down."

Kaitlynn heard some chuckles behind her. Even Big Mama had to join in. They exchanged numbers and agreed to keep in touch. A couple of Kaitlynn's girlfriends came over with the idea that Kaitlynn should bring her family to join them and their families to have dinner.

They all decided it was a good idea and piled in the limos.

Three stretch limos caravanned through town and up La Cienega Blvd. to restaurant row. A mile stretch in Beverly Hills where all the nicest restaurants in town were.

CHAPTER THIRTY

The next morning after Mannish dropped Gloria off at LAX he got a call from Vallawn imploring him to meet with her.

"Where are you going right now?" she asked.
"I gotta drop my truck off at the shop."
"Where at?"
"Over by Big Mama's house."
"Let me pick you up from there."

He thought about those dirty cops and the possibility of getting caught trying to walk down the street from the shop. He had been trying to figure out how he could balance staying out of their reach and eyesight but at the same time check on Big Mama, find his sister and keep Ty under his wing. The answer he had yet to realize.

"Yeah alright, come on. I'ma be on 47th and Main St."
"Okay bye."

Vallawn made it to him in record time. When Mannish got into the car with her she asked him if he was hungry. He told her he was, so they ended up at a black owned spot in Inglewood called The Serving Spoon, where the food is scrumptious and celebrities dine. Most of the stuff on the menu is named after someone that works there. Even the Mexican that cleans off the table and refills your water has a breakfast named after him.

In the middle of their meal Vallawn said bluntly, "How much would you charge me for a kilo?"

Mannish almost drowned with the orange juice he was drinking. He coughed it up and spilled it on his shirt. He coughed for a full two minutes before gaining his composure.

"I'm just saying, you aren't trying to let me be your girl, so at least you can do bizness with me. I got some friends and their men sell drugs but they aren't doing any supplying or nothing like that. I figured if I could get some weight I could sell it to them through the girls and you know, come up."

"What makes you think I got it like that Vallawn?"

"Nigga don't even try to play me like that. People talk, I listen, and for real, the talk is you got more birds flying across town than dudes with pigeon coops. So do I have to ask you again or what?"

"What I want for them you ain't got."

"Aight nigga that's strike one. How do you know what I ain't got?"

"Oh yeah. Where you gonna get $15,000 from?"

"That's strike two. Did I ask you where you got the dope from?"

He couldn't help but laugh. "What's gonna happen if I strike out?"

"See, you wanna play. I was gonna suck your dick after breakfast."

He felt a tingle in his midsection instantly.

"Aight you win I ain't tryna strike out. But it ain't gonna be until tomorrow, I'ma have Ty bring it to you."

"I've been waiting all this time I could wait another day but I ain't doing bizness with Ty, I'm doing bizness with you."

She took a swig of his orange juice, swished it around in her mouth, swallowed and opened her mouth seductively then said, "Bases are empty, you're up to bat, you got two balls. What do you do?"

He felt a surge of blood rush through his dick. He had to adjust his pants.

"You know you talking to Barry Bonds, before the steroid scandal."

When they stepped outside the restaurant Mannish noticed for the first time how dark the tint on her windows actually were. As soon as they were in the vehicle she started fumbling with his belt and zipper. When she pulled his dick out it stood up thick and hard like a full grown oak tree. He reclined his seat back. His eyes closed, his mouth fell open and his mind went soaring into the stratosphere when he felt her full lips and warm mouth engulf him.

Deja 'vu. *She got talent. Oh yeah, she makes erotic sounds too.*

He pulled her head up for a few seconds to get a break from the intensity of her sensational fellatio. His dick was pulsating. She went back down on it and tried to swallow it. A warm healthy portion of nonfat protein rich milkshake shot down her throat. She sucked him clean then pulled some baby wipes out of the glove compartment to finish him up.

He told her to take him back to check on his car. Mannish was disappointed that they weren't nearly finished.

He had been dealing with them for years and had brought them plenty of costumers so he always got priority, even when he would just pop up and needed the entire interior of his lowrider done fast to get ready for a car show.

They told him they had run into some difficulty because of the engineering on the Porsche Cheyenne was new and foreign so everything was situated differently than the average vehicle they worked on. He was glad too because it would be in a new spot the police definitely wouldn't be hip to. Once so many dudes have the same spot in the same type of cars you never know if a cop stumbled across it before or if somebody told something. Then here you come thinking shit is sweet not knowing this cop been around.

Fernando told Mannish to come back the next day.

When they pulled up to Big Mama's house Ty was on the porch getting the low down from Champ who had been scouting out for the ideal spot and found it. The only problem was that it was currently inhabited by a family for the last couple years.

"Yeah, so I kicked the door in and ran up in the joint with two pistols in my hand like Tomb Raider and shit, hollerin' and shit, talkin' bout "Where Co-Co at? I know he here! Somebody betta tell me something befo' I just start ta bussin' up in this mutha fucka." They was actin' like they ain't know what I was talkin' bout."

"Who is Co-Co?" Ty asked.

"Shit, I don't know, I made that shit up. But listen though, I started openin' closet doors and room doors just bussin' as soon as I open the door. Nigga it's bullet holes everywhere. I told 'em I was gonna send my homies that's crazier than me, Murda Mike and Killa Cal and they was gonna find Co-Co if they had to kill everybody to do it.

"Then I got up out of there. Nigga that shit was fun. But anyway I figure in a minute we'll be able to move up in that joint."

Mannish could see how animated Champ was. "What yall got going on?" he asked.

"Nothin', just some stuff me and Champ was talking about doing." Ty answered. Then he said to Champ, "Champ, ay look I'ma holla at you later. Take it easy and next time talk to me first."

"Aight homie but you already know I'm serious about gettin' it." he said, then stumbled on the crack in the pavement on his way down the walkway. Then he stopped suddenly and said, "Oh I seen yuh Momma..."

Both Ty and Mannish sprung up and shouted, "Where!"

"Damn! What's up?!"

"Nigga where you see her at?"

"Damn homie at the swapmeet, but that was yesterday. I was gettin' some fresh white Pro Club t-shirts, she was at the same booth buyin' some boxers and shit. I was high and hungry so I was tryin' to hurry up so I could hit up Micky Ds fa' real."

"She didn't say nothin'?" Ty asked him.

"She said hi but I was on paranoid and shit, I thought she was askin me if I was high. And I'm on probation and shit so I dipped outta there with a quickness, you know it be undercover po' leece in that joint."

Ty shook his head at Champ in contempt for letting Shawna get away.

"Champ." Ty said sternly.

"What's up?" Champ answered.

"I'ma holla."

That was his queue to leave.

"What's going on? Why did yall get so excited like that when he mentioned seeing your sister?"

Vallawn's inquiring mind wanted to know.

"Oh, we just haven't seen her in a lil while that's all."

Then he laid back and thought if the police were anywhere watching they couldn't be sure who was in the car.

For that reason he decided not to get out. Vallawn didn't believe his answer to her question but she didn't press it because she knew that was a sure way to get sent on her way. So she just kicked back.

"Mannish!" Ty yelled from the porch. "I was bout to tell you some of my peoples I delivered to got popped. I don't know what the deal is. I had to knock this one nigga's fronts out for implying I was settin' niggas up, but that could wait cause you got big problems behind you."

Just then Cherise jumped out of her truck and ran up, reached through the driver's side window, grabbed Vallawn by the hair and snatched her out the window. It was a cat fight in the street. Nails were breaking, clothes were tearing and bare tities were jiggling. You could practically hear the Brooke Valentine song "Girlfight" playing as the soundtrack. During the fight a .38 revolver fell to the ground. No one noticed. Mannish watched the fight and smiled for awhile before he took the initiative to break it up. Through his peripheral vision he saw a car fast approaching. He didn't have time to do anything else but run up the neighbor's driveway and hop over the back gate and run into the back door of Big Mama's house.

When he peeked out the front window, he noticed Ty had crept back up on the porch and Cherise was in the back of the police car. One of the officers was talking to Vallawn. Vallawn knew it would better serve her objective if Cherise wasn't charged. She'd just gained some leeway with Mannish and she couldn't mess that up.

Cherise was held in a cell at the 77th division police station for a few hours then released in time to pick up Taj from school. For the rest of the day she was trying to put together some of the things she heard at the station. She was trying to make sense out of some things the officers said.

The next day Mannish picked up his truck from Fernando's.

The whole backseat, although it looked exactly the same, was transformed into a compartment that had the capacity to hold ten kilos or a million dollars cash money the hidden electronic latches that held everything tight and unmovable like a master lock could only be disengaged by pushing the back window defroster button but the engine had to be running (because the police don't search your car with the engine running) and the radio had to be on. Not the CD changer but the radio and it had to be on AM band at that. Needless to say, Mannish was happy with it. Later on in the day he got the phone call he was expecting.

"Ay Man, this Andre.'"

"What's up?"

"You know the police rushed me right after you pulled off. It was like they knew I had something on me. Mannish, I'm always out there and they don't ever fuck wit me, but the one time I got something they run up. If I didn't know better I'd say you called 'em on me."

"I did."

"What you say?!"

"I said, I did."

"Nigaa I'll..."

"Hold up before you get besides yourself. We made a deal, I owe you $90,000 more. You're gonna get five years for the gun, you got that coming fa' sho. Now remember dude I asked you about before you got out the car?"

Andre' held the phone in disbelief. The pieces of the puzzle were falling into place.

"Yeah I remember."

"He's in there somewhere, find him and put that demonstration down."

"When I'ma get my $90,000?"

"I'll drop it off whereever you want after you do the thang."

"You mean the five years or the dude?"

"Do the Dude."

"But I been here a few days and I haven't seen 'im."

"So slap the shit out of some bitch ass niggas and

get moved around til you find 'im, put the demo down, then holla at me." Click.

Mannish and Ty went to Cerritos to pick up some work. When they stepped into the building there was a man walking ahead of them.

Ty said, "Ay Man, I swear that mutha fucka just came out of your apartment. Man I know I ain't trippin.'"

Ty yelled at the man, "Ay you!" The man kept walking.

"Ay, come here!"

Ty chased after him but he had already taken to the stairway and disappeared. They went in and checked their apartment out but couldn't find anything missing or out of place. They put ten keys in a tote bag, loaded the vehicle up and made their way back to the city. Ty dropped Mannish off at Vallawn's house with the kilo he had promised her and continued to make the deliveries of the rest. He smiled to himself thinking about how he had become a celebrity overnight. He had plenty clientele making orders for kilos and delivering them in new whips.

Shit, I'm rollin' a brand new Porsche right now.

He pulled up next to some girls in a silver SRX Cadillac mini SUV. They looked over at Ty. He flashed a cocky smile that said, *I know you want me*. They got caught at a red light. He let his passenger window down. They followed suit, letting their driver window down.

"Where you two pretty girls goin'?"

They smiled and responded. "Home."

"Where that at Ma?"

"We live in North Hollywood. Can I ask you something cause you're cute but you sure look young? How old are you?"

"How old are yall?"

"We're both 24."

"I'm fifteen wit grown man money, grown man whips, grown man ways and grown man dick. Check game, gimme the number."

"I can't do that you're just a baby." she chimed.

"Don't start that shit!" he snapped.

The light changed and the girls sped off. While he was still sitting at the light calling them all kinds of bitches, a brand new Range Rover Sport truck stopped next to him. The back window came down and the head of a girl twice as pretty as the previous girls popped out.

She said, "Hey homie wake up, the light's green, get yuh shit together."

He looked over with a mean mug that quickly turned into a smile when he saw how pretty the girl was.

"Yeah, yeah, you right."

They drove off together talking back and forth.

"Where you goin'?" she asked him.

"I gotta finish takin' care of a lil bizness."

"Can I go?" she said with the cutest look on her face.

"Naw, this kinda some on the low shit."

Seductively she said, "What if I let you fuck me in the backseat of your Porsche on the low?"

He swerved and almost sideswiped the truck she was in.

"Damn daddy, you aight? Lemme' find out you can't even handle the thought of hitting this ass."

"Naw." he said trying to play it off. "I hit a pot hole that's all. But fa' real, I gotta handle something right quick then it's whatever. What's yo number?"

She said, "Area code 3-2-3-2-9-4-1-1-5-6"

He repeated it correctly.

"I'ma hit you on your phone in a hour." he told her.

"Don't get into nothin', or should I say don't let nothin' get into you." then he turned off to his destination.

Thinking to himself. *What was that number? She said 3-2-3-2-9-5 somethin'. Think, 1-1-4-6. 2-9-6-1-1-4-5. Naw, that ain't it. Damn!*

After Ty hit everybody off he picked up Mannish from Vallawn's house.

"How it go Ty?" Mannish asked him.

"It's all good. You know I handle shit. I got a hundred thousand in the stash. In the next day or two I'ma have another fifty. Oh yeah, and boy that got the spot on El Segundo said he need to tell you something he just found out. He wouldn't tell me what though. He said it was yall bizness."

"I wonder what he talkin' about. Maybe he

seen Shawna."

"Uh uh I asked him, he said no he ain't seen her. It wasn't that."

"Oh well, I got other shit to worry about than what he talkin' about right now."

As Ty sat at the light facing northbound on Van Ness, a Range Rover Sport flew across their path headed westbound on Vernon ave.

The girls were bumping their music loud and making plenty of noise themselves like it was a party on wheels passing through. Ty ran the red light, turned behind them and attempted to catch them. Mannish put his hand on Ty's right arm and said, "Never chase a bitch. Especially, them kinda bitches."

Ty tried to explain that he had met them already but forgot the phone number. Mannish squeezed his arm firmly. Ty let up off the gas and made a U turn. Mannish told him to take him home because he didn't feel comfortable going to Big Mama's house. Lately every time he went over there something bad happened. Not only was it risky for him but also for Big Mama's health.

Thank God she was asleep yesterday.

CHAPTER THIRTY-ONE

The next day Mannish laid low while Ty went and picked up some money from a few guys. About an hour later Ty pulled back into Mannish's driveway erratically and parked in the back of the house. All the windows were shot out of the Porsche truck and the body was riddled with holes.

Mannish ran out the back door. "What is it witchu always coming back in some shit!"

Ty hopped out the truck hysterical. "Man! Shit's fucked up! I don't know what's hapnin' but I almost got my wig split twice. I'm bout to go get my soldiers and light up everything! I gotta call somebody to come get me."

"Hold up Ty, slow down. What the fuck happened?"

"Them niggas was tryna have my head on some bullshit!" he said, still anxiety stricken. "Man, fuck them niggas! Man, I don't know what's up but when it's all said and done each one of them bitch ass niggas is gettin' carried by six!" Ty said, pacing quickly back and forth.

"Wait a minute Ty, take a breath."

"Yeah I'ma take a breath aight, a few of 'em."

Mannish wasn't getting through to him. It wasn't working. He took Ty inside, sat him down on the couch. Mannish asked him if he had some weed.

"Yeah."

"Well you need to smoke some right now."

Ty got some weed and a blunt out of his pocket and began rolling it up still cussing and fussing. Smoking was off limits in the house but Mannish had to make an exception today. As Ty inhaled the purple smoke, his mind began to relax. He leaned back as his nerves calmed.

"Okay you aight now?" Mannish asked him.

"Yeah Man I'm cool."

"Now tell me what happened out there."

Ty took a couple of deep breaths, finally he said, "Man I went to my boy Anthony's house on 84th and scooped up that change he had for us. Everything was cool wit him but he told me that Big Ron who I had hit wit a thang yesterday too got knocked soon after I left. I was feelin' lucky cause the D's had just missed me and I got his money already. It's like okay he got problems, but betta him than me right? Anyway I get them chips from Anthony and bounce to the next spot. I pulled up on Twin and 'em block and a bunch of his homies out there but them niggas is mean mugging me so I just call the nigga Twin over to the car. He starts goin' off about me workin' wit the police and shit. I wanted to shoot him in his mouth but I'm thinking I still need to get your $15,000 from this fool.

"Then he said he got busted with the bird and sat in jail all night and had just bailed out a couple hours before I got there.

Now I'm confused, thinkin' damn it sure is mighty hot these days. I'm in a lil daze thinking about all the shit I been hearin'. And befo' I know it bullets is rockin' the truck. I couldn't do nothin' but duck and smash on the gas. I must wasn't thinkin' straight cause I made another stop on the way back here and the cold part about that was my homeboy's baby momma hit the driver's side about six times wit a nine millimeter or something. Man this shit is crazy."

He was amped up again and was pacing back and forth.

"Ty, light that shit back up, sit yuh ass back down, I can't think." Mannish went out to the back and inspected the truck then covered it up and went back into the house. "We gonna just chill and post up right here and wait for Aiyana to come home then we gonna take her car and go to the apartment."

Ty spent the rest of Tuesday arguing and threatening people on the phone until Mannish told him to just cut his phone off.

After he cut his phone off he said, "Man, it's

got me fucked up, outta the sixteen thangs I dropped off, five of them niggas got ran down on like right after I left. Then muthafuckas ain't tryna hear that ain't nothin' happen to the other eleven. I know wasn't nobody followin' me, and you know how I drive, gutta lanes and back streets and shit."

Mannish nervously said, "I got an idea but I hope it ain't what I'm thinking. I read something in a book before like this, but it wasn't drugs. Lord knows I hope it ain't what I'm thinkin', but we gonna see."

Ty didn't ask any questions. If Mannish was ready to speak on it he would have. Mannish's cellphone rang.

When he saw that it was Vallawn he pressed end and ignored her call. It rang again, he ignored it again. Then the house phone rang.

I know that ain't her.

He looked at the caller ID. It said unknown caller.

He answered it cautiously "Hello?"

"Mannish?"

"Vallawn?"

"Yeah, it's me. I called your..."

"How the fuck you get this number?!"

"Boy please, I had this number in my caller ID since you called me from there a while back."

He wanted to say, "Bullshit!" but he couldn't remember if he had ever indeed called her from home. He really doubted it but he had too much shit on his mind.

"Anyway I did try to call your cell first but you

didn't pick it up."

"What do you want?"

"You sure can be mean sometimes. I guess it just be like sometimes huh? I just wanted to tell you that everything's okay but that stuff you gave me I need you to make it hard for me like your dick be when it's in my mouth."

His dick throbbed.

Got damn, why she say it like that?

"Aight Vallawn, I'll talk to you later."

"Bye bye." Click.

When Aiyana and Naj came home Naj ran up and jumped in his arms.

"Daddee!"

"What's up my lil man?"

"Nothin."

"Was you good at school today? You know I gotta always ask your bad butt."

"Daddy, you don't always have to ask me that."

"Why not?"

"Because I'm always good, even when I'm not."

"I understood that, you think you slick. You sayin' you good at being bad."

Mannish put him down and tackled him down to the ground and tickled his tummy and under his arms. Then Mannish kicked it with Aiyana for a while and let her unload the stresses of her day on him. She appreciated his ear even though his mind was elsewhere. Suddenly, he headed for the door.

"We'll be back."

"Yeah, but when?" she asked no one.

She smiled when she heard Aaliyah singing, "Your love is a one in a million. That's what she had been playing when she drove up. She smiled because he was taking her car. He had to come back so she could go to work in the morning, she hoped. On the way to the apartment Cherise called Mannish. He ignored her call. The phone beeped signaling he had a voice message. He checked it.

{you have four new messages and four saved messages.

First new message} "Mannish this Cherise, I really need to talk to you, I'm serious, I love you call me right back."

beep {message erased}

He didn't even bother listening to the other messages.

He was just curious of what Cherise wanted to say. She was his son's mother, he had to make sure she wasn't talking about killing herself or Taj or anybody else. When they reached their destination Mannish circled the block a few times before parking around the corner and casually walking with Ty to the building. They surveyed their surroundings as they entered the building. The area was quiet. They went into the apartment unit, Mannish first with his hand in his pocket finger on the trigger. All was quiet. He went to the closet and took out the bag full of money rolls and the 25 kilos he had left. He threw everything on the bed and told Ty to take 3 kilos into the living room and set them on the coffee table. Mannish took 3 into the kitchen and set them on the table.

"Now what Man?"

"Listen, I want you to take one and unwrap every strip of tape on it and don't use no knife or scissors."

"Why, what we gon' do cook all this shit up?"

"Just do it!"

They both began to unwrap the tape laden blocks of cocaine. After about twenty minutes Ty had a table full of tape, chunks and powder.

"Aight that's one. Damn Man, that shit took a minute. We gotta do all them on the bed?"

"Yeah, you got something else to do?" Mannish responded perturbed.

"Naw, I'm witchu. I was just sayin' though."

"Sayin' what? Do what I asked you to do."

"Can I put a movie on or somethin'?"

"Hell naw, I need you to pay attention to what you doing."

"What am I doin'?"

Mannish threw him a box of ziplock baggies.

"Putting that dope in them bags and throwing that tape in this trash bag and starting on the next brick. And make sure you get it all. Use your ID to scoop the powder up."

Ten minutes later Mannish heard Ty say, "What the fuck?" then yell, "Look at this shit!"

Mannish ran into the living room. Ty was pointing to a small black device hidden under four layers of tape. The four layers were close in color but not the same tape as the rest. Mannish plucked it from the tape and studied it. It was a transmitter.

"Ain't that a bitch!"

The dope was Lo-Jacked. He put that package to the side and told Ty to look in the next one while he went back in the kitchen to continue his search now that they knew what they were looking for. Two hours later they were done and had found that one third of the bricks were tampered with. They filled up a couple of carrying bags with the drugs and sat them by the door. There was no way he was gonna leave them there and risk further trouble. They flipped through the rolls of money. No transmitters. Ten, one thousand dollar rolls lighter than it should've been but no transmitters.

He wasn't surprised because it was evident that someone had been in the closet. He would've been surprised if no money was missing.

Ty grabbed the movies he bought and they left out for what would be the last time. Mannish packed all the transmitters also. He knew he was taking a chance of them zooming in on him with the transmitters and all the drugs in the car with them. If they were caught then he and Ty could kiss that bitch called freedom goodnight.

He got on the freeway and headed east, the

opposite way of the city, until he exited at a truck stop. He pulled up on several trucks that were gassing up.

He noticed they all had different license plates from different states. As he walked pass he flicked the transmitters on top of the trucks until they were all gone. Then he got back in the car and went to the city of Los Angeles. The only safe spot he could think of to hide his load was over Vallawn's. He called her, she didn't answer. Her voicemail picked up.

He tried her again. After three rings she answered.

"Hello."

"Where you at?"

"I'm at Roscoe's Chicken and Waffles with your Baby Momma."

Mannish looked at the phone confused.

"What?"

"Yeah, I had to get up and pretend I had to use the restroom to answer your call."

"What the hell are yall doing together?"

"She called me a couple hours ago and apologized.

She said she overreacted and that I was her only friend and asked me out to lunch."

Mannish was tripping off of the fact that Vallawn and Cherise were together after all the drama Cherise had caused. He forgot why he had called in the first place.

Oh yeah.

"Listen, I need to meet you at your house a.s.a. right now. Tell her something came up."

"Okay Baby, I'll be on my way after we finish eating. I'll just skip desert."

"Did you hear what I said? I said right now, don't even go back in there and sit down." he told her assertively.

"Nigga, you gon' give me some dick when I get there? Cause if you ain't…"

"Vallawn leave right now or I ain't fuckin' witchu!"

"Alright Mannish, damn, I'm leaving right now." Click.

She went back and sat down and cut a small square of the waffle on her plate, stabbed it with the fork and dipped it in the syrup. Cherise resumed her conversation while Vallawn fed her face.

"Yeah girl it ain't even that serious, so we going to be cool and move on or what?"

"You paying for lunch right?" Vallawn asked.

"Yep."

"Well you already know the way to my heart is through my stomach girl."

They both laughed. Vallawn said, "But check it out, I got a movie date with my new nigga and he wanna meet me at the Kodak Theater. We gonna have a few drinks at the restaurant up there then we gonna walk over to the Chinese theater and catch that new Will Smith movie."

"Aight, I'll call you later."

Vallawn took a final sip of her lemonade and left.

When she got to her condo Mannish and Ty got out of the car with the bags and met her at the front door.

"Peep game." Mannish said, "I need you to hold these bags for me cause I'm going through a transition right now. In other words shit done got hot where it was at."

"Oh, well you know it's not a problem with me. You can leave it here as long as you want."

Her cell phone rang. "Hello."

"What's up girl, this Cherise, Did the movie start yet?"

"No we still sitting here talking, with his fine ass." she said looking at Mannish.

"What are yall gonna do watch, a sneak preview or something? Cause I was gonna watch that movie myself but I couldn't find it playing nowhere." Cherise said, matter of factly.

"You know girl you right. He told me I was tripping. That movie haven't even started playing in the theaters yet. He said he's going to make sure he pick something good. she said as she shrugged her shoulders like, Hey once you lie once, you gotta lie again. she said back into the phone, "Cherise I'ma talk to you later."

"Aight." Click.

Pointing to the bag Mannish asked her if she still wanted him to cook one up for her.

Vallawn said, "No. Don't even worry. We

straight."

"Aight then. We outta here."

They pulled off with the music bumping while the video to R Kelly's Trapped in the Closet was showing on all the monitors in the car. But his mind was elsewhere.

What the hell is Cherise up to with her psychotic ass or is she sincere about making up wit Vallawn? You can never tell with these bitches these days. She might take her to the beach tomorrow and come home crying talking about her best friend in the whole world drowned, make all the funeral arrangements, give a speech, read a poem, sing songs and some more shit.

Then he thought about the police and how they found the apartment and got in to do that slick move. *How you gonna Lo-Jack a nigga's dope?*

He was on his way to Big Mama's house to stash the bag of money in the ceiling. When he got there he circled the block a couple times. When he hit Main Street he went up a block and pulled in the lot of the upholstery shop and called Miguel to the driver's side of the car.

"Remember when I brought that big white truck and you put the gun stash in the floor for me?"

"Yeah, that truck was bad homie. I woulda kept that shit if I was you."

"Remember when you said it had Lo-Jack?"

"Yeah, that's what I'm sayin', it had everything homes."

"How did you know it had Lo-Jack?"

 314

"I saw the lil black box under the bottom, and the light would blink and shit."

"Look under this car for me and see if you see one under there."

"Sure homes, hold on."

He dropped down and rolled under the INFINITI FX45.

"Ay homes."

"What's up?" Mannish answered.

"Keep your foot on the brake alright."

"Yeah." he answered laughing.

"Yep, I see it." Miguel hollered from under the car.

"Can you take it off for me?"

"You sure?"

"Yeah, take it off."

He came up with it in his hand. "It was just on with a magnet. They sure don't make stuff like they used to."

Mannish shook his hand and slid him a fifty dollar bill.

"Good lookin' out homes."

Mannish threw it in front of the car as he drove off and rolled over it crushing it into the pavement. They circled the block again for reassurance that the coast was clear before he pulled into Big Mama's driveway behind Kaitlynn's Range Rover. They could tell Kaitlynn was in the living room watching TV because of the glare through the window. They took the bag of money up the driveway and in the back door. Once the money was stashed in the ceiling and they came down to the living room they saw Big Mama sitting in her recliner on the phone.

"Mable, I awredy gots a headache sumpmm terrible an' I caint watch dis movie an' be on da' phone at da' same time. Sos guess what? Uh huh, I talk ta yuh lader, don't call me, I'ma call you, hea me." Click.

Mannish flopped down on the couch and checked out the movie she was watching. His eyes caught the big floor model under the 36 inch TV they were watching. His mind drifted back to when he used to lay right where he was and watch shows like the Jeffersons and Diff 'rent Strokes. He remembered watching Good Times and having a crush on Penny. He remembered when her mother burned her with the iron and how he thought it was real and how he wanted to go protect Penny and shoot her mother with his pellet gun. There was a crack on the tube from one day when he was playing baseball in the house.

He got a thorough ass whooping for that. He thought the trouble he used to get into back then was major but the trouble he found himself in right now definitely redefined his definition of major trouble. He heard Big Mama laugh at something on TV, that snapped him out of it.

Just then a light from a car using the driveway to turnaround shined into the house. Mannish looked out the window and watched a 6Corvette back out the driveway and park in front of the house. A man got out wearing a Cardigan sweater, walked around to the passenger side opened the door and helped Kaitlynn out.

"Momma, why you didn't tell me Kaitlynn was on a date? I thought she was in her room sleep."

"You aint ask, an' I aint gotsta mine dat girl bidness fa' her."

"But she ain't never been on no date before wit no nigga."

"Dat's a nice young man. He da' one whut come ova ta talk ta her afta da' gra'jayshun. But dey aint been gone long."

Mannish opened the window so he could hear them.

"We could've hung out all night." Daniel stated barely concealing his sexual intentions.

"See, that's what we couldn't have done. But I had a good time. My belly is full of some good food and you made me laugh a lot. That's a good thing. I'll consider it my graduation present from you."

"You saying that like this was a one time thing."

"Well relationships lead to drama and drama I don't need so..."

He remained quiet waiting for her to finish her sentence.

She didn't.

He said, "So..."

He stopped short and waited. A pregnant pause. Then she completed it with.

"We can be friends." she paused, then said, "Only if you know how to be a friend."

"You mean friends as in no sex, friends."

"Not necessarily."

"Oh okay consider me a good friend."

"See, there you go."

By this time they were on the porch. He told her about a few websites that he had heard about but hadn't personally checked out yet that were networks for individuals with Masters Degrees in Pyschology. He told her it had chat rooms, tips on jobs, leads and contacts.

Mannish was still eavesdropping, getting completely bored with the content of the conversation. Suddenly, he saw a figure walking fast through the darkness on the other side of the street. He focused his eyes into the night.

"Ahh shit!" he said to himself. "Ay!" he hollered out the window scaring the hell out of Kaitlynn and her date.

"Ay Shawna!" he screamed.

The figure picked up the pace into a sprint.

"Ay!" Mannish hollered again, stumbling over a small table by the window trying to get to the front door.

By the time he got out the house and made it down to the sidewalk she was gone. He jumped into the car and drove around the neighborhood until he saw a patrol car which made him nervous, so he went back to the house.

When he got back inside Ty inquired. "You was chasin' after Shawna?"

Before Mannish could answer Big Mama interrupted, "Boy whut I tell you bout callin' yo mama by her first name? Das yo Momma, she brung yuh lil knucklehead butt inta dis world. You call her Momma. Yuh hea me?!" she reprimanded.

"Yes Big Mama, but she ain't been actin' like no Momma. You my Momma. She out there runnin' around bein' a dopefiend. She run away from the people tryna help her, stealin' money. She ran off with my eleven thou..." He caught himself but it was too late.

"Elebmm thousand dollas, boy where you get elebmm thousand dollars fa' her ta steal?"

She looked directly at Mannish who was looking down and shaking his head. He knew she was about to give him the bizness. He sat down and braced himself for the verbal lashing he knew Big Mama was going to unleash on him. He already knew how she felt.

She feels the streets turned my life to shit and I was dragging my nephew down too. Of coarse I'm the bad guy. She would never understand he was already involved in the street life anyway and I'm just doing the best thing I could by letting him roll with me.

"Mannish!" Big Mama yelled out thunderously. It echoed through the house. It echoed because

Kaitlynn called his name simultaneously from the back of the house.

"Come here, I need help with something please." Kaitlynn begged.

Mannish got up and went quickly to where she was.

"What's up?"

Without saying a word Kaitlynn walked him through the back door.

"What's up, you need me to get something out the garage for you?" he asked.

"No I need you to go home before Momma come out of retirement and beat you and herself to death."

"If I leave she gonna be mad."

"She's already mad. I'll take care of her for you." Kaitlynn said hugging him around his neck.

"I love you sis, I'm gone."

He hopped on the freeway and was home in no time.

He drove all the way to the back and saw the Porsche covered up because it was holier than the average Christian. That was a problem he could easily fix though. Then he thought about the reason the truck was shot up. He went in the house wondering if any of his boys had trouble. He undressed and snuggled in the bed with Aiyana.

I gotta call around tomorrow and see what's happening.

CHAPTER THIRTY-TWO

He woke up to Aiyana gently kissing him on his neck and rubbing on his dick.

"Good morning daddy."

"What time is it?"

"It's time for me to be getting up so I can go to work but I wanna feel my man, no I need to feel my man inside of me." she said while pulling on his arm. "I don't need any fourplay. I'm going to let you slide on that one. Just fuck me Papi."

He rolled over on top of her. She even reached down and guided his morning hard dick into her wet and waiting pussy. When he penetrated her the moist warmth made him harder. He thrust deep into her then pulled it all the way back to the tip. She exhaled a breath. He dropped it all in again. She gasped as if someone had stabbed her in the gut with a knife. Mannish looked into the eyes of his victim. His rhythm picked up and he began stroking her with the rhythm of a jockey on a galloping horse. Then he suddenly pulled out and flipped her over, grabbed two pillows and put them under her midsection for easy access. He slid into her from the back. A minute later her face started to make them funny expressions.

Goose bumps popped up all over her body. Juices squirted out on his legs and some of it gushed down her legs and soaked the pillow. He rolled off. She rolled over on her back.

She said, "Hmmm, that's what I needed cause my students were saying I was a mean lady lately. I gotta go, I'll be late." she said as she floated to the bathroom. "I may not even assign any work today."

While she was in the shower Naj went into the room and jumped on his daddy, not knowing he was naked under the covers.

"Whoa lil man. What's up? How you feel this morning?"

"I'm fine."

"You gonna be good today?"

"Daddy, all the time."

"Good, go see what yuh mommy want."

Naj jumped up and ran out the room and hollered through the bathroom door.

"Huh Momma, you call me?"

Mannish jumped out of the bed and locked the door.

Naj came back and banged on the door. "Dadeee, you tricked me!"

"Who is it?" Mannish asked, while slipping on some sweatpants and socks.

"It's me."

"Who did you say? I don't know anybody named Me."

Naj started laughing. "It's your son Daddy."

"Oh, why didn't you just say that in the first place?" he said after he slipped some pants on. When Mannish opened the door Naj ran in and rammed his head into his stomach.

His father picked him up and hung him upside down by his feet.

Aiyana stepped in, "Mannish don't do that! You might drop my baby on his head or something."

He looked at her like, "Girl stop tripping, I got him." but he put him down anyway to appease her mind.

They left and he went back to sleep. Three hours later he was awakened again by his cell phone. He rolled over to get it from the night stand.

"Hello."

"Mr. Johnson, this is Paul Downing. I left you two messages. You never responded."

"My bad, I haven't even checked my messages in a few days. What's up?"

"Well the message was informing you that there is a hearing today for Jay and it looks like he may be copping a deal. His lawyer is actually very good and since he's cooperating, chances are he's gonna come out alright. But on the other hand you may have bigger worries. The prosecution says their investigation is bearing fruit. There are more details that I can't discuss over the phone. Why don't you come see me in the afternoon, maybe around one o'clock."

"Yeah, I can do that. Listen, try to get Jay's attorney to postpone this hearing for a minute. I sent him a message."

"Okay I'll see you this afternoon."

Mannish called the Porsche dealer and told them to come pick up the Cheyenne and bring a loaner car. Two Hours later a Porsche Boxter was sitting in front of his house and the flatbed tow truck was already in the back preparing to tow the car. Mannish was dressed and ready to go.

He made a few runs then met one of his boys at Earl's Wieners hotdog stand. Earl's had moved up Crenshaw Blvd. to restaurant that used to be called the Chili Factory next to Conroys on Rodeo Blvd. Everything with Mannish's people seemed alright, no one got popped.

He saved the El Segundo spot for last because it was the farthest out the way. But he couldn't make it because by the time he left Earl's Wieners it was time to go see the lawyer. When he got to the building he noticed a sexy, sophisticated black female waiting for the elevator. They boarded together. He thought she must be a paralegal or a lawyer's secretary.

"I bet you win all your cases." he said to her, admiring her backside as she leaned forward to push the button for the 11th floor. While she was still leaned forward she looked back and caught him staring at her butt. Busted!

"I'm sorry I was just um, I..."

"What else would I expect from a man! I mean that is what God put us together here on earth for right?"

Relieved that she didn't get offended he said, "Right."

"And as a matter of fact, I do win all my cases."

"Maybe I shoulda hired you."

"You still can." she said with a sly grin, which made him smile like he was practicing for a Colgate commercial.

"What's your name?" he asked her.

"Erotic...I mean Erica, Erica Caine."

"Maybe I could stop by your office on my way out after I finish my meeting with Mr. Downing."

"I don't have an office and I probably won't be here when you're done because I just came to drop some money off to my lawyer."

"Oh." he said confused. "What do you do?"

"I sell pussy Baby but my official profession is an Exotic Dancer."

She handed him a card as she strutted off the elevator.

It read Sexy Ladies Strip Tease with a Hollywood address. The name on the card said Erotic

Erica. Underneath the name in small letters it said Addicting as Cocaine. Mannish's head was messed up for a minute.

Damn, she was fine.

He exited the twelfth floor and told the Secretary Sherry who he was and who he was there to see. Five minutes later he was sent into the office. Paul looked up toward the clock on the wall. It said 2:10pm.

He said, "You're a busy man aren't you?"

"Sometimes it do be like that, things get hectic." Mannish replied.

Paul opened a folder that sat on his desk.

"I am going to be brief because I am expecting a client momentarily."

Mannish saw four pictures on top of the stack. Two of them he'd seen. The other two were new to him. He looked a little closer and turned them around to face him. He stood up pointing at one picture.

"That's the mutha fucka I seen in the building!"

"What building?"

"An apartment building I had a unit in on the outskirts of the city. You know, like a safe spot."

"You saw him there?"

"Yeah, but I already found out, they bugged my car."

The lawyer said, "Well this guy is one and this is the other guy." he said pointing to the other picture. "These guys, their names are Ramirez and Hunter, there objective is to kill you, period. The other two want to bust you in a way you won't beat. To get so much evidence Mesereau (Michael Jackson's lawyer) couldn't get you off. Speaking of that, there's five guys that got messed up the other day with drug charges and four of them are talking, saying they buy from you."

"What?! I didn't sell them lying ass niggas nothin'!"

"Are you sure?"

"Come on man. I don't even know them faggots! Them are my nephew's people."

"Well these cops aren't going to play fair."

"So now what do I do?"

"Do you have enough money to leave the country and I mean for good or at least until they lose the stiff cocks they have for you, and who knows when that'll be."

"Are you serious? I never even thought about leaving the country before."

"Well that's the only thing I can really tell you at this point especially because there's also another detective out there on your ass. Check with me in a week I should have a picture. One more thing, Jay's court hearing was postponed for a month."

The secretary buzzed the line and told the attorney that his 2 o'clock appointment was there. Mannish left calculating in his head. He had about a half a million dollars and 25 kilos that could bring another $300,000.

He reached into his pocket to get his car keys. He pulled out Erica's card. He threw it on the ground, hopped in the car and zeroed to sixtied to the end of the short block and through the stop sign. He turned a few corners and pulled back up next to where he was parked, opened the door, leaned over, picked up the card and sped back off.

The number on the card was to Erica's cell phone. He called it. She told him she had already left the building and was about to work a few hours at the club on the day shift. She told him to come by.

He needed to take his mind of his dilemma, at least for a minute. So he went to the gentlemen's club. When he walked in, he had to let his eyes adjust from the bright sunny day outside to the significantly darker ambience of the club. He went to the bar to get a shot of Hennessey while he looked around the club for Erica. He found her on the stage doing a slow sensual routine to a slow jam by Neyo. He sat down in a love seat, watched the show and chilled out while the alcohol relaxed his mind. When a drink girl came by and asked him if he wanted something to drink he declined.

"But you have to buy at least one drink sir, there's a one drink minimum."

"I bought two shots when I first walked in." he

said obviously annoyed.

"From which bartender?" she asked like she was going to go ask.

"Get yo ass away from me!" Mannish shouted.

"You don't have to get crazy. I was just..."

"I don't give a f..."

A figure interrupted, stepping in between them. "I got this Cherry."

Cherry walked off. Erica looked at Mannish with one hand on her hip.

"You trouble aren't you?"

"It ain't even like that. But I didn't want nothing else to drink, I already..."

She cut in, "I saw you at the bar." she said that while straddling him.

She began to slowly grind to the music. She held his shoulders and threw her head back feeling the music. She came up and hugged his head burying his face in her bodacious breasts. As she grinded on him some more she felt something hard in his pants.

"Oooh, is that a gun?"

"No."

"Then you're nasty."

"I'm nasty? Girl, you make Superhead look like Martha Stewart."

"It's the Xstasy. You ever fucked a girl on Xstasy?"

"I don't mean to bust your bubble but I haven't, don't and won't every pay for no pussy, before you even get started. God didn't put yall down here for a price."

"Shiiit, look what Eve cost Adam." Erica said with a crazy smile.

Before he could dispute that comment he saw one of the cops that was trying to kill him on the other side of the room getting a lap dance and chug-a-lugging a glass of beer. Mannish sat erect. He stopped Erica from gyrating on him.

"That man over there, he come in here regular?"

Mannish asked her letting his eyes do the pointing. She looked in the direction he was looking. "Yeah, he's DEA and he don't mind paying and he will eat a bitch pussy all night."

Mannish peeled her off two hundred dollar bills. "Ay look Ma, I liked your show. Here this for you. I gotta go, got things to do."

"Alright baby boy." she said kissing him on his nose.

Mannish went outside, looked around and saw the black Grand Marquis. Across the street he saw a grocery store. He ran across the street and went inside.

CHAPTER THIRTY-THREE

An hour later Officer Ramirez came out of the club. He had to adjust his eyes to the sunlight. He got into his car, stuck the key into the ignition and twisted the switch to start the engine. Before the engine could even kick over, three muffled pops came through the back of his seat. Of the two that exited his chest, one lodged in the speedometer on the dashboard. The other cracked the windshield, ricocheted and went through the roof.

Mannish eased out the back door and walked down the street to his car and drove off easy with a smile on his face. A mile down the road he pulled the potato off the barrel of his gun and threw it out the window. He got on the freeway and let the breeze dance across his face. He couldn't believe the cop played right into his fortune like that.

There's a chance I could make it and invest the money without running out of the country like a coward. If I could just catch the other fool that's trying to have my head and make sure I don't get caught with nothing.

Then I just wait for the indictment and try to knock them snitch niggas off one by one or challenge their credibility.

The worst I can get is a conspiracy and if it comes down to it, I'll do the ten years, as long as my money is invested.

Only thing, I gotta figure out is how the fuck do I catch a mutha fucka slipping that I don't know nothing about and a Fed at that. I can't expect him to fall into my hands like ole boy did just now.

The rest of the day Mannish spent riding the freeway thinking. He'd ride an hour in one direction then turn around and come back, then interchange in another direction, thinking. He even got stuck in rush hour traffic but it didn't bother him none, he was thinking. When he got back into the city limits he had a plan. He was going to give it a try and hope that everything went according to the plan. He called Boost and asked them if the model phone he had had the GPS capability. (GPS continuously transmits it's location to a global positioning system satellite. It's accurate within a foot anywhere on the planet.) They answered him he did and gave him the website information. He could check online and see on a regional map where the phone was located.

The first part of the plan involved calling Paul Downing and telling him he wanted to turn himself in.

Paul said, "As of today you don't even have a warrant for your arrest. You are not wanted officially."

"Well get in touch with them fools that's tryna smoke me, Ramirez and Hunter. Tell 'em I know they want me. I know what I did wrong. Tell 'em my conscience is bothering me and I want to talk to them."

Paul was reluctant but agreed. After all he was getting paid to satisfy Mannish's wishes.

"I'ma call you later and tell you were I'ma be."

CHAPTER THIRTY-FOUR

At 11 o'clock that night Mannish called and gave Paul an address and told him to call the detective in an hour and to give it to him.

As he expected Hunter came by himself and drove up in his personal car. The address was to a dopefiend's house in a grimey neighborhood.

When Hunter got to the block he parked down the street. He pulled his sweatshirt off and reached into the backseat to retrieve his bullet proof vest. He fastened it on and put his sweatshirt back on. He checked the bullets in his .38 snubnose then placed it into his ankle holster.

He pulled a black beanie cap down tight on his head.

He stepped out of his car fully donned in black with two 9mm Rugers in his hands. He stuck one in the small of his back and the other one in the pocket in front of his sweatshirt. He casually walked up the street like he was native to his surroundings.

When he got to the house he noticed all the lights were on. He went around to the side of the house and peeked in a window that was barely covered by a tattered old curtain that had seen better days. There were two people smoking crack on a bed. Neither one of them was Mannish. He went to the next window that someone tried to cover with a torn half of a sheet. He saw a boy about four years old, playing with a broken down, filthy Barbie Corvette, still no sign of Mannish. He went around to the back of the house. A pitbull with patches of hair missing and covered with sores looked up when Hunter snuck through the back gate. It looked like the dog was more inclined to run, than to attack. The dog let his head slap back down on the pavement when he realized the trespasser wasn't headed in his direction and was not an immediate threat.

Hunter went to a window with nothing covering it. He guessed they figured no one had any bizness back there to be able to look in. He inched up to the window until he could see in, then he ducked back down.

He had to assess what he saw and prepare his mind to see it again. He inched back up and watched an old lady, at least eighty years old, standing in the corner, asshole naked with wrinkled skin that looked like mounds of melted gum running down her body. She had a crackpipe and a lighter in her hand with paranoia written all over her face. She was staring at the bedroom door. He didn't know whether to be amused or disgusted. But he did realize that he was sent on a bunk run, a wild goose chase. He left the house and headed back to his car.

Hunter didn't see the figure roll from under his car and duck behind some bushes nearby. Hunter pulled off, made a U turn and got the hell up out of the neighborhood.

He was cussing to himself.

I'ma go see that fucking lawyer tomorrow and slap the shit outta him.

Mannish went to Big Mama's house. Kaitlynn had waited up for him like he asked her to. They went into her bedroom and logged onto the internet.

"I lost my phone. Go on this website and see where it's at, it got GPS."

"From the looks of this Mannish, it seems like it's moving."

"Oh I musta left it in my homie's car."

"Alright, you done?"

"No, lemme' see where he goes. If he goes home I might just drive over there and get it."

"Alright, well I'm sleepy. I'm going to sleep." she said, then she showed him how to shut everything down when he was done. After watching the dot travel on the freeway for thirty minutes he realized the cop lived in Simi Valley. (A cop town where they all retreat to after they harass blacks in the inner city allday.) He sat and contemplated the completion of his plan for the next ten minutes until the dot stood still. He watched it stay still for ten more minutes, until he was satisfied it wasn't sitting at a red light or anything like that. He wrote down the name of the street and took notes of the directions and headed out.

When he found the car he parked next to it and pulled out two five gallon gas cans of gasoline.

Once Mannish was done with the gas cans, he loaded them back into the car. Then he slid under the car, drilled a hole into the neck of the gas tank, ran a wire with spliced tips into it then ran the other end to the distributor. He removed his phone he had taped to the frame of the car and disappeared into the night.

Inside the house, Hunter was still pacing and fuming over the failed plot to kill Mannish for payback for killing a fellow officer. Hunter thought he heard something outside. He peeked through his blinds and saw a black Porsche leaving his street. He figured either one of his neighbors got a new car or one of their friends was visiting.

He paced for another thirty minutes.

"I'm tired of this bullshit." he said to no one. "If I wouldn't have missed him that day on Western, this cat and mouse shit would've been over with. My partner should've done his ass right in front of his bastard son.

"I would've squeezed the trigger. And what the

hell is up with Ramirez anyway? I called him on my way down to seal that fucker's fate over two hours ago. He didn't answer his phone and I left two messages. He still hasn't called me back yet."

Hunter's mind went from his partner back to Mannish's inevitable demise by his hands. He got himself so worked up that he needed to rest.

When he woke up Mannish was still heavy on his mind. He was late for work so he decided not to go. He didn't even call in. No shower. He didn't even wanna brush his teeth. His thoughts were only of Mannish.

"That son of a bitch is dying today! I won't eat until after I stand over his dead bleeding corpse."

Hunter stomped out of the house. When he got to his car he smelled a faint aroma of gasoline. Upon closer examination it looked as if gas had spilled down the side of his car, under the gas cap.

"Shit! Don't tell me somebody stole the little bit of gas I had in there." he said, remembering parking it on a quarter of a tank last night. He opened the door pissed off and sat in the car with one foot still out on the ground.

He stuck the key in and turned the switch so the electronic gas hand could register. It said the tank was full.

"Full?" he said, turning the key to start the engine.

The distributor sparked.

BOOOM!!!

CHAPTER THIRTY-FIVE

Mannish was at home when the breaking news interrupted any and everything anybody was watching. The newscaster said that they were identifying body parts from as far as two blocks over.

A battered and bruised neighbor got in front of the camera and said, "I was on my way to meet a client when I noticed my neighbor, Mr. Hunter come out of his house cussing about something. Then he got into his car and it just exploded. It was like something you'd see in a mafia movie or something you'd read in a book, but this was real. The blast threw me face first into the brick wall along my driveway."

Mannish turned the TV off and rolled over still dressed. He needed some rest. In the afternoon he rolled over to answer his cell phone. It had rung a few times earlier but he ignored it. This time he was tired of hearing it ring.

"What up?"

"What's up Mannish?" It was Vallawn.

"You call me earlier?"

"No, but I called you yesterday and the day before and the day before that too just like I did the day before that. I was going to go look for you today if you didn't show up. What are you doing?"

"Nothin', chillin.'"

"Why don't you come over here?"

"Because I got a lot of shit to do today."

"You just said you weren't doing anything, besides I got something for you."

He automatically thought about her fantastic head job. But at this point, that was the last thing he felt like doing. But he had to keep in mind that she had 25 kilos of his over there.

"Okay I'ma come thru and see what you got for me."

"Alright Mannish, I'm going to hold you to that. Just call me when you're on your way so I can be ready for you."

"Ay, I'm telling you now I don't know when it's gonna be."

"But sometime today right?"

"I don't know. I'ma hit you later."

"Okay I'm not trying to rush you or anything. Just call me okay."

"Okay Vallawn." Click.

He rolled out of the bed, went and turned the shower on and undressed. But before he could step in, his phone rang. He ran into the room to answer it.

"What up."

"You betta stay away from Vallawn!" Cherise yelled at him.

He hung up in her face. He wasn't in the mood. She called back but he didn't answer. When he got out of the shower his phone was telling him that Cherise had left a message. He checked it.

She was yelling, "You think it's a joke! I ain't playin'! You know what nigga, I gotchu!"

The message after Cherise's threat was from Will. He said he needed some stuff but he wanted Mannish to bring it because he had something important he needed to talk to him about.

Mannish called Vallawn back and told her he'd be there in an hour. He got dressed, went and sat down to eat lunch at M&M's Soul Food Restaurant on Centinela Ave in Ladera.

An hour and a half after he talked to Vallawn he turned the corner of her block. He parked and got out. He bounced up her stairs but before he could ring the doorbell, the door swung open. She stood her cute ass in the doorway with some curve hugging jeans on, some white Air Max Nikes and a t-shirt that said *Just Say No To Drugs*. Her hair was pulled back into a ponytail. She looked outside and seen the Porsche Boxter.

"Boy you change cars like socks. No wonder..."
"No wonder what?"
"Huh?" She was thinking, shaking her head.

"I thought you would've been in the Cheyenne or the FX."

"What difference it make?" he said instinctively locking the door behind him.

"No difference Mannish, sit down." she said as she pointed to the bag on the couch and said, "There's the drugs you left over here a week ago."

He gave her that *Damn, why you say it like that?* look but didn't say anything.

Vallawn continued, "You know for the last week Cherise has been over here so much wanting to hang out and you weren't answering my calls. I started thinking that maybe she was running interference for you. I think somehow she found out about me. I thought maybe you felt the heat and took what you had and made a move out of the country or something."

Her saying that scared the shit out of Mannish. Not only what she was saying but how she was saying it. There was a totally different presence about her. She had a persona of authority. Just then his phone vibrated on his hip. He looked and saw on the caller ID that it was Cherise. He had more reason not to answer than to answer, but for some reason he did. He pushed the send button.

"Hello."

"Mannish, a hard head make a soft ass! I told you to stay away from her. Look outside!"

He got up close to the window and looked out. There were no less than twenty cars of all types stopped in the street with their doors flung open and DEA agents taking position and creeping up to Vallawn's door. He heard a helicopter circling the area. He turned around to come face to face with a .40 caliber pistol.

"You are under arrest Mantrell Johnson, get on the ground!" Vallawn said assertively.

The phone was still to his ear. His jaw was hanging.

"Mannish!" Cherise yelled into the phone for the fourth time finally getting his attention.

"Huh?" Mannish answered, shocked stiff.

"Go out the upstairs bathroom window!" Cherise said into the phone.

"Get on the ground now! I'm not going to tell you again!" Vallawn barked.

There was a lot of noise outside. The agents banged on the door. It sounded like it almost came off the hinges. It startled both of them. But Mannish took that second of distraction and rushed her. He big fisted her with two heavy blows to the face. She was out cold before she hit the floor. The door came crashing in as he dashed upstairs to the bathroom. He locked the door and went straight for the window with no other option. He was maybe thirty feet up plus the ground was crawling with agents. He heard feet stomping up the stairs. One leg and the upper half of his body was already outside the window before he even saw the rope hanging from the roof. This was the time for all those pullups he did in jail to payoff.

He hoisted himself up to the roof where a ladder made of rope was descending, hanging from a helicopter. He didn't know what the fuck was up but again he had no other option. When the ladder was within reach he grabbed it and worked his climb game to the top and the helicopter took off. Mannish sat down and tried to calm down as his chest heaved up and down. Sweat wet his face and shirt.

Cherise said, "I told you nigga, I gotchu."

Mannish was speechless. The pilot asked where Mannish wanted to go. He wanted to hurry up and get rid of Mannish so he could collect on what Cherise had promised for the risk he took. Mannish got out of the helicopter near the L.A.X. airport.

"Dependable Travel Agency. How can we make your arrangements easier?"

"Yeah, I wanna take a flight to Costa Rica ASAP."

"And when will you be returning sir?"

"Never!"

CHAPTER THIRTY-SEVEN

The old lady with the long gray braids hanging out of the little black beenie cap, slowly managed her way down the block and up Big Mama's walkway pulling a cart lined with black plastic, making it impossible for the agents in the van up the street to see inside. Halfway up the walkway the old lady stumbled on the big crack in the cement landing hard on the pavement. Her basket rolled backwards and tumbled on the sidewalk spilling its contents.

An assortment of oranges, cantelopes and bananas spilled out onto the ground. She painstakingly picked herself up and then her fruit. The agents felt compassion and a compelling to help but that was out of the question, it would blow their cover. It took her all of fifteen minutes to get it together. Then she made her way back up the walkway and then the stairs. She rang the doorbell then took a seat on the porch to rest. Someone answered the door but the agent couldn't make out who it was. The screen door was obstructing his view. The old lady and someone exchanged a few words then someone held the door open to let her in.

"Hey Steffans." One of the agents in the van said to the other one while logging the time of the visit.

"How long do you think we're gonna be posted up watching the house before the director realizes the fucking dude isn't coming back around? He hasn't even communicated with anyone in his family."

"Well we've only been out here for a week. I've been on a case where I sat and watched a house for eighteen months and then the guy shows up like everything's super. And he was genuinely surprised when we cuffed and stuffed his ass. It's going to payoff even if he never comes back. That's eighteen months paid vacation in the van. Shit, I could practice playing my guitar and write a Country Western album."

"I see what you mean and your right. I'm going to bring a portable DVD player and a bunch of National Geographic DVDs tomorrow. How's Officer Dupri doing?"

"They sent her to Seattle to have constructive surgery done to her face. You know that fucker crushed the skull bone around her eye socket."

"That's terrible cause that was one fine chick."

"Don't count her out yet, they've got one of the best working on her. But I already heard she's going to be transferred to Kentucky afterwards."

"What about her kid?"

"What kid?"

"You know, the kid, her daughter Shani."

"That wasn't her daughter. Her name wasn't even Shani. I think it was Lakina. That's Agent Janet Griffin's baby. Janet's on a big case up north so Dupri borrowed the little girl for effect. I bet you think that was her mom's house on 2nd avenue too huh?"

"No. I knew that wasn't, but I'm still thinking about her being transferred. Damn another fine piece of pussy I let slip through my fingers."

"I didn't." Steffans said matter of factly.

Agent O'Brien swung his head around and looked at his expression to see if Steffans was serious. He saw that he was.

"You always get the good ones."

"Hot chicks want that entertainment. They want you to sing to them. Well every chick wants you to sing for her, but you want to sing for a hot chick. Them fat and lonely bitches you be fucking are the only ones who care to hear about that animal kingdom shit." Steffans said laughing.

O'Brien scratched his head with a pensive look on his face. Thinking *I might have to get a guitar.*

While still pondering on it, he picked up his pen to write down that the visitor was leaving an hour and a half later. The old lady still had the cart but without the black plastic lining it.

"It's filled with colorful material, looks like clothes." O'Brien told Steffans while pulling out the binoculars to zoom in.

She descended the stairs eventlessly, then stumbled on the crack in the walkway and tumbled down flat on her front. The basket tumbled over her back and dispensed all its contents into the street. Again she was burdened with the task of picking herself up and her belongings.

O'Brien wrote: [The colorful clothing turned out to be 2 quilts. She dusted them off, folded them back up and put them back into the cart. When she was about 50 yards up the block the suspect's nephew ran outside and caught up to her, said a few words to her and helped her with her cart back to the house. He helped her into the suspect's sister's vehicle, a Range Rover. Then he got into the driver's side and backed out of the driveway. We are aware he has no driver's license but that is a trivial offense in relation to our primary objective. The grandmother probably told him to take her friend home. The Range Rover turned the corner. We maintained our position and watched the comings and goings of the house.]

The Range Rover took Broadway to Slauson and got onto the 110 Fwy South, interchanged 105 Fwy West then exited Sepulveda. Where you would make a right to go to the airport they made a left, drove up a few blocks, parked and went into the back door of the Hacienda Hotel.

They went into room 308 unnoticed. While Mannish took the wig off, got out of the old clothes and showered, Ty cut slits to remove the stacks of money they had sown into the quilts with Big Mama's sewing machine. When Mannish came out of the bathroom Ty already had the $500,000 stacked on the bed.

"It's fucked up how shit turned out." Mannish said, "I gotta get outta dodge, damn! I always hoped it would turn out different. It really do be like that sometimes I guess. It is what it is. Yall got a hundred grand at the house. You the man of the family right now Ty. You gotta make sure everybody straight. And stay clean. They gonna be watching. I gotta go out here and make this money work for me and still try to follow my plan. Who knows I might stumble across a connect on that coca in Costa Rica."

Mannish transferred the money to a duffle bag. The plan was to catch a red eye flight at 1 o'clock in the morning to Costa Rica. He had about ten hours to kill so he stretched out on the bed and checked the messages on his phone.

{you have 27 messages,.first message.}

"This is Paul Downing, please give me a call."

Some of them were messages from days prior.

beep {message erased, next message.} "Mannish you some shit. I gotchu nigga."

That was Cherise. That message amused him.

beep {message saved, next message} "This is Paul..."

beep {message erased, next message}

beep {mesage erased, next message}

beep {message erased, next message}

beep {message erased, next message.} "Ay, this Will, I got all new numbers, I left 'em on your voicemail earlier. Call me right away Dog. I gotta keep it real wit you"

beep {message erased, next message}
beep {message erased, next message}
beep {message erased, next message} "Hey this Vallawn, I want you to come over and.."
beep {message era...}
beep beep beep beep beep {message erased, next message.}
"Mannish, this is Shawna. This is my third message. I need you to come by but don't bring anyone not even my son, he don't need to see me like this. I've been on that glass dick heavy Man, and I haven't ate in I don't know how long. Call me at 547-1212 that's 323 area code."
He called right away.
Mannish said. "Ay Ty, this yo Momma."
"I know my money gone by now so fuck what she talkin' about fa' real!" Ty responded angrily while Mannish listened to the phone ring.
"Hello."
"Shawna?"
"Yeah this me."
"Where you at?"
"The Magic Carpet Motel on Century."
"What room number?"
"112."
"I'm on my way."
"You by yourself, right?"
"Yeah."
"Okay, hey!"
"What's up?"
"I'm sorry for this."
"It's alright." Click.

"Come on, let's go get yo Momma. She all fucked up on that shit."

"I already knew that."

"Maybe seeing you will make her realize she needs to straighten out."

"Yeah whateva."

Ty kicked the duffle bag under the bed and they left.

Mannish drove. By the time they reached the motel Ty had decided that his mother was dead to him. He didn't even want to see Shawna.

"Ay yo Man I ain't getting out."

"Aight. I'll be back then." Mannish said, getting out of the vehicle and going up and knocking on the door next to 111. It just had a 2 and the bottom piece of a 1 on it.

Shawna opened the door then stepped out of the way.

Mannish walked in. A man snuck from around the back of the building with a pistol in his hand. Moving quickly he ran up behind Mannish. Ty saw something moving fast out of the corner of his eye and looked.

"What the fuck!" he said to himself grabbing the door handle of the truck to get out. Before he could barely exit the vehicle three shots caught Mannish off guard. Two bullets came out of his chest and one blew out of the side of his jaw. He slammed face forward into the floor.

Ty ran into the room with his gun drawn. Shawna sat on the bed frozen. The killer was on his knees digging through Mannish's pockets.

"Mutha fucka!" Ty screamed. Travis, Shawna's husband looked up. Ty looked him deep in his eyes.

~FLASHBACK~

"Where yall taking me?" Travis asked.

"You going to Never Never Land fool." J Stone answered.

"Why? I don't owe yall no money. I was tryna spend $200 I just got from my wife with yall."

"Ain't nobody said you owe us shit. But I'm gonna keep that two hundred though thanks."

"Why yall gonna kill me? Yall can keep the $200 and I promise you I'll spend money everyday, big money. I'll bring customers, good customers."

Chuck cut in and said, "Nigga shut up! Stop cryin' like a bitch. We bouta get paid today. We don't need you to bring us shit no more. We bouta split up a kilo as soon as we get back. All we gotta do is off yo lame ass."

J Stone commented, "Yeah homie, that nigga Mannish is aight and he got much dope. I'm tryna be on that nigga team."

"Mannish is paying you to kill me?" Travis asked.

"Didn't I tell you to shut the fuck up? I woulda kilt yuh punk ass fa' free but yeah he payin' and nice too. He probably want yuh sorry ass out of his sister's life, cause she do whatever yuh dumb ass say."

Travis was quiet for the rest of the trip. They were really going to kill him this time. They got to the beach and pulled up near the pier where they could throw his body into the water.

"We still gotta mix the cement and put his feet in the bucket." Chuck said.

"Damn, we gotta wait for it to dry and shit. We shoulda been letting it dry on the way up here." J Stone responded.

"Ain't no use in talkin' bout it now. Let's get to it."

They pulled up to a dark part of the pier. As soon as they put the car in park Travis kicked the back door open and dived head first off the ledge and into the water. J Stone made like he was going to go in after him. Chuck grabbed him by the arm.

"Oh you ain't gonna catch no crackhead."

"I'ma tell Big Will you ain't let me catch 'im."

"I'ma tell 'im you tied the rope like a bitch."

"Nigga I tied that shit tight. I was a Boy Scout."

"Nigga when? You been in and outta Juvenile Hall all yuh life."

They turned on the interior light and looked in the back. The rope laid on the backseat obviously cut with something. Then they noticed a broken glass crack pipe on the floor.

"Damn!!" they said at the same time.

"Listen." Chuck said, "Let's not say shit and just get this dope."

J Stone responded logically, "You right."

They headed back to get their pay. When Travis heard the car drive off, he pulled himself out of the water and stood there soaking wet looking into the night.

Mannish, you bastard. I'ma get you for this.

I unloaded my clip into the both of them, Travis and Shawna.

"Now you could be a better mother." I told her.

I guess cum was thicker than blood. I thought.

I dug into Mannish's pocket and took out the Hacienda room key.

I pulled off in the Range Rover as the sirens in the distance were getting louder.

CHAPTER THIRTY-EIGHT

Big Mama's heart gave out and she died when she got the news of what happened to my momma, her daughter Shawna and my uncle, her son Mannish.

The End

BE LIKE THAT SOMETIME part.2
SOMETIMES IT IS WHAT IT IS
Available Now!
bebpub.com

Hope You Enjoyed The Ride.
Comments Are Welcome,

Biz-e-Bee Book Group
8549 Wilshire Blvd. #139
Beverly Hills, CA 90211
323-439-1222

The Last Big Momma

Be Like That Sometimes

www.ingramcontent.com/pod-product-compliance
Lightning Source LLC
Chambersburg PA
CBHW071300110426
42743CB00042B/1117